"LIFE IS A JOURNEY OF DISCOVERY—AND CHANGE IS THE CATALYST"

So welcome change into your life and reap its rewards: freedom to be yourself, absence of conflict, a growing sense of well-being and self-confidence, and most of all, happiness and joy. Happiness and joy are what living should be all about. They're yours for the seeking, the doing. Change is the ticket—and it takes courage to change.

—Dennis Wholey

THE MIRACLE OF CHANGE
The Path to Self-Discovery and Spiritual Growth

"Dennis Wholey has developed a reputation for putting a microphone in front of famous people and getting them to talk about their most personal problems. . . . *The Miracle of Change* . . . [offers] insights from more than sixty people on how they faced their most difficult challenges."

—*The Detroit Free Press*

"Inspiring stories. . . . *[The Miracle of Change]* may . . . provide the guidance or inspiration you seek."

—*The Portland Oregonian*

"Dennis Wholey is a recovering alcoholic who knows what inner fortitude it takes to turn a life around completely. Change is the ingredient that adds zest and meaning to anything we do. Here is a fine companion for those who want to move forward on the path of self-discovery and spiritual growth."

—*Values & Visions*

Also by <u>Dennis Wholey</u>

The Courage to Change:
  Personal Conversations About Alcoholism

Are You Happy?:
  Some Answers to the Most Important Question in Your Life

Becoming Your Own Parent:
  The Solution for Adult Children of Alcoholic and Other
  Dysfunctional Families

When the Worst That Can Happen Already Has:
  Conquering Life's Most Difficult Times

THE MIRACLE OF CHANGE

THE PATH TO SELF-DISCOVERY AND SPIRITUAL GROWTH

DENNIS WHOLEY

POCKET BOOKS

New York   London   Toronto   Sydney   Tokyo   Singapore

The following pieces are used by permission: Excerpt from The Tibetan Book of Living and Dying by Sogyal Rinpoche, copyright the Rigpa Fellowship; "The Prayer for Protection" by James Dillet Freeman by permission of the author; excerpt published in Radical Grace, the newspaper of the Center for Action and Contemplation, Albuquerque, NM (505) 242-9588, by Father Richard Rohr, O.F.M., founder, reprinted with permission; Reflection by Amalie H. Frank by permission of the author; "Footprints" copyright © 1964 by Margaret Fishback Powers by permission of Harper-CollinsPublishersLtd; prayer by Thomas Merton is taken from A Seven Day Journey with Thomas Merton (Servant Publications, 1992) and used by permission of Pax Christi USA; Meditation by Rabbi Joseph Telushkin by permission of the author; quotation by Linus Mundy by permission of the author and publisher; "After a While" © 1971 by Veronica A. Shoffstall by permission of the author; quotation taken from the Big Book of AA with thanks; "Maturity" from Ann Landers—permission granted by Ann Landers and Creators Syndicate; "Grace Prayer" used by permission of Wings of Spirit Foundation, 6757 Arapaho, Suite 711, Box 345, Dallas, Texas 75248 (972-233-2992); "To Look Back" by William S. Cohen from A Baker's Nickel, by permission of the author.

POCKET BOOKS, a division of Simon & Schuster Inc.
1230 Avenue of the Americas, New York, NY 10020

Copyright © 1997 by Dennis Wholey

ISBN: 0-671-51890-9

First Pocket Books trade paperback printing April 1998

10 9 8 7 6 5 4 3 2 1

POCKET and colophon are registered trademarks of Simon & Schuster Inc.

Front cover photo by Valder-Tormey Photography/Picture Perfect

Printed in the U.S.A.

THIS BOOK IS DEDICATED TO
THE NEXT GENERATION

Richie, Michelle and Ashley
Corey and Katelyn
Allie and William
Jessica and Maggie
and Elias

ACKNOWLEDGMENTS

The making of this book required the participation, talents, and efforts of many people who deserve my deepest personal thanks and public recognition.

I want to express my appreciation to the many generous contributors who trusted me, believed in the concept of this book, and shared their experience and wisdom. It is their book as well as mine; I hope they are as proud of it as I am.

I am extremely grateful to my editor, Tom Miller, for his enthusiasm and commitment to this project and for his excellent editorial input. Tom has stretched me as a writer and offered important and creative suggestions in the organization of the material.

I was blessed early on to benefit from the meticulous transcription work and extensive word processing skills of Michael Nine. His dedicated effort, positive spirit, and good humor during the preparation of the first draft of this book were terrific.

In the later stages of the book, I was incredibly fortunate to be in the gifted hands of word-processing wizard Marlon Fixico. His fine work—including transcriptions and the exacting work of the final draft—support, and warmth made a world of difference.

In my THIS IS AMERICA office, I thank former producers Amy DeLaureal, Dan Rabbitt, and Regina Pierce, who all helped out along the way; special appreciation goes to Andrew Murray for his effective research assistance in the final hours; and thanks also to the staffs and crews of THIS IS AMERICA and DENNIS WHOLEY: AMERICA.

Some other folks I want to acknowledge are: Ponda Weakly, William

Winston, Rick Hamilton, Hamilton B., G. Wayne Smith, Suzi Montes de Oca, and Skip Smith.

At the offices of the contributors special thanks to: Tom Eadie, Judith Dickie, Bjorn Amelan, Ellen Jacobs, Gail Clark, Alexis Prida, Bette Mandino and Matt Mandino, Lisl Cade, Barbara Semedo, Carmen MacDougal, Greg Bailey, Patti Ruiter, Ginnie Stodghill, Walter Miller, Tracy Thornton, Lyn Paulsin, Sue Burkhart, Matthew Rich, Carolyn Holt, Carla Shell, Barbara Chapman, Ruth Collins, Maya Labos, Barbara Fant, Amy Crouch, Ebon Robinson, Deborah Nelson, Mary Ellen Rouiller, Susie Godfrey, Sathi Pillari-Colucci, Ann Cullen, and Amy Morris.

This book has been quite a journey for the inner circle—so family members I want to thank are: my dear mother, Jerry Wholey, and her sister Nonie Wholey, Ann Wholey, Nora and Peter Corrigan, Elsa and Tim Wholey, Midge and Skef Wholey.

I also express my deep gratitude to my close friends for their terrific support along the way, especially Craig Cullinane—and Steve Lee, Father Ed Pritchard, Steve Baron, Bill Trombley, the Reverend John Knight—and the Murphy and Hutchins families of Michigan (and Georgia) who are so special to me.

I wish also to express my appreciation to the following people at Pocket Books and Simon & Schuster: managing editors Donna Ruvituso, Donna O'Neill, and Kathleen Stahl; Pocket Books president Gina Centrello; Tom Miller's editorial assistants Amanda Reid, Kevin Maynard, and Dan Slater; and publicist Stephanie Hubbard.

I also thank senior editor Nancy Miller for her special eleventh-hour efforts to make this book a reality.

Finally, I am ever so grateful to my agents, Richard Pine and Arthur Pine, for their commitment to my work over the years. This is our fifth book together; they help and encourage me in many ways above and beyond the call of their professional obligation. I also offer sincere thanks to Lori Andiman and Sarah Piel, of their office.

If I have omitted anyone who should have been thanked, I apologize. A book is a complex undertaking and if there are any errors, I ask your forgiveness. Please let me know so I can make amends—and corrections—in future editions.

THE CONTRIBUTORS

Claudia Black, Ph.D.
Les Brown
Mary Higgins Clark
The Honorable William S.
  Cohen
Wayne W. Dyer, Ph.D.
Betty J. Eadie
Albert Ellis, Ph.D.
Mary Fisher
Michael J. Fox
Millard Fuller
Reverend Joseph Girzone
Shad Helmstetter
Arianna Huffington
John Jakes
Judith Jamison
Bill T. Jones
Tracy Kidder
Dennis Kimbro, Ph.D.
Lonnie MacDonald, M.D.
Harvey Mackay
Rebecca Maddox
Og Mandino
Kelly McGillis
Michael Medved
Pia Mellody, R.N.
Andrea Mitchell

Thomas Moore
Georgette Mosbacher
Dennis O'Grady, Psy.D.
The Honorable Hazel O'Leary
James and Salle Merrill
  Redfield
The Honorable Ann Richards
Sogyal Rinpoche
Theodore Isaac Rubin, M.D.
Tim Russert
Pierre Salinger
Laura Schlessinger, Ph.D.
Natalie Shainess, M.D.
Martin Sheen
Cal Thomas
Nina Totenberg
Tommy Tune
Jack Valenti
Andrew Weil, M.D.
Betty White
Rabbi Harold White
Armstrong Williams
Marianne Williamson
Judy Woodruff
Zig Ziglar
And Members of
  Twelve Step Programs

CONTENTS

Contents

CONTENTS

CONTENTS

12. WISDOM 253

There is nothing stable in the world—uproar's your only music.

—JOHN KEATS

If nothing changes—nothing changes.

—ANONYMOUS

1. CHANGE

All is change; all yields its place and goes.

—EURIPIDES

Change is not made without inconvenience, even from worse to better.

—RICHARD HOOKER

LIFE IS A JOURNEY OF DISCOVERY—AND CHANGE IS THE catalyst, the energy source, that propels us toward self-acceptance, unconditional love for others, appreciation of life, and a relationship with God.

Personal growth is at the heart of living. However, since human beings by nature seek security, one of life's greatest continuing challenges seems to be finding the courage to change. We are frequently offered the opportunity to change. More often than we'd like, circumstances beyond our control force us to leave an existing state of affairs—our "status quo"—and muddle through an uncomfortable time before arriving in a new situation. Even if we initiate the change ourselves, the transition process is difficult. In brief, change is the spiritual movement from holding on to letting go to getting there and starting all over again.

While it's easy to write glibly about lumping change with death and taxes as givens in life, there is something ironically symbolic in the "Jekyll & Hyde" song lyric: "The only thing constant is change." Not only is change everpresent, it also always seems to involve a mixture of good news/bad news—or the other way around. Even if we live happily with the same partner working at the same job for years, there will be plenty of significant changes to absorb in a lifetime. While change often produces happiness and joy, change can also hurt, especially when it's not wanted. All change includes elements of loss. That is what makes it so threatening. Since

3

change temporarily takes away our security blanket, our safety net, it's normal that fear, frustration, hopelessness, and even low self-esteem are often the short-term price we pay.

Intellectually, we know all that. But it's our denial of the predictability of change and misunderstanding of its very positive purpose that prevent us from welcoming change with grace, humility, and enthusiasm when it comes into our lives. If we *really* grasped what change was all about, we wouldn't shrink from it and cry, "Why me?" We would embrace change, gently ask, "What's next?" and enjoy the adventure to follow.

Some of the most dramatic changes in my own life were triggered by my recovery from alcoholism. Becoming an author is a good example.

A couple of years into recovery I was hosting my PBS show, *LateNight America*. One night—in the middle of an interview with another recovering alcoholic, comedian Sid Caesar—the thought occurred to me how easy it was not to drink once I got the hang of it and how terrific my life had become because I had quit drinking. The idea came to me that it might be helpful if I could gather together in one place—the pages of a book—a group of well-known recovering alcoholics who would relate their experiences, collectively saying, "There is life after alcohol."

The Courage to Change: Personal Conversations about Alcoholism was published a dozen years ago. While on promotion tours for the book, I talked on an intimate level with people all over the country. Many shared their own recovery stories with me— on planes and trains, at book signings and after speeches, in restaurants and hotel lobbies, and on radio and television call-in shows.

A number of times, however, I was surprised when folks volunteered that while they had no problems with alcohol or drugs themselves, reading *The Courage to Change* had helped them get through other stressful changes such as being fired, getting a divorce, having heart surgery, losing a parent, or coming out as a gay man. While it felt good to know that these readers were helped, it was a long time later that I finally realized a deeper common nerve—other than alcoholism—had been touched by that book, and that there was a real need for a more general look at courage and change. I put the idea on the shelf—until now.

The Miracle of Change is the collective work of more than sixty people who have come together to help you live a richer life, an easier life, a happier life. They share the fears and frustrations, as well as the benefits and rewards, of change. You may already know some of the contributors; others you'll be meeting for the first time. They will offer you their experience and wisdom in navigating many of life's most frequent transitions. The changes they discuss range from daily routine to personal crisis. The struggles and challenges they share—from birth to death—show the amazing breadth of human experience. While each participant is a unique individual, as a group they confirm that we all are very much the same. The number of major changes we must handle during the course of a lifetime is staggering. We *all* deserve enormous credit for just making it through life.

If you are reading this book in search of help to get through a change with which you are now struggling, I hope you will find some deeply inspiring stories and wonderful professional advice here. Long before this book was finished, I was quoting contributors' thoughts and reading sections of the text to friends and family members who were (among other things) quitting smoking, changing jobs, starting a new career, or dealing with a relationship problem.

In putting this book together, I compiled a list of some of the most important principles—the common denominators—of change. They will be elaborated on throughout the book, but I'll introduce you to them now and offer a quick thought or two on each.

1. Change creates fear (but the fear can be overcome).

That's true. It's the nature of the beast—of us, human beings. It's the way the good Lord designed us. Fear is a normal human reaction when our security is threatened. The greater the change, the greater the fear—but the fear doesn't have to be paralyzing.

2. Change is hard (but it's doable).

A lot of change is about giving up or losing something or somebody you like (or love). Accepting loss is difficult. Making a change is difficult. Life is hard, but whatever the challenge, it's not the end of the world. In fact, change leads to a new beginning and something wonderful will come of it.

3. Expect change (and enjoy it).

Life is packed with joy; it's also full of disappointment. We often don't get what we want or whom we want. Events overtake plans; so plan the action, don't plan the results. Change makes life exciting and fun.

4. The only person you can change is you (and nobody else).

Keep trying if you want to, but people will prove to you over and over again that they will do exactly what they think is best for them. No offense, but change is not about fixing them, it's about changing you.

5. Courage is action (in the face of fear).

No fear, no courage. Action and fear must coexist to qualify. Courage is moving forward *despite* the fear—and you can do it.

6. Change is really exchange (so go for it).

Only with hindsight do we come to realize that what we gain through change is usually much better than what we lost or gave up.

7. Change is possible (even if it doesn't feel like it).

Life isn't fair and change often hurts like hell; but people have handled the loss of a loved one, being fired, tragic illness—even quitting cigarettes. Others have survived, even benefited from these changes. You can too.

8. Don't attempt major change alone—do it with an ally.

If you're going to change, the first step is to get the support of someone you trust. It's probably going to be three steps forward and two backward; so get the help you need to get through major transitions.

9. The answer may be acceptance (and not action).
You may have to bite the bullet and accept some things exactly as they are—unchangeable. If that's the case, take a deep breath, yell, and start changing your attitude.

10. Change is a process (not an event).
Change is about the getting, the going, the moving from here to there. Change is even the turmoil, the upsetness, the middle part. The goal is not even the big payoff; it's what you experience and learn getting to it.

Going to college isn't about history and chemistry facts and figures. It's about learning systems, discipline, responsibility, self-starting, discovering who you are, living with others, building character, and choosing a career.

In a similar way, change isn't about external events, it's about the internal making—and maturing—of a human being. Change is about self-discovery and spiritual growth.

THE GIFT OF COURAGE

The ocean seems to be the apt metaphor for change. There is an ebb and flow to change. It drifts in and out of our lives, sometimes gently like the tide—and other times like the crashing waves during a storm. If we were superhuman, we would have no need for bravery when traveling through troubled waters. But we are human and change provokes great discomfort. Yet we discover, much to our surprise and often with the help of others, that deep within us there is a magnificent gift of strength that will pull us or push us through our changing times. This power is courage. We all have it. You have it.

During life's most difficult times, the courage we need to face change is already there. Our challenge is to seek it, find it, and use it. Discovering how to tap into that reservoir of courage is the subject of this book, and learning how to face our fear and navigate change is its substance. The book's goal is to offer you a true understanding of how change works and a deep appreciation of the miracle of change in your own life.

HOW IT WORKS

I have arranged the book's chapters to showcase the process of change. Early chapters deal with loss, action, acceptance, fear, stress, and the spiritual significance of change. Faith, hope, and courage are absolutely necessary to maneuver through change, and each virtue is examined in depth. Later chapters are devoted to self-discovery and the rewards of change. Wisdom on personal responsibility makes up the book's final chapter.

Sometimes I'm asked how I chose the book's contributors. Some are friends or guests I have interviewed on television; others I got to know about by reading; and some were suggested to me. As you will discover, all of the contributors are drawn to the subject of change; and all see the book as an opportunity to help others going through change. Like the pieces of a mosaic, the wonderful and varied voices of the contributors touch on the major themes of change, including relationships, raising families, jobs and career, success, failure, loss, vices and character defects, health issues, death, and faith in God.

I love talking with people about who they are, what they do, and why they do it. I was amazed as I got into the conversations for this book to rediscover what a deep and rich subject change is. People approach change so differently. Some of the people in this book handle change with confidence and optimism; others, predicting the worst, resist change with everything they've got. Regardless, you'll be inspired with the amount of courage people muster when facing difficult challenges.

I asked the contributors how they got through change, what they've learned about change, and what were the positive results. In my conversations with the psychiatrists, psychologists, and therapists—experts who study human behavior—my questions focused on "Why is change so difficult?" "What advice can you give someone who is trying to change?" and "How does change fit into our lives?" Their advice is invaluable. Except for only a few interruptions from me—I have edited out my questions—I have tried to step off to the side and let the participants talk directly with you. A few of the book's contributors offered essays in lieu of a personal conversation, including some Twelve Step program members I invited to participate.

LIVING THE SERENITY PRAYER

In *The Courage to Change* some of the most powerful wisdom came from anonymous people in recovery.

Millions of people, of course, use the opening lines of theologian Reinhold Niebuhr's famous Serenity Prayer when dealing with life's changes:

God grant me the serenity
To accept the things I cannot change,
Courage to change the things I can,
And the wisdom to know the difference.

Who better to walk us through courage, acceptance, wisdom, serenity, and the miracles of change than those whose programs have adopted this prayer as their own and who try to live its message daily in their lives. Since membership in all Twelve Step groups is anonymous, the uplifting essays are signed with the writer's first name and last initial only, in adherence to one of their program's most important principles: "Anonymity is the spiritual foundation of all our traditions, ever reminding us to place principles before personalities."

FINDING THE COURAGE TO REALLY CHANGE

Twelve Step programs play a huge and successful role in helping people quit alcohol and other drugs and stop compulsive behaviors; however, since addictions and compulsive behaviors mask pain that is symptomatic of other personal problems, these also need attention. To quit alcohol or drugs or stop "acting out" compulsively is frequently only the first step. Major change is called for in the lives of most recovering alcoholics and addicts. It certainly was in mine—and continues to be so.

MY OWN JOURNEY

It was fun to let my mind wander as I was writing this section to review some significant changes in my own life. I encourage you to go down memory lane yourself to appreciate the many changes you've experienced—and how they've shaped your life.

Leaving home in Rhode Island and going away to Catholic University in Washington, D.C., was the first big change in my life. Not many weeks after landing there, I switched my major from math (don't ask!) to speech and drama. I moved to New York after graduation and changed my career path from theater to broadcasting. I often wonder how my life would have turned out if I had pursued my original goal of becoming a director in the theater.

I began my broadcasting career as a guide conducting tours around the radio and television studios at 30 Rockefeller Plaza in New York City and eventually became the guide trainer. During the next couple of years, I worked as a director for the NBC Radio Network and as an assistant producer on a weekly WNBC-TV documentary show. After those production jobs, I left my behind-the-scenes work and went on air, first as a producer/interviewer on listener-sponsored radio, and then with public television. Commercial broadcasting jobs as a morning television talk show host took me out of New York City to Cincinnati, Detroit, and Washington, D.C. I lived in the Detroit area for the better part of sixteen years. During those years, I worked in both commercial and public television.

THE WORST TURNED OUT TO BE THE BEST

My whole world changed when I quit alcohol and Valium. Few people live a life with a before and an after. Sobriety was a second shot at life for me. At the time I thought admitting to being an alcoholic was the most horrible and humiliating thing I could experience. I saw myself as a total failure and my life as a complete disaster. Of course, as is so often the case, it turned out to be the best thing that could have happened to me. I've continued to discover over the past sixteen years that the more painful the change, the greater the rewards.

In recovery, I've put together and hosted five national television series. I've had the incredible opportunity to interview many of the most important national figures of our time from every walk of life. I've toured the country, appeared as a guest on many of the major network radio and television talk shows, and traveled the world. I've moved to Washington, I'm in excellent health, own my home, and have wonderful friends. These exciting things happened as the direct result of not drinking. The most important changes I've made, however, are on the inside. That's probably true for everyone since it's our humanness with which we really struggle and where we really do change the most.

At the top of my list I'd have to say I've learned to love myself: I'm pretty comfortable with who I am. That wasn't always the case, but today, I'd rather be me—with whatever problems I have—than anybody else I know. Growth in self-esteem, self-acceptance, and self-forgiveness were hard-fought-for, hard-won. I know today that I am good, capable, lovable, worthwhile and important.

In the past, I used other people to try to prop myself up; but I learned that "other-esteem" didn't work at all. At this stage of life, I'm a different person in how I relate to others. Since I'm more secure, I'm more open and more comfortable in expressing my feelings. By being freer to tell others who I am, I'm more able to connect with them, love them, and contribute to their lives.

For too long a time, fear, anger, worry, and depression ruled my life, motivated my actions, and caused me pain; but I look at life in a new way today. Nowadays I'm much more of an optimist and see more of the good that life has to offer—even accepting that I'm a very imperfect person in a very imperfect world.

The biggest internal change for me has been the movement from fear to faith in God. To realize that I can't control life (and the people in it) has been a shock (which I seem to keep on learning); but it's also meant that I could give up my job as GENERAL MANAGER OF THE UNIVERSE. The simple God-line for living I try to use is: "I can't, He can, let Him."

At some point along the way, I discovered a couple of life's truisms: that the journey of life is inward, not upward—and that all change is really for the better, regardless of how painful it is at the time.

Life isn't a spectator sport: it requires being deeply and actively involved at all times. Change is the process that challenges us and pushes us to the next level of living. To be happy requires not only effort, hope, faith—but also the willingness to move on when faced with change.

So welcome change into your life and reap its rewards: freedom to be yourself, absence of conflict, a growing sense of well-being and self-confidence, and most of all, happiness and joy. Happiness and joy are what living should be all about. They're yours for the seeking, the doing. Change is the ticket—and it takes courage to change.

MEDITATION

I have resisted change with all my will—
Cried out to life, "Pass by life and leave me still."
But I have found as I have trudged time's track
That all my wishing will not hold life back.
All finite things must go their finite way.

I cannot bid the merest moment "stay."
So finding I have no power to change change
I have changed my self. And this is strange.
But I have found when I let change come,
The very change that I was fleeing from
Has often held the good I had prayed for,
And I was not the less for change, but more.
Once I accepted life and was not loathe to change
I found change was the seed of growth.

—JAMES DILLET FREEMAN
Unity minister, author, and poet

There is a certain relief in change, even though it be from bad to worse; as I have found in traveling in a stage-coach, that it is often a comfort to shift one's position and be bruised in a new place.

—WASHINGTON IRVING

2. ADVENTURE

An adventure is only an inconvenience rightly considered. An inconvenience is only an adventure wrongly considered.

—G. K. CHESTERTON

True miracles are created by men when they use the courage and intelligence that God gave them.

—JEAN ANOUILH

As I was writing this, a friend called from Colorado. He had moved from Washington to Boulder literally hours ago. So determined was he to get there that after a brief stopover in Pittsburgh, he had driven the fifteen-hundred-mile distance in two days.

He had given his decision to move a lot of thought over many months. It hadn't been easy. He was leaving a good job, giving up the excitement and fun of living in Washington, saying good-bye to close friends. His motivations for moving were to enjoy an outdoor and sports-related life, to seek more interesting career opportunities, and to find romance. He also felt, as do other bright young people who come to D.C. for a while, that he had outgrown his "Washington time."

I was glad to hear from him so soon; and having been talking to people about change for this book for months, I was not surprised at the content of his call. His first words were, "Oh my God, what have I done? What the hell am I doing here?" This was his jumping-off point for forty-five minutes of anxious thoughts and feelings that were predictably centered on looking at what he had had in Washington, all that he had given up, and what (little) he had now in Colorado.

Moving to a new city where you know almost no one is a very difficult experience. Thank goodness he had one good friend there.

ALL CHANGE IS EXCHANGE

So much of the pain of change can be linked to negative emotions that are immediately triggered whenever we lose or give up something important to us. My friend who had just moved was up on the high wire without a safety net, at least for the time being. His losses hurt, negative thinking had taken over, and his fears and regrets had kicked in. In situations of change, for some of us, the mind is a terrible thing to have.

I'm fond of the old saying "When one door closes, another door opens." It's often true; but it is also almost impossible to think of, let alone believe, when wrestling with the shock and initial stages of major change. That's the time when life is at its bleakest and everything looks hopeless. However, when I look back on the changes—and losses—I've been through, I see that even though I gave up something or something was taken away from me at the time, what I got in return was better. When we have moved from the immediate trauma of change and have become more emotionally available, new people and experiences will come into our lives. Through the change process, we know ourselves better; and we enjoy life more fully because of the very change that is causing problems for us now. French novelist Anatole France says it this way: "All changes, even the most longed for, have their melancholy; for what we leave behind us is a part of ourselves; we must die to one life before we can enter into another!"

∽

Behavioral researcher **Shad Helmstetter** outlines the major categories of change, explains why change is so hard, and tells us about the rewards of change:

LOOKING FORWARD TO CHANGE

IT'S FASCINATING THAT SO MANY STRESSES AND PRESSURES are tied directly to change. If you are a person who is feeling anxious, tense, or insecure, you almost have to ask yourself, "What is the change I'm going through right now?" "What is the change that is coming?" or "What is the change I'm hoping for?" If you ask yourself those questions, you'll probably get closer to the real answer quicker than if you ask yourself, "What am I feeling?" or "What's wrong?"

Change usually falls into one of the following seven major areas:

- Loss
- Separation
- Relocation
- Change in relationship
- Change in direction
- Change in health
- Personal growth

When you ask a group of people in an informal survey, they tend to say that change that is forced upon them is the most difficult to deal with because they don't have control in the matter. However, if you give them some time to think about it, most folks will change their mind and say, "Wait a minute, the kind of change that I have the greatest problem with is really the change that I'm trying to create myself." While it depends on the individual, if you're talking about broad averages, there is almost a comfort in change that comes from someone else— from the boss, the company, or some external situation. As a result, people give up a lot of responsibility and allow change to happen to them.

GETTING RID OF PROGRAMMED FEAR

If I were counseling people, I would work with the kind of change that people want to generate themselves but can't. Something stops them: probably fear. I wish there were some more complex answer. It just gets down to that belief that "I can't do it," "I'm not capable," or "I'm not good enough." That fear can always be traced back to programming. Your long-held beliefs, or programs, vote very strongly when you are anticipating a change. If those programs say, "This isn't going to work for me," the chances of getting through that change successfully are very low.

People would take positive steps to change whatever lifestyle or habit might be holding them back and navigate through it much more successfully if they could get rid of their "I can't do it" automatic programmed-in fear. If 77 percent of an individual's programs were wrong, negative, or false, you would probably find that person saying "I can't" 77 percent of the time. That figure is based on work that was originally done by Viktor Frankl. I think that's a low statistic. Look around you at the people who are struggling. When people are failing, we know those people got bad programs along the way. Unfortunately, there are many people who have few positive programs to help them.

There are also people who are clearly programmed to look forward to change, to deal with it more positively, and to find joy and opportunity in change. When you deal with change well, greater self-confidence and self-esteem are its reward, and your chances of dealing better with your next change increase.

—*Shad Helmstetter*

~

It is only in adventure that some people succeed in knowing themselves—in finding themselves.

—ANDRÉ GIDE

~

To acknowledge the discomfort that accompanies all major life transitions and to appreciate the roller coaster of conflicting emotions we feel as we adjust to change is to have learned an important lesson about this inescapable aspect of life. Yet however troublesome changes may be as we are living through them, we are almost always surprised in retrospect at the positive outcomes these negative situations bring. According to film critic **Michael Medved,** two difficult events were "absolutely necessary" for the course his life has successfully followed:

IN YOUR GLORY—RIGHT NOW

A GREAT RABBI WHO WAS A TEACHER OF MINE SAID THAT every day that he looked in the mirror and saw more gray hairs in his beard and on his head was an occasion for thanking God. He believed God set the world up to remind us of that principle of change. You cannot remain static. Time is fleeting; change is a given.

Little kids hate change. They want to eat the same thing every night. "No we don't want anything else. We want macaroni and cheese. No we don't want anything spicy." I used to want hot dogs every night when I was young. Children really resist the idea of moving the furniture in their room, let alone switching from one room to another.

My wife and I have been talking about moving. We've lived in the same house since we've been married and I lived in it for ten years before that. Whenever we talk about it, my eight-year-old pipes up and says, "We're not moving." Basically, it's a healthy response. Kids are dealing with the reality of such tremendous physiological, psychological, and intellectual change in their lives they absolutely don't want any external change added to it. They've got enough to deal with. The process of change is for the most part scary. It's occasionally exhilarating, I guess, but the biggest changes are the biggest stress producers.

The most meaningful change I've had to tackle is having children. I was thirty-eight when Sarah, our first child, was born. That was a huge change. In a whole slew of ways it was a bigger change than getting married.

THE POSITIVE REWARDS OF DIFFICULT CHANGE

I have been particularly allergic to change for most of my life, partially because my parents made two big moves when I was a kid. Both were wrenching for me, particularly the second one, when I was a junior in high school. That was a nightmare. I was an adolescent and all of a sudden I had to go to a brand new school. It was the one time when I really had a tough time getting along with my parents.

I was two years ahead in school, so I didn't have my driver's license. In a California high school that means absolutely zippo in the way of social life. What are you going to do? Are you going to have your mother drive you? It just doesn't play. It got better, but the first semester in the new high school was just horrible.

My parents had moved to San Diego from Philadelphia when I was six. I had grown up in San Diego in the same neighborhood with the same kids in elementary school, junior high, and the first year of high school. I loved it there. I was fairly successful and well accepted. When my parents moved to West LA, it was a different world.

I often look back on all of it because my whole life and career have been based upon that change. My first book, which ended up being a best-seller, was about my new high school in LA. The truth is I could not have written a similar book about my old high school back in San Diego. The LA high school had been selected by *Time* magazine as part of a cover story on American youth. Looking at that article ten years later gave me the idea to do *What Really Happened to the Class of '65?* That was my class at Palisades High School in West LA. I was motivated to write the book in part because of my position as an outsider looking in at this peculiar high school world. At the time it was happening, however, this fourteen-year-old was resisting, screaming, protesting, and angry.

The same kind of thing happened with my divorce. I got

married at twenty-three and then went through a divorce eleven years later. Thank God there were no children involved. I emphatically didn't want the divorce, wasn't prepared to handle it, and it took me by surprise. I had a typical arrogant male attitude—"How could anyone be leaving me?" I thought we had such a perfect marriage. In retrospect we didn't. At the time, I felt, "This is a train wreck and I'm crawling out of the wreckage." However, literally within weeks after my ex-wife left me, I met Diane. I don't want to sound corny about it, but every day since has been sunshine. I would never have known what I had missed in life had I not made Diane's acquaintance and had the inestimable privilege of marrying her. We've just celebrated our tenth anniversary. My ex-wife and I had hoped to have children and it just didn't happen. Diane got pregnant fairly shortly after we were married.

I had a friend who had been divorced and very happily remarried; he took me for a walk around the block one night during the first week I was alone. He said, "Look, keep in mind that 99 percent of the time, divorce is the first act towards a happy marriage." He gave me the statistics, which are quite impressive. Most people who go through a first divorce do get remarried. Most of them rate their second marriage as better than the first. Shaw said, "Second marriage is a great triumph of hope over experience."

CHANGE IS INEVITABLE

Courage is one of those things that you can recognize in other people. Maybe you can recognize it in yourself in retrospect. I don't think courage is a quality that we're ever conscious of when we're doing something courageous. I don't think people on the battlefield say, "I'm now going to be courageous. I'm going to be brave." They just do what they have to do. I don't think that people in points of moral confusion who stand up and take risks say, "Look at me now, I'm going to do something courageous."

E. M. Forster writes in *Where Angels Fear to Tread,* "Death destroys a man, but knowledge of death saves him." The recognition that our time is limited, that change is inevitable, that change is a basic principle of life, is our salvation. We change to come into this world, we change to go out of it, and we change every moment in between. That knowledge is the saving grace we have as human beings.

The phrase "having it all" is really destructive to people's happiness. No one can have it all. Human beings have problems. Part of our legacy as human beings is a certain amount of trouble, worries—the Yiddish word is *tsouris*. I must have said to Diane twenty or thirty times how fortunate we are that our daily dose of *tsouris* comes not through our children or each other. I see the faces of my children and my wife and I think, how fortunate I am.

One of the things I've tried to learn from Judaism and from my wife is that when you think of yourself or anybody else "in their glory," that's this moment, that's right now. That's me at this very moment looking out at an absolutely gorgeous spring day where everything is greener in California than I can ever remember because of the tremendous rains we had here, holding my little boy, who has buried his little blond head on my shoulder and is fiddling with my neck right now. The springer spaniel puppy, who's just turned six months old, has put his head on my foot. I'm middle-aged, I'm forty-six, I'm "in my glory." This is the moment; this is it.

CULTIVATING AN ATTITUDE OF GRATITUDE

Gratitude, it seems to me, is the absolute key to coping with change. All you need is that one word, that concept. When you look in the mirror, feel grateful for those gray hairs. We all have so many reasons for total and profound gratitude. We're the envy of the world, and yet our gratitude is so seldom expressed. Expressing gratitude for every moment, for this moment in which we are in our glory, seems to me the one most reliable, uplifting, and enriching way to accept and deal with change.

—*Michael Medved*

༄

Attitudes are more important than facts.

—KARL MENNINGER

Focusing on the negative brings fear, worry, anger, and self-pity. Dwelling in a state of gratitude and love promotes feelings of security, calm, optimism, and success.

Some years ago I was angry and frustrated with my lack of success in finding sponsors for a new show I was trying to produce. I called a close friend and asked him for his advice on whether I should send out more proposals to potential sponsors. "How many have you sent out already?" he asked. "I guess about seventy," I said. "How much money have you raised?" he asked. "Nothing so far," I answered. I'll never forget his response: "Well, do what you think is right, but I think the answer is NO."

He went on to say that I had given it my best shot, had come up empty-handed, and the timing for the project didn't appear to be NOW. He suggested I set the project aside for a while—not give up on it forever—and write another book. I did. A year later I went back to the project and within six weeks of pitching the program, I received a pledge of full sponsorship for a year. When the answer is clearly "NO," it's time to bite the bullet and let go. That's very easy to say; it's a hard lesson to learn.

Change is the law of life. Those who look only to the past or present are certain to miss the future.

—JOHN F. KENNEDY

∾

Only in retrospect do we clearly see that one thing in life leads to another. Our goals and efforts to attain them surely matter. Proceed with confidence and positive expectations but be willing to accept the results—whatever they may be. Dance legend **Judith Jamison** reflects on her philosophy of life:

I Put the Past Where It Needs to Be

MY LIFE HAS BEEN GOING IN A CERTAIN ORDER AND I HAVE very little to do with it. My parents put me in dancing school and I loved it. I was scared to death at my first performance. Nobody tells you that when the curtain goes up and all the lights are in your eyes, you won't be able to see. But there was a big audience response and I thought, "Oh, this is kind of nice," even though I was a nervous wreck. Then I got the hang of it and got very serious about dancing.

I studied dancing through the age of seventeen and then went off to Fisk University. My parents wanted me to go and Fisk offered me a scholarship. There was a dance club, but I'd been dancing all my life, so that wasn't enough. I said, "I need to go to a school where I can dance," and I ended up going to the University of the Arts back in Philadelphia, which was really turning out teachers, not dancers. The goal was to get your degree and join a faculty someplace. I didn't know what my goal was, but it wasn't that. So I just kept taking classes and Agnes de Mille, who was teaching a master class, saw me dance and invited me to do a ballet for her with the American Ballet Theater at Lincoln Center.

After that ended I worked at the World's Fair pushing buttons on the log-flume ride. Then, all of a sudden, I was in an audition for Harry Belafonte. I was dressed in classic tights and was a very pristine ballerina. Everyone else had on fishnet tights, stiletto heels, and wigs and lashes that would cause a hurricane. I was terrible. But Alvin Ailey was sitting on the steps and I didn't know he was there. I went right past him to a phone to call my mother for some encouraging words. Three days later Alvin called me and said, "Join my company, please."

Alvin Ailey revolutionized dance in America. As a principal dancer in his company, I made a contribution to what he did. He changed dance not only for the audience but for the dancers too. Alvin brought a humanity to dance that wasn't there before. He was saying dance is a wonderful tapestry in which everybody can participate. He also changed the way dancers think about dance.

Because of him, they understand they must bring who they are as people to the stage and not just do a bunch of steps.

As an artistic director now myself, I've come full circle. I see myself on the other side today and I recall Alvin looking at me back then the way I look at dancers now. Nothing has changed in that regard. The way Alvin loved us is the way I love my dancers today.

USE FEAR TO PROPEL YOU

I am here and I'm dealing with the present. Sometimes, I look back and I marvel. What has been going on in my life is overwhelming. I say, "Thank you." I put the past where it needs to be so I can continue to change, to make steps, to keep going forward. I don't rest on, "God, I've come a long way."

Part of what makes my life so exciting is the innocence I put on myself. There are some things I don't know and other things I don't want to know. I'm not carrying any extra baggage with me, so it clears a path and I can do what I have to do. Thank God I have a sense of humor. I have to laugh at myself a lot. Otherwise I think I would implode.

I lost my Dad just days before we opened in New York. I've now lost both of my parents. What were they here for in the first place? Wasn't it to plant my feet on the ground? Did I come this far to fall apart? Those transitional situations punch you in the stomach and knock the wind out of you. Sometimes I need that in my life to get along. If you have fear about what the next thing is, don't let it traumatize you. The fear should propel you.

DON'T BE AFRAID TO FALL

I just had auditions. One hundred men showed up for the audition; I needed one. One hundred and sixty women came to the audition; I wanted two. So they get nervous. I tell them to breathe and I say, "Fall, but show me that you've got something going for you, show me who you are." That involves taking it to the max. So all of a sudden you're down on the floor even with all your training. So what? Get up. A person whose life has no falls? I can't imagine that. I've had many falls myself. Don't be afraid to fall.

We've all been dancing since the beginning of time. We're always in motion, even if we think we're not. If you feel static, then you've got a problem. If I'm dissatisfied with something or not accomplishing what I want to, the first words that come out of my mouth are, "I need a change."

—*Judith Jamison*

∾

Life is either a daring adventure or nothing. To keep our faces toward change and behave like free spirits in the presence of fate is strength undefeatable.

—HELEN KELLER

Most change involves loss and that can include losing material things. I've made money and lost it; I've had to move from places I loved living in; and I've been let go from several broadcasting jobs. Program directors and station managers change schedules, cancel shows, or replace talent. Looking back, those experiences hurt like hell. When they happened, it felt as if my world ended. A couple of times it took many months for me to get over my humiliation and hurt pride, work through my anger, and face my fear about the future. In bad times I relied on friends and family for moral and financial support.

I know the pain of those on the receiving end of the brutal news of job termination. In this age of corporate "downsizing," automation, and forced early retirement, too many good people have lost their jobs though no fault of their own.

∾

Men, unfortunately, seem to invest too much in what we do and what we have as opposed to who we are. Consequently, when the external validation of a job or possessions is gone, we are doubly lost. **Rabbi Harold White** relates a unique personal experience with material loss, change, and inner value:

RECYCLE YOURSELF

I OFTEN TAKE A LONG WALK IN THE MORNING. IT'S A REAL turn-on because I can identify the various shrubs, trees, flowers, and birds that I see along the way. My students ask, "What does that all mean?" I tell them that what it means for me is that life unfolds daily moment by moment. I learned that from a wonderful teacher I had, the late Abraham Joshua Heschel, at the Jewish Theological Seminary of America in New York City. Rabbi Heschel said that what was needed most in the world was a sense of wonder, a sense of radical amazement, a sense of surprise. Looking at life that way has kept me very young, more than anything else. People say, "You're young because you've dealt with college students for twenty-five years." No. What's kept me young is the attitude that life constantly unfolds and offers something new every moment.

Young people are very directed and they plan their lives out with long-range goals; as a result, they burn out easily. Many young people are also very bored. They don't know how to take life a day at a time. That's terribly important.

I used to be the way they are. When I was younger, I programmed my life in such a way that at thirty-five I wanted to be here and at forty I wanted to be there and at fifty I wanted to be in some other place. I don't do that anymore. One of the wonderful things about growing older is the ability to let go of that long-range programming and enjoy life as it comes.

In my younger years I was a collector. I met many interesting people. I collected art, I collected antiques. I traveled a great deal and took many photographs. One evening someone said to me at a dinner party, "Rabbi, you must be an interesting person because of the art and the antiques you've collected and the people you know." I said, "I would rather you look at me not knowing anything about these things which are ancillary to me and say, 'Indeed Rabbi, you're an interesting man.'"

Something tragic happened shortly thereafter. I owned a

house in the country and it burned down. My entire home—
and all of my art and antiques—went up in smoke. Yet I felt
liberated. It was as if I had been cleansed by fire. No longer did I
have to be known by those things which were external to me.
Now I could be identified by who I was. I tell young people,
"Don't seek an identity through that which is external. Look
inside."

Probably the course I like teaching most is Job. Prior to the
beginning of the tragedy, Job is judged by his sheep, his cattle,
his children, and his wealth. Job loses all and he must turn
inward. At the very end of the drama, Job says to God, "I repent:
I know that I am but dust and ashes." Job reaches a basic
humility. In turning inward, Job finds himself.

I can pride myself on my articulation, but that is an extension
of my ego. I tell my students, "I'm best when I'm not articulate,
I'm best when I can't find the words." In fact, the most
profound moments of my life are those when I really can't
express myself and I have to remain in silence. According to Dr.
Heschel, the response to the confrontation of the Holy Spirit is
not to wax eloquent, but to say "Wow!" and think "That's
wonderful!"

The people who are fascinating to me are people who are
interested in discovering themselves, recycling themselves, and
growing.

—Rabbi Harold White

∽

Delighting in the adventure that change produces is
characteristic of those who can approach change with optimism. A positive attitude make change a pleasant experience
for actress **Kelly McGillis:**

CHANGE IS AN OPPORTUNITY

I SEE CHANGE AS EXCITING—AN OPPORTUNITY TO BE EM-
braced. I may have come to that way of thinking because of what

I do for a living. Being an actress and traveling so much, I'm confronted with change every time I start a new job. It also has to do with my outlook on life. I believe I can perceive the world either negatively or positively—welcome each moment, or run away from it.

For the most part New York had been home, but when I met my husband, Fred, I was working and on the road. We moved to California for a while when I got pregnant, then we lived in Florida for several years, and now we're in Washington. I like moving. I like to change. If I'm in one place too long, I tend to stagnate because I'm not challenged. It's my creative side coming out. Each time we moved, we both enjoyed it. We look forward to making new friends and trying to assimilate into a new community. It's a little bit difficult with two children, but our kids seem to be pretty used to it since they've been all over the world with us already. Kids have no problem making friends and we make friends with their parents.

Sure I miss my own friends, but we live in an age of technology and airplanes: nobody is too far away. Most of my good friends don't live anywhere near me anyway. They live in California, New York, Vermont, and Canada. Most of those friendships take place on the telephone and through letters, visits, and vacations. Although I like to have a sense of community where I live, my friends are my family. My best friend is my husband and my two next closest friends are my children.

The most anxiety-ridden part of moving is finding a place to live that we can make work for us. This move to Washington was great fun. We had a lot of boxes in storage because we lived in a small house in Key West. It's been wonderful to open those boxes, find things I had forgotten about, and put them around the house here. I have such a sense of familiarity with those objects that it doesn't matter where I am. A book that means something to me, a special photograph, or some beautiful drawing paper that a friend gave to me all create wonderful memories that I bring with me.

Houses are transitory. If I had the attitude "I have to live in this house for the rest of my life," I'd be living in the past. I choose to view change as a wonderful learning process that will take me to the next level of my personal growth.

Life is about change. Nothing is constant. It's continually

evolving. Look at the cycle of the seasons. We're a part of that natural balance too. It's egotistical and narcissistic of some human beings to think they're not part of nature.

I have a strong spiritual life and I'm fascinated with theological dogma. A lot in Buddhism, Christianity, and Judaism has been helpful to me in how I look at life.

Buddhist ideology teaches living in the moment, in the here and now, not in the past or future, and living each moment to its fullest. It's a difficult thing to do and I have trouble with it because I have children and worry about their future.

I've had dramatic change happen in my life because of both terrible events and wonderful events. The tragic events have been the more difficult to deal with, of course, but they have not been insurmountable. Out of those adversities I learned the most, grew the most, and gathered a more positive outlook on life. Even though the journey may have been dark at times, there always was tremendous light. Most of it centers on having faith. I believe in God and I believe that things in life work out the way they're supposed to.

As a parent one of the lessons I'd like to pass along to my children is not to be afraid of change. Change ultimately is a good thing: we can't stay where we are forever. We shouldn't allow fear to interrupt growth or make us stop living. My children must have learned some of that already because when we moved here—away from the house in which they grew up, their friends and family—it wasn't difficult for them at all. They were not dwelling in that past.

Their example was a wonderful lesson for me. No matter where I am, all I have to do is to live in the present moment and enjoy the experience.

—Kelly McGillis

∾

He knows not his own strength that hath not met adversity.

—BEN JONSON

∾

Perhaps a current relationship, job, or person is causing you unhappiness. That hurt may motivate you to try to bring about a healthier and happier situation in many ways. However, sometimes the only option is the door and it's necessary to say "I'm leaving," "I quit," or "I must end this." **Liz M.** tells us about such a circumstance in her own life. Many of us can relate to her story:

TRUST THE PROCESS

I WAS ONCE TOLD A STORY ABOUT A MAN SWIMMING ACROSS a pond. He had a rock in his hand and as he tried to swim, he was sinking both under the weight of the rock and because he could use only one hand to pull himself through the water. People gathered around the pond and they watched him as he began to dip under the water, coughing as he emerged.

"Drop the rock!" someone shouted. But the man just kept lurching through the water. Soon, he was splashing and beginning to sink. "Drop the rock!" someone screamed more loudly, in case the man couldn't hear. But the man didn't drop the rock and he started to go down and stay down. "Please," everyone shouted. "Please, drop the rock or you will drown!" The man looked once at the shore and right before he disappeared from sight forever, he answered, "I can't! It's mine."

I will swallow many mouthfuls of water before I am willing to change. The easiest changes for me are the ones in which fate lands on top of me like some metaphoric piano and my job lies simply in accepting and adjusting. Motherhood happened that way, unplanned but unparalleled. My mother's death, too, involved no decisions on my part. Mourning and grief and altered circumstance all arrived in succession without my instigation.

But when it comes to making a voluntary change, I will endure the worst circumstances, suffer the most miserable fools, swallow the bitterest anger, nurse the sharpest resentments. I will wear clothes a size too small, glasses a prescription too weak, shoes beyond the cobbler's aid, just to preserve my comfort with the devil I know. I'll make a contract with misery if there is just a whiff of the promise that I can control the outcome of events. Until I can't.

The day inevitably comes when the part of me that wants health more than sickness, or joy more than sorrow, or serenity more than turmoil wakes up and demands I pay attention. Finally, I am willing to try something different, mostly because the pain has become too much even for me to continue. Sinking is the only alternative. Then, and only then, do I surrender.

But surrender marks only the starting point in the process. One day a few months ago I was at work and as I sat in a meeting with a man who had dedicated himself to neutralizing my position in our company, I looked out the window and saw the spring sun wash over a baby in a stroller who was crossing the street a few stories below. I saw my alternatives in an instant; I could stay and fight for my job or I could leave and push my baby through the spring air. Yes, I had to work and contribute to paying expenses, but I could find something else to do. Something less high-powered, something less tense.

I went home and told my husband that after months of complaining and anguish I felt it was time to call it quits at the job. He was thrilled. He'd been upset by my struggle to maintain the job and bored with my constant complaints. He backed me 100 percent.

I had no excuses now. Supported, freed, surrendered. Then, I panicked. Fear bored into my heart like a hungry worm in an apple, gnawing through my resolve and faith. I turned in on myself and began second-guessing my decision. I bargained, reasoned, and equivocated. I projected poverty, disgrace, and, in the corner of my ears, I heard the snickers of those who I just knew had always wished me ill. What had happened to my beautiful vision of the future?

I had been sober long enough to know self-centered fear when I saw it—even when the canvas was my own mirror. I also know that the first weapon I pick up against fear is my mind—which is like fighting a dragon with a toothpick. My mind cannot fix my mind and my fearful mind surely can't wipe out my fear. So I turned first to my sponsor and then to my husband.

My sponsor helped me with an inventory and my husband with my self-obsession. It's hard to have a happy marriage when one person is a lunatic. I wore out his patience, which brought me to my senses. But I still needed more.

After a hiatus of several years, I went back to a therapist looking for someone to help organize the clutter of fears and hopes. And I talked to others who had dropped out of the high-powered career world and who still had arms and legs and lives intact.

Yet I continued to cling to my fears. I just knew in my heart of hearts that we couldn't afford to live without my income. This sure knowledge threatened to sink me even more than the politics of the job I was leaving. Finally, I prayed. I had prayed for direction and seen a child's baby carriage. Finally, I realized I just had to pray for that simple promise offered in the third step: that I could be taken care of if I would just trust the process.

It all came down to an attitude of trust and conviction of faith. The actual steps of change aren't steep; they are easy to take. But I needed my husband, my program, and my God to be comfortable and secure as I stepped out into the unknown.

—Liz M.

∽

We live in an incredibly fast world. We are assaulted with change in every aspect of our lives. The pace is dizzying and the stress can be overwhelming. A concerned psychoanalyst **Theodore Isaac Rubin** says that because of all this external activity, personal change may be much more difficult to achieve. Dr. Rubin says that while humans are adaptable, "Nowadays, you have to have courage to change, to move:"

OUR CULTURE IS SPINNING

THE EARLY GREEKS REALIZED THAT PEOPLE ARE DRIVEN IN two directions. On one hand they want to maintain a status quo, because the status quo gives them a sense of identity, and on the other hand they really have an urge to change, to move. In the last several hundred years there's been a traditional culture in which we stand still. Unfortunately, we're beginning to have a culture of movement where people want to move just for the sake of moving. The result is that some institutions are being neutralized and others are crumbling. Nowadays a great many people are developing personalities that almost require constant change in order for them to feel comfortable.

The very progress we've made in electronics, computers, and television has made for a devaluation of stasis, of things remaining the same. The rate at which information is offered is so rapid that there is almost no point of absorbing anything. That's why intellectual enterprise is devalued. People feel that everything exists in short bytes of time. When businessmen talk about plans for the future, they don't mean a year or two, they mean three or four weeks.

A camera salesman was complaining to me recently that he buys cameras of a particular make and six weeks later the manufacturer is putting out a new camera that's more advanced than the ones he's still trying to sell. The rate of change itself has increased incredibly in all respects. This makes for an enormous change in terms of personalities. Relationships are fragmented. People think if it takes a long time, it's not worth anything. On television you see a leader who's very important and they cut him off after two minutes.

HAPPINESS IS A KIND OF INNER PEACE

It's hard to be happy in a society that confuses high stimulation with happiness. Forty years ago, do you think you could have convinced anybody to go bungee jumping? Do you think you could have convinced people to go parachuting for fun? Or go hotdogging down a ski slope doing three somersaults before you hit the snow? Risking your life is seen as a form of happiness.

Happiness is a kind of inner peace and we confuse inner peace with deadness. On prime-time TV, nothing is brutal enough. Tune in your average talk show, and one is more grotesque than the other. Do we really have this many dysfunctional families in the United States? Our values are twisted, most relationships are adversarial, and too many people are worried about getting their piece of the action. The demise of the educational system of the United States is a demise of a whole culture.

There is a tremendous dissatisfaction with the quality of people's lives. If this were not true, we wouldn't have so much clinical depression. We wouldn't have so many teenagers committing suicide. We wouldn't have the breakup of relationships on every level.

It's not just divorce—friendships are no longer what they were. Twenty years ago, you invited friends to the house. That's no longer true. Now we see each other in a restaurant where we can't talk because there is so much noise. The social order is such that people have gotten more distant from each other. In this technological world people will sit in their houses and not do anything.

Our culture is spinning. As a consequence, we have considerable anxiety over which way to turn and we are terrified of the unfamiliar. It's instinctual; it certainly exists among all other animals and it exists among humans. However, I see people who would rather hang on to a whole set of things that produce depression than feel better by changing. They're afraid of what's new, and adaptation takes *courage*.

—Theodore Isaac Rubin, M.D.

∾

MEDITATION

If there is nothing in your life to cry about, if there is nothing in your life to complain about, if there is nothing in your life to yell about, you must be out of touch. We must all feel and know the pain of humanity. The free space that God leads us into is to feel the full spectrum, from great exaltation and joy, to the pain of mourning and dying and suffering. It's called the Paschal mystery. The totally free person is one who can feel all of it and not be afraid of any of it.

—FATHER RICHARD ROHR, O.F.M., IN *RADICAL GRACE*

REFLECTION

The good word for today is CHANGE. One thing that we can always depend on in this life is change. Nothing ever stays the same for very long. The tree, in just standing there being a tree, also changes. Just look about and you will observe this phenomenon.

Actually change is a blessing. We tend to want things to stay the same. We prefer not to move out of the neighborhood in which we have lived for a long time. We are saddened when someone dies and leaves our life experience.

But think, what would life be like if everything remained the same? There would be no progress. We would still be living in caves.

So today, think about change and think about it as a great blessing. It is through change that we develop and become finer people. It is through change that we move into new and exciting experiences. It is through change that life is an adventure rather than a bore.

Welcome change. See it as an opportunity to better use the talents that you have. Tell yourself, "Doors are opening into new and wonderful experiences for me."

Love the changes that come into your life.

—AMALIE H. FRANK, MINISTER
Community on the Hill, Washington, D.C.

EXERCISE: TAKING A GRATITUDE WALK

You may be going through a change right now that hurts. When you are feeling angry, hopeless, upset, or fearful—all predictable feelings associated with change, gratitude may pull you through. When I was so frustrated looking for sponsors for my television series and coming up empty-handed, a friend suggested that I take a "gratitude walk." He explained that the idea was to get out and breathe some fresh air, relieve the stress through exercise, and force myself to focus on all the good things I had going on in my life at that moment. He told me to begin "counting my blessings" with the fact that I had a roof over my head, feet to walk on, and eyes to see where I was going. Those three made for a pretty impressive start. If you're struggling with accepting change you don't want, you might try a gratitude walk yourself.

The first time I ever tried it, I actually counted the positives in my life on my fingers as I walked. I got to sixty-four things for which I was grateful without pausing. I remember coming back to my apartment and tossing my keys on the desk. They landed next to my list of sponsor rejections. After looking at the list and weighing it against my blessings, I saw that the balance was clearly in my favor. That's usually the case.

∾

There is a time for departure even when there's no certain place to go.

—TENNESSEE WILLIAMS

Change is at once the death of that which was before.

—LUCRETIUS

3. ACTION

The test of any man lies in action.

—PINDAR

Change means movement. Movement means friction.

—SAUL ALINSKY

PAIN AND SUFFERING MAY BE LIFE'S WAYS OF SOFTENING US up for change. We are wise if we let them lead us. Just as fear can alert us to impending danger and protect us from harm, pain can also serve as a positive warning signal. Doctors are trained in medical school to look at pain as a symptom. They are specifically taught *not* to treat the symptom but to use it to discover the real cause of the pain. After the diagnosis, it is hoped, the correct treatment will be prescribed. While physical pain may send us to a doctor or hospital, mental or emotional pain should prompt us to seek out a friend, family member, mentor, support group, therapist, or member of the clergy for help.

Painful emotional symptoms tell us our lives need to change. Unhappiness, sleeplessness, loss of weight, anxiety, headaches, fear, feeling "stressed out," sudden anger, addictions, and compulsive behaviors are all symptoms and signals that should not be ignored. The more pain and suffering, the more we should acknowledge some problem or situation that needs to be changed.

We may have actually invited into our lives the troubles that are causing us grief. We may be forced to abandon goals, break off a relationship, or make radical changes in our daily activities. We may need to change our own actions and attitudes to bring about peace of mind. We may need to accept some unchangeable situation or person exactly as is. Perhaps we've created a mess for ourselves because of some glaring character defect or shortcoming such as anger, dishonesty, or grandiosity. The courage to change—**the strength to take action in the face of fear, danger, or hardship**—can apply to all kinds of situations: getting married, beginning a new job, quitting smoking, leaving an abusive relationship, accepting a difficult in-law, offering forgiveness, learning patience.

Change is part of the human landscape and random change is always around the corner. There is nothing we can do about it. It *happens to* us, from the outside in. A parent dies, a company downsizes, a friend moves away. This kind of change calls for huge doses of acceptance, activity, and gratitude for what stays in our life—and for realizing that time heals.

The other kind of change is voluntary, from the inside out. This is change we choose: joining a gym, switching careers, buying a house. Since we make it happen, we have some control over the timing and the process. We know what kind of change we're trying to produce and the goal we want to accomplish. However, even voluntary change, such as starting a weight loss program, going back to school, or seeking a new job, triggers fear and stress.

∾

All of the behavioral professionals agree: **don't attempt major change alone.** Enlist some help to assist you through the change you want or need to make. There will be plenty of times when you will doubt your decision, waver in your resolve, or fall backward once the change process starts. So the first action step is to get help. This is enormously empowering. You won't regret having an ally as you successfully move toward your goal. Psychologist **Albert Ellis** says that although people demand that change be easy, it isn't:

CHANGE IS HARD

THE MAIN REASON PEOPLE STAY IN JOBS THEY HATE, RELA-tionships that are abusive, friendships that are critical, and continue to smoke and drink addictively is low frustration tolerance—things must be easy. They say to themselves, "Even though it's desirable for me to change in the long run, it's going to be very hard in the short run, and therefore I'll do it tomorrow, I'll do it tomorrow, I'll do it tomorrow."

The other reason for procrastinating about change is fear of failure. "If I change, I must have a guarantee that it will work out, everything will be fine, I will succeed, and people will love me. Since I don't have that guarantee, particularly in a new situation, I'll do it tomorrow or I won't do it at all."

A subheading under the fear of failure is fear of disapproval, which means that if you leave the drunk you're married to and marry another person, she or he may not love you enough; or if you leave your job, the new boss may get on to you. You never have a guarantee that the people in those new situations will care for you as much as people around you do right now, including the one who is beating you.

It is very important for someone who's contemplating change to understand the "why" of all this. People had better see that they believe, "I must do well, I must be approved of and things and conditions must be the way I want them to be immediately." They'll rarely change without seeing that they are unrealistically demanding conditions that rarely exist. Once they give up those demands, it still will be hard to change because they are habituated to their current scene. It will also be difficult to change unless they acknowledge that they are really demanding that change be easy.

Now, it is human to stick with what is known. You choose to drive a car with or without a stick shift. You know it, it's easy. You're habituated to it. You're successful. Most of the things you do you know how to handle. People do what comes easy and what's guaranteed rather than what's hard even though it would give them even greater pleasure and greater success down the road. Most people are short-range hedonists. They go for the pleasure of the moment rather than look into the future.

Most people change when forced to—when conditions or people put a gun to their heads and make them change. The majority of alcoholics stop without AA or without therapy because life becomes too painful. The majority of smokers quit once they get emphysema or something close to it. I have one client who's been smoking for forty-five years. He's already got asthma and he can hardly walk up one flight of stairs. His doctor showed him he's going to kill himself. So pain motivates him and other people to change. Just focusing on the thought of the pain can also kick people into gear to change.

—*Albert Ellis, Ph.D.*

❧

One starts an action
Simply because one must do Something

—T. S. ELIOT

Today, I know when I *have* to change. Usually some reoccurring discomfort or pain tells me that it's time. When the evidence has broken through my denial and the handwriting on the wall tells me that change is in the air, I know I cannot stay where I am. Even though I may procrastinate, I must act. It's only a matter of time.

It wasn't always so simple for me. I used to have to be dragged kicking and screaming by those closest to me—skillful professionals included—to begin to understand that some change was called for; and even then, I would argue with them and not follow their advice. I thought if I worked the problem harder or if I just tried to do things another way, I could get a different result. Of course, I couldn't and didn't.

Certain signals tell me when to take action, when to let go, when to get out, when to move on, when to change. I've learned to respect those warning signs and trust my feelings. Most of the time, after giving troublesome situations my best shot, I'm now able to act in a way that saves me wear and tear, effort, energy, and sleepless nights. Usually what I'm trying so hard to protect is my security, sometimes my total sense of self. By being willing to change when change is called for, I become freer and more secure in the long run.

❧

The willingness to make the "hardest decision" of her life

and set out on a different course of action brought about lasting and personal rewards for business executive **Georgette Mosbacher:**

TAKE THAT FIRST STEP

TAPED TO MY DESK IS A NOTE CARD WITH THE QUOTATION from Anaïs Nin: "Life expands or shrinks in direct proportion to one's courage." I keep it on my desk to remind me of the rich rewards of change. Ironically, life is continual change and change is the force that continues life. What I know deep in my heart is that the greatest lessons of my life and my greatest skills are a direct result of changes that occurred with or without my choice.

My father was killed by a drunk driver when I was a child. My mother had only a high school education and no work experience. Because she was left with four children, some people voiced concern that we children might have to be split up. Over my dead body was that going to happen. Even though I was only seven years old and the eldest of four children, I resolved the very night of my father's death that I would do whatever it took to keep us all together.

The death of my father turned our family upside down. But we all pitched in; my mother, my brother and sister and I did what we could do. I took over the care of the house and the kids and continued to do so throughout junior high and high school. I worked every kind of job you can imagine and held on tight to my dreams. From that experience, I learned that life is not certain, there are no guarantees, and the status quo is only momentary. Most importantly, I learned I can stand tall and straight and succeed even in the deepest, roughest waters.

Sometimes the path of change is not clear. I was married to an abusive alcoholic who also happened to be my boss. I was trapped in a horrible situation that threatened my emotional well-being and physical safety. I knew I had to get out of that marriage but I was terrified—if I left my husband, I'd lose my job, my income, my friends, my contacts, my place in the world.

Finally, one night, I made the hardest decision of my life—I left him. He'd punched me hard in the face after several drinks. I grabbed my purse and I ran out into the night bleeding from my nose, my cheek swelling fast. Later, when I walked out of the emergency room, I stepped into the center of my own life. I lost everything when I divorced him, but I secured the best thing life has to offer—possession of my own life.

Every change toughens you. Fear is only fear. That's all it is. Fear of failure and fear of the unknown are always defeated by faith. Having faith in yourself, in the process of change and in the new direction that change sets, will reveal your own inner core of steel.

Changes that occur whether it's your choice or not require the same effort. Taking that first step to overcome fear with faith and commitment will propel you forward. The first step is always in the right direction. You put one foot in front of the other and all the other steps become easier.

The benefits that change brings last your whole life. When you rise to the occasion to face the challenges of unwanted change, you do new things you thought you couldn't do. Change is such a nifty teacher. Suddenly, your hidden talents and skills are laid out before you like priceless treasures. Navigating down the road of wanted change, you become all the proof you need.

Strangely, change can bring profound security and happiness. Security and happiness are never external; they are always with you because they are inside you. Security and happiness come when you take control of your life and take the risks necessary to make your dreams come true.

My husband, Robert, is an avid and accomplished sailor. Every day I luxuriate in the gift of life-lessons that I've learned sailing with him. The first lesson I learned is that the wind changes all the time. The seas can be calm and smooth and they can become furious. Sometimes you can prepare for a wind change, but more often, you can be caught in the grip of a ghost-storm that sneaks up behind you, catching you unaware and unprepared. Robert has taught me that the critical moment for a sailor is when you decide either to take the helm during the storm or to go below deck.

Storms can whip up suddenly and they can move in slowly, but storms always pass. And suddenly, you find yourself wrapped in the most beautiful sunset you've ever seen. You guided the boat through the darkest hour and you were still at the helm when the sun burst through the clouds and warmed your face. That is the beauty of change.

—*Georgette Mosbacher*

∾

Discomfort and dis-ease signal a call to action. To address the pain, something must happen either externally in the way of action or internally through acceptance—or perhaps a combination of both. Insight begins the change process. Deciding on a course of action, making a commitment, taking steps toward the goal, and finally making the change are all part of the package. Only in hindsight do we see that there is a very predictable formula to change.

Positive results may come quickly or slowly. However, some benefits—including relief from anxiety, the satisfaction of moving, and an enhanced sense of self-worth—will be felt immediately. Those feelings will be pleasurable and empowering. And remember, every time we navigate a change, it becomes another building block for greater confidence in handling the next change. Change can be learned like anything else.

∾

Some of us have pushed life to the max and endangered our lives in the process. A brush with ruin, defeat, or death gets our attention as nothing else can. Life in these circumstances demands *total* change as a price for another shot at life. Author **John Jakes** is unequivocal: "I didn't have an A or B choice; I had only one alternative:"

LIFE IS A PRETTY GOOD MOTIVATOR

THE SIGNIFICANT CHANGE IN MY LIFE OCCURRED AFTER I was hospitalized for a heart attack. I assume the heart attack was finally caused by twenty-plus years of high-level stress in the publishing business—cranking out books against deadlines and touring. I had a cholesterol problem for several years, and that was under control with medication, but I must say I had let myself get drastically out of shape. I was grossly overweight—by 40 or 50 pounds. My wife and I were on an 80 percent healthy diet but the other 20 percent was dangerous. It was the Saturday night desserts, when they bring out the chocolate tray at the restaurant and I'd say, "Well, why not?"

I went up to Antioch College in Yellow Springs, Ohio, at the end of July to teach at their writers' workshop. Actually, I took on too much extra duty, conferring with students, reading their manuscripts, and giving the keynote address. It was hectic, but it seemed enjoyable at the time.

When it was over, we went back into nearby Dayton, where we'd lived for a number of years, and spent Saturday with some of our closest friends. We went out to dinner that night, and for the first time in my life, as I parked at the restaurant, I locked the keys inside my rental car with the motor running. The stress bells were ringing pretty hard that night. We flew home the next day to Hilton Head Island and, as usual, I had a couple of drinks on the plane. I got back home feeling what I thought was severe indigestion. The pains persisted until about twelve-thirty at night, when I got up and put on my shorts and T-shirt. I almost got in the car to go to the hospital but the pain seemed to mitigate so I didn't.

I had things checked out by my doctor the following morning but he could find no evidence of a heart attack or any problems on the cardiogram. Of course, cardiograms aren't very good in showing heart damage. So, I went back home and lo and behold that night the pain started again. My wife, Rachel, drove me to the hospital at three A.M. An hour after I got to the emergency room they did some arcane blood tests and found that there had indeed been a heart attack.

I was very lucky. I learned afterward the devastating statistic that one third of all heart attack victims never get up off the floor. I was astounded. They shoved me into a hospital in Savannah, my cardiologist did an angioplasty, and it came out all right. Now, I'm well past the six-month critical relapse time for angioplasty.

After about a week, my wife and I took off and went to the mountains of North Carolina to an inn to figure out what the hell was going on, because this was the most significant event in our lives. It was very evident that things had to change. Almost every significant causal factor in heart damage had to change, and I had most of them. So, to begin, I went into a really good cardiac rehab program in our local hospital. The three-times-a-week graduated exercise program was electronically monitored. My wife and I immediately went on a no-fat diet or as close to it as you can get without becoming a hermit. Most importantly, I spent the fall not working very hard but sitting out on our dock on Calibogue Sound, looking at the water, enjoying the warm weather, and trying to figure out how I was going to change the stress level.

The only way I could make a change work was to tell myself, once and finally, there was no other option. I had no alternatives. I had to take another course or risk dying a long time before I wanted to. I didn't have an A or B choice; I had only one alternative.

The choice was between stupidity—continuing the kind of life I had let creep up on me—and doing what I knew I had to do. That seemed to work. I took a three-by-five Day-Glo red card and a big black marker and I wrote, stealing from the current Ford advertising campaign, "Job No. 1: Get Healed." That's on my desk at home and it's caused some fairly serious rethinking of my work burden. I don't intend to give up writing but I'm going to try to go a little more slowly or at least not let the inevitable business pressures get to me quite as much as they did. That decision that things had to change filtered down into my head in the two or three weeks after the hospitalization. The only way to make the change work was to realize there was no option. No way out. No multiple choice. Only one way.

A year ago if you had said, "Well John, you've got to exercise three days a week," I'd say, "Well, yeah, if I get my work done."

Now if I get my exercise done, I'll work. The health requirements now are first, and work comes next.

THE REWARDS OF CHANGE

I've had outstanding success, and hope played a big role in creating my new lifestyle. I've lost 50 pounds. My cholesterol has dropped 50 points, even though I'm still on medication. I think I have even succeeded in ratcheting down the internal pressure. I'll never conquer that completely, but at least I'm aware it's a problem. I seem calmer and less concerned by outside stresses. In one of the books I read, the very telling point was made that stress really comes not from outside events but our perceptions of those events and how we react to them. I have tried to apply that in my daily life. When I get in a traffic jam, it's not the traffic, it's me that's going to make it a heart pounder. That perception has had a calming effect on the day-to-day quality of my life.

I feel great about myself today because I don't have a belly on me. I've been forced to buy almost a completely new wardrobe in sizes that really look good, and I am physically stronger than I have been in twenty-five years. I can schlep bags through an airport as though they were feathers. I couldn't have done that twelve months ago. Several friends said to me, "You no longer have anything to prove, so quit worrying," and that attitude has helped me approach my work in a somewhat calmer way. When I have the kids and grandchildren around, I enjoy them more than I did before the episode. I'm not exactly thrilled that I had a heart attack, but nevertheless, I think it was a blessing in disguise. Life is a pretty good motivator.

—*John Jakes*

For some, the elevator is going down very fast and it is only a matter of on what floor we decide to get out. Unfortunately, for others of us it's a long and painful ride down before we hit the panic button and change.

∾

Much harder to initiate and sustain is action born out of a dream and a determination to do, to achieve, to be. This kind of action requires total dedication and commitment. Determination, willingness, and performing the work needed—as opposed to wishing, dreaming, and talking—create results and get you where you want to go. The enthusiasm and spirit of bestselling novelist **Mary Higgins Clark** shine as she recounts the story of her goals, efforts, early failures, and ultimate writing success:

HAVE FAITH IN YOURSELF

I WAS DETERMINED AS SOON AS WE WERE MARRIED TO learn how to be a professional writer. My husband Warren said, "Sure, but just don't break your heart." It took six years before I sold my first story, but I was sure I was going to make it. You have to have faith in yourself and you have to work at your craft. I had eleven stories in the mail by the time the first one sold.

Today people sometimes say to me, "I was the editor of the school paper and everyone said I was going to be a writer and I was planning on becoming a journalist and I got married but I know I could write a book and I will write one . . . when I learn the computer," or "when I get a nice quiet room," or "when the kids grow up," or "when I retire," or "when the dog dies." One set of excuses is replaced by the next. I say, "Stop right there. It is never going to happen." When they say they don't have time, I say, "Look, if you are a morning person, get up an hour before the rest of family; if you're a night person, stay up an hour later." You can make the time, even if you're very busy, if you really, truly want to write. The people who become professional writers not only have a talent, but a compulsion. They must write. They are not happy if they are not writing. There is a need, a hunger. You feel as though you haven't brushed your teeth if you are not working on something.

I was always writing. I sent out some short stories when I was in high school. I always kept a journal, which is something writers tend to do. I thought of myself as a short story writer; but during the sixties, when Warren died, and there was no market for short stories, I took a job writing radio shows. But I missed the printed word so much that I had to make that big decision to try a book. I told myself that a book was twenty short stories strung together with the same characters.

My first book went nowhere; I say it sold seventeen copies. But it was a triumph for me. It proved I could write a book and then I wanted to write one that would sell. I made the big decision to try suspense and I suddenly wandered into my pot of gold.

—*Mary Higgins Clark*

∾

There can be no acting or doing of any kind, till it be recognized that there is a thing to be done; the thing once recognized, doing in a thousand shapes becomes possible.

—THOMAS CARLYLE

∾

If there is a change you are wrestling with, get a piece of paper and a pen or pencil. **Dr. Albert Ellis** will guide you through a terrific exercise. I've used it several times myself. He says a daily review of what you write may be helpful in bringing about the results you desire. It was for me. Dr. Ellis also reveals the three basic irrational ideas that get in the way of change:

WRITE IT OUT

I ENCOURAGE CLIENTS OF MINE TO DO A COST/BENEFIT ratio and to write it out. Suppose you're smoking because you are focusing on the pleasures of smoking. You think about the pains with horror. Now if you write down all the negatives to smoking, of which there are about twenty—from the expense, to turning people off, to possible lung cancer—and you go over the negatives many times, you think them into your head instead of thinking them into the ground. Most people suppress them or are only vaguely aware of them. They don't focus on the negatives; they only focus on the immediate gratification of smoking. So you write down your list of disadvantages and make yourself go over those negatives five or ten times a day until you really believe they will happen—because they probably will. You can also list the pleasure of giving up smoking and the pains of continuing.

Suppose you want to change a bad characteristic or feeling, say anger or rage. You would put down the disadvantages of feeling the rage. You show yourself that the rage is going to give you high blood pressure or ulcers, or get you fired or a divorce. Remember, however, rage is a pleasure—that's why you don't want to give it up. Rage and anger are pleasurable because you get to put people down. "That son of a bitch is no damn good." So you—temporarily—feel better about yourself. Rage does you no good, however, so you'd focus on the harm you do to yourself and others.

THE BENEFITS OF THERAPY

Good therapy would teach you to change when you're screwing yourself, and therefore you'd better change *for you*. As a therapist I would give you unconditional acceptance and teach you there are three basic irrational ideas:

- I must do well or I'm no good.
- You must treat me well, or you're no damn good.
- Conditions must be easy or the world's no good.

There is never a reason for an absolute "must." No matter how desirable something is, you don't have to do it and people certainly don't have to treat you well or else they always would, which they obviously don't.

In therapy, I'd show you that most of your fears are self-generated, such as, "I will be no good if I fail" or "It would be awful if I lost my job." I'd show you what your nutty idea is and how to challenge it.

There is no way to change but work and practice, work and practice. You can't change just by saying, "Oh yes, that's right." You have to work your ass off to fight those "shoulds" and "musts." Push yourself and change your behavior while you are changing your thinking.

When you stay in a rotten situation or you're addicted to something, you're certainly not very effective. In the long run that behavior does you in. Change makes you more productive and more efficient; of course, in the long run, it enables you to enjoy life much, much more.

—*Albert Ellis*

The Serenity Prayer is a connecting thread in this book. Faced with a difficult situation at work, **Jan D.** offers a line-by-line interpretation of how she is working the prayer in her life right now:

CHANGE COMES THROUGH GOD'S GRACE

FOR ME, AND MANY RECOVERING ALCOHOLICS, THE SERENIty Prayer stands above all prayers. Here's how I'm using it now.

God grant me the serenity. My first request is to always ask for a peaceful state of mind (an attitude adjustment). If I am in turmoil, I cannot think or act clearly. Yoga, meditation, AA meetings, laughter, walking, talking with a close friend or therapist, retreats, theater, music, repeating the Serenity Prayer, and more laughs are a few of the ways to change my perception of any situation and calm my anxious mind.

To accept the things I cannot change. For over ten years I have worked as a public relations executive. Currently, I work for a boss whose style is my total opposite. We are oil and water. After a year, it's obvious to me we cannot work together. I have neither the stomach nor the nature for office politics. Her hardball approach to management has worn me and other staffers down. After numerous attempts, it became clear I could not resolve this. I hoped it might get better on its own. I went through different stages of surrender.

My first choice was to leave. *Flee* is actually a better description. Whether it was a relationship or a job, I always escaped. "Who needs it anyway!" I would say.

Here I stand today in sobriety in the midst of a dilemma. Should I leave a job I love, which provides me many benefits—financially and socially—because of a personality conflict. The advice of my AA friend, Tom I., was, "When you are in conflict, the first thing you must do is *nothing;* the second thing to do is *nothing rash;* and the last thing to do is just sit tight and *review the situation.*"

The courage to change the things I can. Why not be proactive instead of reactive? I enlisted a few trusted associates for their advice and help. I believe in our product, and what the company represents. If values and principles are similar, the chances of working problems through are better. Principles over personalities. Courage, timing, judgment. *We will intuitively know how handle situations which used to baffle us,* our AA literature tells us.

I do my homework. Through the help of associates, I develop a proposal, based on the current needs of the company. I line up my support. My recommendation for reassignment will not cost any money, nor will it cost anybody their job. I lobby some of the key executives. *Past experience* provides me the *courage to make changes.* I ask to be part of the solution rather than part of the problem.

Change comes through God's grace. Amazing grace. Grace comes unexpectedly. What we could not do for ourselves is being done for us, as the promises of AA predict.

As I write this story I do not know the outcome. I take it a day at a time. If circumstances remain the same, I will return again and again to the Serenity Prayer's simple message: First do nothing. Secondly, do nothing rash. And lastly, again review the situation.

And the wisdom to know the difference. "Wisdom," said one top CEO, "is nothing more than experience." When I am emotionally in turmoil, change cannot take place. When I believe I am being guided by a divine force for ultimate good, my fears subside.

I offer this from the famous unattributed poem, "Desiderata": *Whether or not it is clear to you, no doubt the universe is unfolding as it should.*

—*Jan D.*

∾

Marketing genius and businessman extraordinaire **Harvey Mackay** outlines the commitment necessary to achieve change, success, and the positive results that flow from it:

PRACTICE THE RIGHT CONCEPTS

A GOAL IS A DREAM WITH A DEADLINE. MEASURABLE, identifiable, attainable, specific, in writing. Pale ink is better than the most retentive memory, which means, write your goals down. I dreamed about being on *The New York Times* best-seller list. I wanted to join other successful authors. So what did I do? I sent my assistant down to the newsstand to buy *The New York Times*. She typed in *Swim with the Sharks Without Being Eaten Alive* on *The New York Times* best-seller list and pasted it up on my door. I looked at that for seven straight months, every morning and every evening. I was visualizing. I was believing in myself. And it happened. The book came out in 1988 and has sold 4 million copies in eighty countries, and has been translated into thirty languages. It's selling five thousand copies per week nine years later. I've always believed that whatever you want to accomplish, whatever your capacity is, you will reach it if you practice the right concepts. "Practice makes perfect" is not true. "Perfect practice makes perfect" is.

Let's take tennis. Let's say you play eight days a week or you practice eight days a week. If every time you hit the ball, you're pulling up, which is a weakness, you put a ceiling on how good you can become. So here we go. Number one, you have to have a good instructor and stay with him or her. Number two, get a little audiotape recorder and record everything that's said. I've had lessons for over twenty-five years and I still have the tapes. Number three, visualization is very important; ask the instructor to take pictures of you. Number four, ask the instructor for the best three books that have ever been written on tennis, both its mental and the physical aspects.

Want to be creative? Go around with creative people. Want to be a good runner? Go around with marathoners.

If you want to become a good tennis player, go around with good tennis players. Then enter some club tournaments. They're very important to get the idea of competition. And of course, it's essential to keep in good shape. Watch tennis tournaments on television. Go to tennis tournaments, and go with a pad. Write down your thoughts, because 50 percent of what you've heard you'll forget in three hours. That's what you do to become a good tennis player.

Whatever your capacity is, whether it's golf, tennis, public speaking, or selling, you will reach your capacity and you will be successful if you practice the right concepts over a long period of time. The ideas I've described—I've practiced them all. I have a mentor. I take the notes. I have pictures taken. I enter the tournaments. I'm lucky enough to have a number one ranking, and I'm playing the senior tennis circuit.

Most of all, I'm having a good time.

—*Harvey Mackay*

∾

EXERCISE

When you have a few minutes, grab paper and pencil and see what you come up with in the following exercise. It could produce some startling changes in your life. It did in mine.

FIFTY THINGS TO DO BEFORE I DIE

In a provocative article, a special to *The Washington Post* and published under the headline above, author Wendy Swallow Williams writes:

Most of us muddle through life, making compromises for the good of our families or our jobs, passing up opportunities, not taking time for what is really important to us. Building a list of 50 things you want to do before you die can help you concentrate your limited energies and resources on those things that matter. Just writing the list can help you sort through priorities. When I wrote my list I filled up the first twenty blanks quickly, but then began to think carefully before adding things that were not a driving need. When I looked at the list later I saw some startling things.

∽

Courage is only an accumulation of small steps.

—GEORGE KONRAD

4. ACCEPTANCE

Always fall in with what you're asked to accept. Take what is given, and make it over your way. My aim in life has always been to hold my own with whatever's going. Not against: with.

—ROBERT FROST

IF YOU ARE STRUGGLING WITH SOMETHING RIGHT NOW, it's probably because that something is not the way you want it to be. (That something could also be a someone.) It's human nature to want the world to go *our* way. Everybody does. Unfortunately, a great deal of life is getting a *no* answer to our wants and desires. Even though we know this is true, some of us try to control every detail of life and attempt to make other people and circumstances conform to our personal agenda.

Sooner or later we must accept life's reality that we can't change anyone—ever—and trying to change situations that can't be changed is even crazier. As much as I understand the theory, I often mistakenly believe that if I give the problem another dose of my very best willpower, tolerance, or hope, the situation will change and conform to what I want.

As far as this matter of trying to change what you can't, a bumper sticker I once saw addressed the right question: WHAT PART OF "NO" DON'T YOU UNDERSTAND? When we make unreasonable demands on ourselves and others and try to get the world to bend to our agenda by the force of will, we often create more, and more serious, conflicts.

Our worlds are very small. They consist of only a few places: where we live, work, play, and pray; and only a few people: our partner, family, circle of friends, co-workers, and acquaintances. To be truly happy, I've learned, I must accept my present circumstances as they are, accept myself as I am, and accept the people around me as they are. On top of all that, it's also necessary—though incredibly difficult—to accept that God's got a plan that is unfolding every day exactly as He wants. Our mission is to go where God wants us to go and do what He wants us to do. The headaches arise when our plan bangs heads with His plan. God's plan is usually obvious. When you are looking down an avenue and all the lights are green, that's a pretty good indication of where you should be headed. If things are not proceeding in a good orderly direction, if events overwhelm plans, if the lights are red; the answer is no and the solution is acceptance.

Things are often not going to go the way we want them to go, people are often not going to do what we want them to do, and we are often not going to get what we want to get. Anger, frustration, resentment, jealousy, and envy are the painful results of our failure to accept people and things as they are.

When things don't go our way, it's not that life is unfair; life just is. But when disappointed, we may wallow in self-pity, blame others for our misery, and play the victim. It's the baby in us that says, "I want what I want when I want it." However, happiness is not about getting what you want, it about wanting what you've got.

❧

I dance to the tune that is played.

—SPANISH PROVERB

My friend Michigan psychologist Jack Gregory used to say, "Whatever has happened, should have." He'd explain his bit of cleverness by stating "specific circumstances come together at a particular point in time to produce the results they did."

When faced with events not to our liking, we ultimately must accept the things we cannot change. "To endure without protest" is the essence of acceptance.

Happiness doesn't come from having the world change itself to accommodate us: it comes in accepting the world as it is. It's about living life on life's terms.

Radio and television correspondent **Nina Totenberg** has a

terrific philosophy about change. She says, "I've been a great advocate for changing if you're not happy doing whatever you're doing. The whole point of being a human being is to be able to look around and figure 'this is not working' and try something else. I'm a pretty stubborn person too, and it pays to be stubborn. Being pigheaded is good when you're looking at life's overall goals. It's not good when you're talking about whether to see a certain movie or whether or not to go out to dinner. That's stupid. Be pigheaded about life's big things. They are worth it."

However, a single event can change our lives. With no say in the matter, we may be challenged to adjust to the very worst that life can force upon us. Nina Totenberg knows the hardship and pain of major adversity and the acceptance necessary to meet it:

I ALWAYS BELIEVE IN HAPPY ENDINGS

A WEEK BEFORE MY HUSBAND FLOYD FELL, WE WENT TO A wedding. It was a big, formal, elegant affair. I had on a new dress and we both looked great. I can remember thinking, "Life is pretty good to us."

It was a horribly icy and snowy winter. On the day they shut down the city of Washington, Floyd went out to brush off the car. He was planning a fiftieth birthday party for me and wanted to make the final arrangements. His feet just went out from under him and he fell and hit his head. Three brain operations and two months later, he got out of intensive care. He was in rehab for two months more and then he came home, just barely able to walk with a walker and terribly frail and exhausted. It took him pretty much of eight months before he had really finally come back.

He gave me the delayed party a year later and we had a wonderful time. Four days later the doctor called me and said he'd found shadows on Floyd's lung. Just when he finally looked like his old self, they found a lesion. He had an operation that was successful. There was no spread at all and no chemotherapy was needed. But then his lung collapsed and he's been in intensive care for five weeks. He's lost every pound I put back on him, all forty of them. He never complains and the nurses all love him. He thanks them for doing awful things to him. He has much more courage than I do. I just do what I have to do; there are really no alternatives.

J. Edgar Hoover once tried to have me fired because I wrote a profile on him. I was a young reporter trying to do a good job and he didn't like the piece. I was lucky; *The National Observer* stood by me. People told me I had courage to stand up to him. What choice did I have?

As a reporter you have ethics: you don't give up your sources and you go ahead with a story even though it's going to make people mad. Obviously, in real life you care for your husband. You don't abandon him because he's sick. It's not a matter of ethics—I love him. It doesn't take an enormous amount of courage. I suppose I could go try to hurt myself, but that wouldn't help him or me.

I have obligations to my husband. For four months I went to the hospital once, twice, sometimes three times a day. For the last five weeks I've been going again. However, this time I'm not as hospital bound; I just can't be, nor would it do any good. I go every day, but usually only once.

It makes me terribly sad for my husband and for me. Maybe I would be angrier if he were younger. A good deal older than I am, he is, without a doubt, the kindest person I know. I think of all the mean people who deserve to have something bad happen to them and nothing does. That doesn't make me mad, it just strikes me as terribly unfair. Everybody loves him because he's such a gallant person. I just can't get over his courage and spirit. You always know somebody in your life who's like that, but you're not usually married to him.

THE LOVING SUPPORT OF FRIENDS

One thing that has come out of this is that my husband found out he has so many friends. People really love him. He probably did not know until the accident how much people cared about him. Me included. He knew I loved him but I don't think he understood how much. I knew I had a lot of good friends but I didn't know how good and how many either.

People say what a dreadful place Washington is. You find out who your friends are when you fall from power and nobody's there for you. I have not found that to be true. People I barely knew have leaped into the breach and called repeatedly asking, "Is there anything I can do?" or "Can I take you out to dinner?" People really have extended themselves above and beyond the call of duty. I didn't really know many of our neighbors all that well, but they have pitched in unbelievably. I don't buy into the notion that this is a heartless, money-grubbing, power-hungry community. At least not the community of my friends.

I guess I always have had faith that things would work out all right. I always believe in happy endings. I don't like movies with sad endings. Even when I look at the country, it's always had a pretty happy ending. McCarthyism got beaten back. Watergate didn't kill the country. Even Vietnam, although it came close, didn't destroy us. I still believe in the goodness of most of us, and my husband has taught me never to give up. He never gives up. Never. He probably wouldn't be alive if he did. When people told me he wouldn't walk, I didn't tell him, because he wouldn't have believed it. And he did walk.

—*Nina Totenberg*

∽

When dancer, choreographer, and director **Tommy Tune** and I talked for this book, he was on tour in San Francisco with his Broadway-bound musical *Busker Alley*. He was starring in the show and I caught him in his dressing room between an afternoon rehearsal and a nighttime performance. "The show needs more work," Tommy told me, "but we'll make it." He was excited, happy, and optimistic.

All the hard work had paid off. I saw the show in Baltimore, just one more out-of-town city before previews and opening night in New York. "The show is terrific," I told Tommy during a backstage visit after the performance. It was the truth. I think every member of the audience who left the theater that night—after a long standing ovation for Tommy and the cast—felt the same way.

A week or so later, I heard that Tommy had broken his foot in Tampa on stage during the show's final number. The entire production had to be canceled. I felt sad for him and everyone connected with the show. All the effort, all the anticipation, and now no Broadway. Instead of smash reviews, it was another situation requiring Tommy's total acceptance.

Ironically, acceptance had been the subject of our conversation for this book. Tommy had told me that many years earlier as he was beginning to set his sights on a dance career, he had to make a major adjustment in his goals. That decision didn't pivot around accepting something that had happened, but rather the acceptance of who he was.

Some of us spend a lifetime banging our heads against a wall, convinced that our way is the only way. Tommy Tune figured out there was another way:

DIFFERENCE IS A GIFT

I WANTED TO BE A BALLET DANCER. I TRAINED AND I WAS good. Then around the summer between junior high and high school, I started growing and I grew and grew.

I woke up one morning and I was in agony. My parents rushed me to the hospital. My mother was ringing her hands and crying. They thought I'd contracted polio. After the staff completed all kinds of tests, the doctor said, "I have good news for you, you have growing pains." That's all they could figure out. Then he took a Ticonderoga pencil and a rubberband and said, "Now this pencil is your bone and this rubber band"—and he put it around the eraser and stretched it, but he couldn't get it to the point—"this is your muscle. Give it a little time, do your stretching, and keep taking your dancing. That muscle is going to fit that bone and you're going to be fine." And I am.

I returned to the studio that fall, climbed the steep and narrow stairway, went into class, and regarded myself in the mirror in my tights. As a result of all that growth, I had to take a personal assessment. I said, "Tommy Tune, you're going to have to be some other kind of prince; you can't be that one in Swan Lake, you can't; look at you." (I have filled out compared to what I looked like then.) That was a real moment of realization, so I said, "You're going to have to be some other kind of prince, because you don't fit that role."

Then my mom took me to see *Easter Parade* at our local theater. There was this guy that looked real tall and skinny but he wasn't wearing tights; he was wearing clothes and I said to myself, "Oh, I bet underneath he looks real skinny in tights too, but he's wearing clothes." So I thought, "Okay, Fred Astaire!" And I've been dancing around in my pants ever since.

When you have to take an assessment of yourself and realize that you're not going to be pruned and watered and grow in the way that you thought, you become a palm tree instead of a boxwood. You say, "Well, what's appropriate? Where will this tree look best?" I was born to dance and when you've got to dance you've got to dance. That was the overriding thing. It was the dance that saw me through. That's the God-given gift; that's the God thing.

I was born with that. My parents said I danced before I walked. I would crawl into a room and the radio would be on. I would get up on my legs and dance. Then the music would go off and I would go down and crawl to the next destination. I hadn't figured out how to perambulate but I knew how to dance. If it's something in your human heart and spirit that you have to do, you will, with help, figure out a way to do it.

I never dreamed of being a featured player or a star or anything like how my life has worked out, and for which I'm very grateful. I went to New York to dance in the chorus of a Broadway show because they didn't wear tights on Broadway, they wore clothes, costumes. I went to my first audition and discovered much to my surprise that all the dancers were all very compact in stature.

I'm six feet six and a half inches. I am not built like a chorus boy and that was a big shock to me. I had arranged for how I was going to look in life, but I hadn't figured out the height thing in comparison to everybody else so I really stuck out. That was a big, "Oh, my gosh."

I got hired because I was good, but then they would say, "Oh my God, he's so tall, though. We hired him, but now what do we do with him? Well, let's give him that special part. Give him that cross-over. He can talk, so let him say that line. We'll let him be one of the members of that trio. It gives it a character thing."

I was doing that when the talent scout for 20th Century Fox saw a George Abbott show I was in called *How Now, Dow Jones*. I got a call at the theater: "You're that tall guy who's in the show who wears the straw hat?" I said, "Yes," and the woman said, "I'm casting the movie of *Hello, Dolly!* Gene Kelly is directing it, and we want to fly you out for a screen test." So the fact that I stuck out in the wrong way worked to my advantage.

It's about using flaws to your advantage; the freak factor is not necessarily a bad thing. It can be good thing. A lot of the types of people that end up in show business have a little of the freak factor in them—if not physically, then mentally, or in their speech or something. There's another angle to this I like to think about: the difference is a gift, not a liability. It's all in how you use it.

On my passport is written *Showman Optimist*. That's my basic philosophy. When a symphony orchestra plays, there are bad notes. I don't care how good the symphony is, or how great the conductor is, people hit clinkers. Are you going to focus on the clinkers or are you going to celebrate the success of the whole symphony? The fact that you're living is proof that you have a symphony to play.

—*Tommy Tune*

❧

Some years ago, I read a magazine article in which provocative questions were posed to get readers to help them discover what was really important in their lives. If you answer these few important questions honestly and accept and act on your answers, they could change your life.

Whatever direction your answers are leading in, you should be following!

What would you do if you knew you had only six months to live?
Would you spend your time with the same people?
Would you work at the same job?
Would you live in the same house (city, or country)?
If money were no object, what would you like to be doing?

∾

Our mortality may be the ultimate acceptance lesson for all of us. I've learned to identify what's important—and to do it sooner rather than later—from friends who are HIV positive or living with AIDS. The reality of death often leads to decision and action. Confronting her own terminal illness, artist and activist **Mary Fisher** decided how and why she wanted to live her life:

CREATING PRIORITIES

MY PRIVATE LIFE HASN'T CHANGED ALL THAT MUCH. I'M still a busy person; I'm still a mom, and I'm still an artist. I believe artists grow with their work and I certainly have. My work now is very reflective of where I am. My art's a combination of handmade paper, photographs, and my speeches. Giving an image of what I'm trying to say is my way of speaking out. My message is that we need to love each other, be honest with each other, and live in reality.

If it can happen to me, it can happen to you. When I found that my husband Brian was HIV positive, I knew that our biological son, Max, and I needed to be tested. My husband and I were divorced at the time but we went through this painful time together. I found out I was positive. Then we tested Max and found out he was negative, which was a great relief to both of us.

July 17, 1991, is a date I'll never forget. I still didn't believe that it could happen to me. Denial. It's understandable. It's protection. The denial that I have a hard time with today is our social denial of AIDS. It's only a gay disease—that's not true. It's only a drug user's disease—that's not true. AIDS is a disease of all of us. It belongs to every person and we are going to pay for this disease on every level if we don't take action. It is an avoidable epidemic. We need people to speak out about making AIDS a priority. Leadership on every level is crucial.

I had some general fear about how people were going to react, but the truth is there was a bigger picture for me and that focused on my children. It was about me standing for something. It was about being open and honest and wanting to create a model for my children.

When the test came back positive I said, "Well, there must be something else You want me to do." Something has taken over and allows me to do things for the greater good. I don't think it's all about me. Integrity is something my children need to learn and I am their model at this point. AIDS has made me public. AIDS has brought together a lot of pieces of my life. I would still teach my children the value of people and that we should celebrate our differences. I've always felt that. It's just that I have a larger, broader audience now to say this to, and maybe I can make a difference. What a model that would be for my children! I don't think I've changed as much as I've figured out a way to use the gifts I have.

HOW DO YOU WANT TO LIVE?

I was faced with my own mortality. It's at that moment you know you can't save your life. It's then you decide how you want to live. What do you want the quality of your life to be? That's when you start creating priorities and even if you felt the values before, felt the integrity before, and felt the love before, it all becomes more intense.

Being in the AIDS community, I'm constantly confronting death. I'm constantly brought up against what death means. We need to teach our children about death and dying—that with life comes death. I don't know that I would have talked about that as openly, clearly, and as honestly as I do now.

Elisabeth Kübler-Ross talks about anger, denial, bargaining, depression, and acceptance—the stages of death and dying. I think it's an ongoing process.

I'm taking medication three times a day and that reminds me I'm positive. I'm trying to create a different world for my children and in so doing, to create it for your children as well. They are my motivating force.

When I feel strong, I can give more intensely than I did before. There's been something that has opened up for me so that I can help others. Would they have listened to me about love if I didn't have AIDS? I don't know, maybe not. It's given me an opportunity to make a difference.

SOMEONE WITH AIDS WILL TOUCH ALL OF OUR LIVES

AIDS is not a priority in Washington. It's an avoidable epidemic that nobody wants to talk about. So my guess is they don't want to avoid it very much. They keep confusing it with values. It's just not the reality. Soon every person will know someone who is HIV positive, someone who has AIDS, or someone who has died or is dying from it. I don't see the priorities being created that would make all this change. I don't have the kind of belief in our system that I did as a child.

But I do have faith in God. I have a great belief and hope in my fellow humans that they will make a difference. If something good has come out of this, I'm glad. Then I've done the right thing.

—*Mary Fisher*

❧

A man's dying is more the survivors' affair than his own.

—THOMAS MANN

❧

A few years ago, I compiled the book *When the Worst That Can Happen Already Has: Conquering Life's Most Difficult Times.* The book looked at how people coped with major adversity.

Some of the most difficult times of change we will face will involve the deaths of those we love. Best-selling novelist **Mary Higgins Clark** knows all too much about this painful kind of change:

GET ON WITH LIFE

THERE HAS ALWAYS BEEN AN UNDERLYING CURRENT OF sadness in my life. Any child who loses a parent early on as I did misses that parent for the rest of her life. My mother died when she was eighty-one, and of course I miss her too. But she was very sick and she really wanted to go at that point. It's quite different when you're eleven years old and your father dies. Then, when your father's early death is later repeated with your own husband and you see that your own children are not going to have a father either, it's really horrible.

My father had run a successful Irish pub but the Depression was in full blast and his business started to go bad. He had to get up at seven in the morning to do much of the work that he used to pay other people to do. He came home for dinner every night but he worked seven days a week and I don't remember a single evening of my life that he didn't go back to work. He was a devoted father—on Sundays he took us for a ride in the car—but then he still went back to work. The poor guy wore himself out at age fifty-four trying to support a family.

One night I said goodnight to him. The next morning, like a good Irish Catholic girl during the month of May, I went to Mass. When I came home there was a police car at our house and people standing around. My little brother was out in front and I said, "What are you doing up so early, lazy bones?" He said, "I think Daddy's dead." My father had died in his sleep of a heart attack.

His death changed my life. There was a great sadness. My mother had enormous faith. We didn't have money. There was only two thousand dollars in insurance and that was it. My mother changed the dining room into a bedroom and rented rooms for the next four years, but she still couldn't keep it up and we lost the house. She then moved seven rooms of furniture into a three-room apartment, convinced she was going to get her house back one day.

My husband Warren and I got married the last week of 1949. He proposed on our first date. I had always known him. From the time I was twelve, I had a heavy crush on him. He lived around the corner. He was nine years older than I; to him I was a kid.

We were married only ten years when we were told he was lucky if he made it to the door of any room. Even though his heart was strong, his arteries were clogged. In those days all you could do was take nitroglycerin. So over five years Warren had three heart attacks and the third one took him.

ACCEPTANCE AND ACTION

A month after Warren died, I bumped into a friend who asked how I was. I said, "I'm fine." And he said, "You seem to be taking it very well." I replied, "If I didn't take it very well, would it change the circumstances?"

The best remedy for grief is hard work. Volunteer for something, go to school, get a job. A friend of mine lost her husband and her son within four months. It was dreadful. She is very well-off but she got a job as a secretary. Her boss once said to her, "You live in Saddle River, don't you? I hear that's a pretty expensive area." She said, "Oh, I live on the wrong side of the tracks." She has more property than anyone else in Saddle River, but the job was good for her, because at the time, she says, "I just had to get out of the house, I had to be busy." She said it really worked. The worst thing in the world is to sit and look at the four walls even if you can afford to. It works to keep yourself busy.

Losing people you love requires having acceptance. When I was sixteen, my brother, who was in the service, died. He was only eighteen and we were very close. That was a big toughie. My other brother died in an accident when he was forty-two.

It doesn't mean you won't always have a strain of sadness, but it also doesn't mean that you can't have a great deal of happiness. It's not fair to children if they have lost one terrific parent and the other one turns into gloom and doom. Warren had such a wonderful sense of humor. Our house was filled with laughter. He used to say, "I don't worry about leaving you to raise the kids. You could be put in Detroit naked at midnight and by seven in the morning you'd be fully dressed honestly with a hundred bucks in your pocket." When he died, I thought, I am not going to take that from my kids. Our children have great senses of humor and they are fun. And they still speak of Warren thirty years later with tremendous love.

Rose Kennedy said, "My life has been a series of agonies and ecstasies." I had nothing like she had, thank God. I've certainly had many, many happy times. If you have experienced pain and loss, it makes you more understanding of other people's suffering and even more generous.

I've always loved the story of King David. When Bathsheba gave birth to their first child and the child was dying, David lamented, tore his hair out, and prayed day and night. Finally he heard the servants whispering. They were afraid to tell him the child had died. David said, "While the child lived, I could hope that heaven would relent; now I must accept it." He bathed and ate and went in to comfort his wife; a year later she gave him a son whom they called Solomon.

I do think you can storm heaven; but once you've lost, you pretty much have to pick up the pieces and put a smile on your face. Nobody knows what tomorrow is going to bring and sympathy wears pretty thin if you're always moaning and lamenting. People playing the victim role are defeating themselves because they don't get on with life.

Life goes too quickly. My friends and I say, "Hey, wait a minute, we're still doing the Lindy, what happened?" One of our group says, "Look at those old people," and then we realize we're older than they are. We get too soon old, and too late smart.

—*Mary Higgins Clark*

&

The truth shall make you free.

—JOHN 8:32

Sometimes we attempt to live our lives by meeting the demands, expectations, needs, and wants of others rather than accepting who we are, being ourselves, and acting accordingly. "To thine own self be true" is excellent advice. It's the only way to live a happy life. Real happiness comes from surrendering to what is—if we can't solve our problems by changing them, we must learn to live with them.

∽

It takes grace and humility to know, accept, and love ourselves and appreciate that each one of us is a single unrepeatable mystery of God. **Craig C.** talks about the pain of not being true to himself and the changes he's made to achieve that goal:

LISTEN TO YOUR INNER VOICE

FOOD FEEDS THE BODY. KNOWLEDGE FEEDS THE MIND. Change feeds the soul. I see change as an opportunity to learn about myself and to extend the boundaries of my world. I haven't always felt so enlightened about change. It has haunted me in my life. It has brought me moments of intense anguish and despair.

I am a gay man. When I was young the mere thought of not being able to have a wife and children living in a house in the suburbs with a trim little lawn drove me to near hysterics. I would have done anything to keep that dream alive. But I couldn't. The pain of not being true to myself became too great. I wish I could say that coming out of the closet was a bold act. In truth, it was very selfish. I did not want to suffer the pain of lying to people or sneaking around anymore. I was running out of the energy I used to keep up my facade. Change was thrust upon me and I was forced to comply.

Paradoxically, when I walked through the fear of living my life as a gay man—as nothing more nor less than I honestly am—I became free. My old belief system crumbled as I began to realize that my life wasn't limited anymore. I also knew that if I could walk through that fear and emerge better for my actions, I could do anything—anything, that was, until the next time change started knocking on the door of my soul, telling me I had more growing to do.

The fears began again and the vise grip I had on the status quo got tighter. And I was forced one more time to walk through another seemingly impossible situation. This time it was addiction to drugs and alcohol.

I still was not being true to myself. I was hiding behind a joint or a beer, still so afraid that the world would see the real me. When my life on drugs got so bad that I was again lying and cheating and stealing, the pain drove me to change.

I believe we all have an inner guidance system that tells us what is right or wrong for us. The more I used drugs, the more that inner voice was crying out for me to heal. I couldn't dump enough anesthesia on that voice to shut it up. I could always hear it. Thank God, I finally listened to my inner voice and I got sober and quit using drugs. It was scary as hell. I was again leaving behind the constructs of my current world to begin once again in a strange new reality. In many ways, getting sober was very much like coming out of the closet: I began a beautiful, intimate relationship with my true self.

Change for me is the fertile soil of spiritual and emotional growth. As I continue to walk through the changes in my life, some big and some small, I am beginning to develop faith through the experience. Change can be painful and grueling, but I know it is ultimately necessary if I want to evolve as a spiritual being. Being committed to building my self-esteem and growing spiritually and emotionally is the least—or possibly the most—I can do for myself and for the world.

—Craig C.

∾

Og Mandino, the late dean of inspirational writers, shares his personal experience with adversity and the miracle of change:

At Peace with Yourself

WHENEVER SOMETHING BAD HAPPENS, JUST LEARN TO SAY, "That's wonderful. That's great." Back away from it and say, "Let me see what seed of good I can find in this adversity that has just hit me." How many times in your life has something happened to you that at the time seemed absolutely terrible, but when you looked back ten years later, you found yourself saying "Thank God that happened. If that hadn't happened, this wouldn't have happened and that wouldn't have happened, and I wouldn't be where I am today."

The lowest point in my life was when I was thirty-five years old, standing outside a pawnshop in Cleveland in the rain with no coat. It was freezing. It was November. I saw a handgun inside and there was a little tag on it that said $29. I had three wet ten-dollar bills in my pocket, all I had in the world. I thought, "Hey, there's the answer to all my misery and problems. I'll buy that gun, get a couple of bullets, and go back to that mangy room where I'm staying. I'll put the bullets in the gun, put the gun to my head, and pull the trigger. I'll never have to face that miserable slimeball failure in the mirror again."

I don't know what turned me around. I didn't hear voices speaking, angels singing, or harps playing. I joke about it now and say I didn't even have enough guts to buy the gun. Even that takes some kind of courage. I wandered up the street in the rain and went into the public library. It was warm, it was free, and it was dry. I stumbled over the rows of books that are in every library— the books on success: how to achieve it and how to hold on to it. I found Napoleon Hill, W. Clement Stone, Maxwell Maltz, and Dorothea Brande. I began to read those books.

Gradually, over time, my life began to change. I wandered across the country, but I was spending more time in libraries and less time in barrooms. In a library in Concord, New Hampshire, I found a book by W. Clement Stone and Napoleon Hill called *Success Through a Positive Mental Attitude,* and it changed my life.

Parents say to kids, "You're never going to amount to anything. You'll never make it." What happens? We spend the rest of our life working very hard to fulfill what mother or father said to us. They pushed our "kill" switch.

Years ago I bought a very expensive automobile. Besides a burglar alarm, it also has a kill switch that turns off the power going to the motor. If a burglar breaks into your car, he can't start the motor if you've pushed that switch.

One morning I went out to start my car and nothing happened. The windshield wipers went back and forth. The lights went on. The radio played, but the motor didn't turn over. So I called my dealer. He asked, "Og, don't you remember you have a kill switch?" Well I couldn't find it so they sent a young man to the house. He flipped the carpet over and said, "It's right here, sir." He pushed it and said, "Try the key now." Of course the motor started. I had accidentally stepped on the switch through the carpet.

Many parents accidentally push our kill switch and we spend the rest of life not being able to do anything except go through the motions. We'll never achieve anything because they told us we wouldn't.

Back in the 1940s when Winston Churchill was the number one man in the British empire, he addressed an Oxford graduating class. When the great man stepped up to the microphone—usually most commencement addresses are long and very dull—Churchill looked out over the crowd of young faces and said, "Never, never, never, never, never, never give up." He turned and walked back to his seat. That was all he said.

Success depends on the degree to which you are at peace with yourself. If you have people around you who love you and you have peace with what you're doing, it doesn't get any better than that. We look everywhere for happiness, forgetting that it's in our own little plot of land. We have our own acres of diamonds but we don't know it. Somebody has to shake us up to make us realize it.

—*Og Mandino*

༄

A friend was singing the praises of a Tibetan master he'd heard speak and whose writings he had studied. **Sogyal Rinpoche**—perhaps the most well known and respected interpreter of Buddhism to the West—was coming to speak in Washington. Was I interested in going? was the question. I was and I went.

Sogyal Rinpoche's ninety-minute talk in a packed church was spellbinding. He touched on many topics including "impermanence" with humor, warmth, and gentleness. After his very spiritual and stimulating talk, there was such a demand for his tapes and literature that his most famous book was sold out by the time I moved to the front of the line.

I easily tracked down *The Tibetan Book of Living and Dying* at a local bookstore. It's a very important book. One of its themes is that meditating on death changes your life. This is a brief excerpt from the book which Sogyal Rinpoche has generously contributed to this work:

THE TRUTH OF IMPERMANENCE

I ASK MYSELF OFTEN: "WHY IS IT THAT EVERYTHING changes?" And only one answer comes back to me: *That is how life is*. Nothing, nothing at all, has any lasting character. The Buddha said:

> *This existence of ours is as transient as autumn clouds.*
> *To watch the birth and death of beings is like looking at the movements of a dance.*
> *A lifetime is like a flash of lightning in the sky,*
> *Rushing by, like a torrent down a steep mountain.*

One of the chief reasons we have so much anguish and difficulty facing death is that we ignore the truth of impermanence. We so desperately want everything to continue as it is that we have to believe that things will always stay the same. But this is only make-believe. And as we so often discover, belief has little or nothing to do with reality. This make-believe, with its misinformation, ideas, and assumptions, is the rickety foundation on which we construct our lives. No matter how much the truth keeps interrupting, we prefer to go on trying, with hopeless bravado, to keep up our pretense.

In our minds changes always equal loss and suffering. And if they come, we try to anesthetize ourselves as far as possible. We assume, stubbornly and unquestionably, that permanence provides security and impermanence does not. But, in fact, impermanence is like some of the people we meet in life—difficult and disturbing at first, but on deeper acquaintance far friendlier and less unnerving than we could have imagined.

Reflect on this: The realization of impermanence is paradoxically the only thing we can hold onto, perhaps our only lasting possession. It is like the sky, or the earth. No matter how much everything around us may change or collapse, they endure. Say we go through a shattering emotional crisis . . . our whole life seems to be disintegrating . . . our husband or wife suddenly leaves us without warning. The earth is still there; the sky is still there. Of course, even the earth trembles now and again, just to remind us we cannot take anything for granted . . .

Even Buddha died. His death was a teaching, to shock the naive, the indolent, and complacent, to wake us up to the truth that everything is impermanent and death an inescapable fact of life. As he approached death, the Buddha said:

Of all footprints
That of the elephant is supreme;
Of all mindfulness meditations
That on death is supreme.

Whenever we lose our perspective, or fall prey to laziness, reflecting on death and impermanence shakes us back into the truth:

What is born will die,
What has been gathered will be dispersed,
What has been accumulated will be exhausted,
What has been been built up will collapse,
And what has been high will be brought low.

—*Sogyal Rinpoche*

∾

Life has no other discipline to impose, if we would but realize it, than to accept life unquestioningly. Everything we shut our eyes to, everything we deny, denigrate or despise, serves to defeat us in the end. What seems nasty, painful, evil, can become a source of beauty, joy and strength, if faced with an open mind. Every moment is a golden one for him who has the vision to recognize it as such.

—HENRY MILLER

REFLECTIONS

If God told you exactly what it was you were to do, you would be happy doing it no matter what it was.
What you are doing is what God wants you to do.
Be happy.

Life works when you choose what you've got.

—WERNER ERHARD

PRAYER

The Lord is my light and my salvation;
whom shall I fear?

The Lord is the stronghold of my life;
of whom shall I be afraid?

—PSALM 27:1

5. SPIRITUALITY

There is one spectacle grander than the sea, that is the sky; there is one spectacle grander than the sky, that is the interior of the soul.

—VICTOR HUGO

The most spiritual human beings, assuming they are the most courageous, also experience by far the most painful tragedies; but it is precisely for this reason that they honor life, because it brings against them its most formidable weapons.

—FRIEDRICH NIETZSCHE

I WAS RAISED AS A CATHOLIC; BUT I REBELLED NOT ONLY from my parents, but also from religion, prayer, and church when I left home and went away to college. There came a very long stretch in my life when I tried to run my own life. While there were a few successes along the way, there were many miserable failures. For too many years, I went at life alone. I lived like a figure in an Edward Hopper painting. Today I not only believe God exists, but I have also come to know and experience that He's in charge and He cares.

A spiritual life is our evolving relationship with God. The minor changes and major life transitions that occur in our lives are all leading us closer to Him. Our confrontations with change rid us of our self-centeredness and selfishness and teach us about love and humility. As we travel through our own "seven stages of man," we move from self to others to God. (Even if you say you don't believe in God, perhaps in some corner of your heart you want to believe. All God asks is willingness and open-mindedness. He'll do the rest.)

In the course of our spiritual growth we experience an internal shift in the way we relate to the world. We move from pessimism to optimism, from hostility to hospitality from me to you, and from fear to faith.

Each of us has one or two very special gifts. To be happy it is necessary that we use those gifts to fulfill ourselves and make the lives of others better as well. Part of our life's mission is to uncover our talents and do the job God created us to do.

∾

At least for me, there is some comfort in knowing that throughout history the great philosophers, religious leaders, and saints have wrestled with questions about God. The struggle of faith is the struggle of man. **Father Joseph Girzone** invites us to examine a gentle and perhaps new vision of a God-centered life:

THE STRUGGLE

LIFE HAS TO BE A STRUGGLE, OTHERWISE WE'LL NEVER grow. Struggling helps us to understand things more deeply and develop our vision. I don't think we can mature if we don't struggle.

A person who is by nature fearful or insecure resists change almost violently. For a person who is comfortable and free, it's easy to be open to new values, new ways of looking at things, and to adapt what you've learned to new experiences.

I don't think anybody feels totally adequate. That's why it's so necessary to have a relationship with God, a partnership with God. It's not a make-believe thing. Jesus said, "When you accept me as your friend, my Father and I come and live within you." He comes to live within us as a friend, as a partner, so He can share His life with us and so we can share our life with Him. One of the most beautiful things about our relationship with God is that God respects the freedom He's given to us. He's a God of options. In other words, if you say to God, "Well God, what am I supposed to do?" I think Jesus would say, "What do you want to do? I gave you free will so that you can make your own decisions. So you say, "Well, I would like to do this. I don't see anything wrong with it." I think Jesus would say, "Well, let's give it a try. If we find out it's a mistake, we'll make some little changes here and there and see if you can make things work out." That's the way God works with us.

God has a beautiful overall plan and I think He very gently—without violating our freedom—makes suggestions. That's where God's grace is so marvelous. He has to compete with a whole batch of other things that we may feel drawn to, but He's a master at suggesting to us different courses of action, different ways of doing things.

WHAT WOULD JESUS DO?

If we approach life from a legalistic or philosophical point of view—"Which is the better thing to do?" or "What should I do?"—we can get terribly, terribly mixed up. Even when it comes to a specific issue, we can get confused. "How should I treat this poor person approaching me on the street? If I give this person money, he's going to use it either for drugs or for a drink anyway, so why should I give it to him?" Then you think about it. "Well, here's a poor person. Everybody else feels comfortable taking a drink. Why shouldn't a poor person have a right to use his money to buy a drink? Why should I discriminate against this person because he has nothing?" So you go into a big philosophical argument with yourself just to give a person a quarter.

The simpler way of approaching it is: "What would Jesus do?" All of a sudden it becomes very, very simple. If the poor person does have a need for something to eat and you happen to have some food with you, you might share the food. If you don't have any food, you might just give him or her a little something. Or you might want to stop and talk to the person for a few minutes. "What would Jesus do?" or "How would Jesus treat this person?" If we ask ourselves these questions frequently during each day, it reduces our whole life to real simplicity. Our lives are sometimes very, very difficult because we come across all kinds of situations and we don't know how to respond to them.

Ask yourself, "Well, what would Jesus do?" Now there's something that happens inside of you that helps you instinctively know how Jesus would respond. That's the way we can approach a lot of moral issues. But you have to spend a good part of life becoming acquainted with Jesus and developing your partnership with Christ through your own prayer life so that your understanding of Jesus is well developed and not just your own instincts telling you something.

God always responds to any human being who reaches out to Him. We're all His children. He created each one of us with infinitely tender love. No matter who we are, we can develop a partnership with God.

Life is so fragile. We hang on to life by a thread. You step off a curb at the wrong moment, you're finished. Some friends of mine were on a plane last week and there was a violent storm. Everybody felt they were going to crash.

Once we realize how frail, how tenuous our existence is, it's instinctive to cry out to someone who can rescue us, who can save us. Our false pride totally disappears when we're desperate. We reach that point frequently when we see a loved one threatened or when our own future, our stability, our financial security, is threatened. We know there's no other human being who is going to be able to rescue us. We know we can't rescue ourselves in this crisis situation, so we instinctively go to God. When the chips are really down and there is nothing left, we naturally go back to the realization that there's a God who created us and we all depend totally upon Him.

WE EACH HAVE A JOB IN THIS UNIVERSE

God created each one of us to do a little job in this universe, with many, many people depending upon our accomplishment of that little job. All kinds of wonderful things happen in our world and in the community around us because of our fulfillment of that little job. God gave us all the gifts, virtues, talents, and circumstances we need to fulfill that little job.

All the rest of our personality is defective and inadequate. That's the way God made us and it doesn't bother Him one slight bit. People who live with us don't like it, but it doesn't bother God that we are inadequate in many aspects of our life. He didn't intend to create us as little gods. Once you reach that point when you realize that God created you special—to do a very, very special job for Him—you do the best you can with those shortcomings. "God made me the way He did and He did not make a mistake."

From that point on we can begin to develop a solid, healthy basis for our personality. When we look in the mirror we can say, "I like what I see, because that's God's gift to me. I know I'm not perfect. I can't overcome all these weaknesses that I know are in me, but I can do things that are positive. I can notice the pain, the hurt, the heartaches, and the troubles in other peoples' lives, and I can help others. I can try to get closer to God in my own personal life. I can be a good person in a lot of ways even though I'm very, very weak."

We limp, physically, emotionally, psychologically, spiritually, and it's okay. In God's good time He gives us the grace to outgrow these limitations to a greater or lesser degree. It's that constant growing that is important. We never arrive at total perfection, but we are struggling and constantly growing. Growth and change are synonymous. People who are too conservative stymie their ability to grow. They refuse to let themselves change and that's the greatest obstacle to the Holy Spirit working in their souls.

THE GIFT OF EXPERIENCE

I went through a period of many years of the most horrible depression when I was in the seminary. It started when I was around sixteen years old.

I used to be able to spend time thinking about God and meditating and praying. Then after I was sixteen the bottom dropped out. I couldn't pray and I couldn't feel God's presence anymore. I would wake up in the morning and say, "Oh my God, not another day." That depression went on for almost twelve years. I didn't lose my faith, but I had a very difficult time feeling that there was a God. During that time of struggle I wanted to give up the seminary, go home, and get married. Every time I thought about doing it, something kept telling me, "No, stay, don't give up. You're going through this so you can understand the pain, the hurt, and the anguish of people's lives, so you'll be able to help them later on."

Looking back on that pain and depression, I realize that at that time I learned more about myself, more about God, more about people, and more about life than I did during any other period of my life. My greatest period of growth took place during those twelve years of horrible depression. I don't think I could ever go through it again, I don't think I could go through it now. But at the time, God gave me the strength and it was a very powerful learning experience.

On my first assignment after being ordained, the other priests in the house didn't want me there; that was heartbreaking. After I joined the Albany diocese, I left the Carmelite Order but I was treated as an outsider. In other places where I was stationed, there were a lot of community problems, so I was asked to join the Human Rights Commission and eventually became head of it. There was a jail riot I had to mediate. There was also turmoil in the school system and it was very dangerous. All of those things were stressful. My health started to fall apart and finally, I had a heart attack.

Looking back on it, however, I can now see that practically every major experience I went through in my life was an intimate part of the preparation that was necessary for the writing of my book, *Joshua*. It's almost as if everything was perfectly coordinated to give me the experiences I needed to be able to write in a way that could touch people's lives and make Jesus real for them.

The questions posed by *Joshua* are: If Jesus were to come down to earth today, how would his life unfold on a day-to-day basis? How would we as individuals relate to Him? How would we accept Him?

When God created human beings, He placed in their hearts and souls needs to be fulfilled. When Jesus came down to earth, the message that He taught responded to those deepest needs. What I try to do in *Joshua* is develop a portrait of an authentic Jesus. So when people meet Jesus in *Joshua,* what He does and says responds to the needs in every human heart.

Those deep needs we have are to know that we belong to God in a very intimate way, that God is very much a part of our life, that we are not evil, that we are good, that God loves us as He made us, and that He did not make a mistake. He knows we are weak, He knows are we frail, but He also sees all the goodness that we have interwoven with our weaknesses and our frailties. He loves each of us with a love that is immense and immeasurable. He is always by our side, He's always in our heart, He is our partner and will always go through life with us hand in hand. We are never alone. He's always with us. People desperately need that message today because people feel frightfully alone on this planet.

OPEN YOUR HEART TO GOD

People in the course of their life's experience realize, "I really don't have anybody I can totally depend on." I think people want to believe in God. A relationship with God starts when you open your heart to Him. You place yourself in God's presence. You feel God's presence all around you and it's very emotional. It's so overwhelming that no matter what you're doing or where you're going, you sense that God is there and it has an effect on you physically and emotionally. You find yourself thinking about God all the time and it's a beautiful experience. It's also a fun experience as God draws you closer and closer into this relationship with Him. Then you find yourself doing things that you think would be pleasing to God, as you would find yourself doing things that would be pleasing to someone that you love very deeply.

This exciting experience happens in quite a few people's lives, but you have to prepare yourself for it. You have to be able to take some quiet time each day and spend some time reading the Bible, reading the Gospels. Open your mind to allow Jesus' presence and allow God's presence to become part of your life. Once you open your heart to God, then God becomes a part of your life. That experience is available for everybody.

As your partnership with God grows and develops, the benefit of it is that you see your whole life becoming very simple. You no longer have to worry, "What am I going to do tomorrow?" "What am I going to do with my life?" All that struggle stops because you place yourself in God's hands. The other benefits are the tremendous peace that settles over you, and there is a sense of joy.

—*Father Joseph Girzone*

∾

The weekly best-seller lists of books tell us a great deal about what is of interest to Americans. For more than two solid years, **James Redfield's** book *The Celestine Prophecy* has been a fixture on *The New York Times* list. His latest book, *The Tenth Insight,* appeared on the list immediately upon publication. Both novels have spirituality as their theme, as do the packed workshops and lectures by James and his wife, **Salle Merrill Redfield:**

THE GOOD LIFE

James
Anyone who has read my books knows they're about finding your own sense of spirituality within, your own definition of spirituality. We're at an age beyond gurus now. It's not about giving your power to some charismatic figure.

The Celestine Prophecy, The Tenth Insight, and other books put into words what a lot of people are already sensing and perceiving. These books are creating a new vocabulary of the spiritual search. We've been asking for a long time, "Isn't there more to life?" At this point in the nineties, we are starting to pull together the answer to that question: "Yes, there is." There are some definite ways that we can find more fulfillment, have a sense of peace, and have a sense of mission. We're in a consensus-building process. It's a dialogue from which we're exploring what it really means to live the spiritual life. We're going to have a new idea about what the good life is.

Salle
In 1989 I went through a divorce. It was life changing. Eventually life forces us to go within. It may be a divorce; it may be the loss of a loved one or the loss of a job. It's partially the result of aging, maturing. But it's also because historically our society has progressed to a point where we see through the material. We want fulfillment at a deeper level. There's a great wave of exploration going on now. People are turning to religion and spirituality:

James

Just the whole idea of a new millennium puts us in the frame of mind to think cosmically. Western society has reached a point of critical mass. The old materialistic Newtonian world view is in transition. It's shifting into a new spiritual way of life. People are seeing their lives as an adventure unfolding. That changes everything.

Salle

It's important for us to remember that we do have a mission, a higher purpose. Sometimes we do have to let go of the old ways in order to achieve it.

James

The yearning for fulfillment is really a memory of "Hey, I came here to do something special. All that's happened to me in my whole life is preparation." When we start to see ourselves as a historical figures, we become more tuned to coincidences that seem to be leading us. Suddenly we're on a path where we can actualize our mission.

All the mystics say that transcendent experiences exist. They've been described in hundreds of ways. Each of us in our own way is opening the door, going out, and looking for this experience.

—*James Redfield and Salle Merrill Redfield*

∾

Faith without good works is dead.

—JAMES 2:26

∾

Many talk the talk, but don't walk the walk. After years of wandering, actor **Martin Sheen** rediscovered his faith and identified his "true self." In an interview Martin told me, "As soon as I accepted that life was tough, as Dr. Peck tells us in *The Road Less Traveled,* and it's supposed to be tough, then it wasn't tough anymore, it was life. When I accepted that, it was a great relief and a great joy. Of course, I also had to accept responsibility for knowing. I think that's the beginning of real maturity."

His thoughts were initially offered in a speech in August 1995 at the National Press Club in Washington, D.C.:

WE ARE NOT GOD, WE ARE OF GOD

I HAD BEEN RAISED CATHOLIC—ONE OF TEN CHILDREN. MY parents were both immigrants, God rest them. My father was Spanish, my mother was Irish.

My real name is Ramon Estevez. I created Martin Sheen at the time I began my career in New York. In 1959 there was a great deal of prejudice against Hispanics and I thought I would sidestep the whole issue and reinvent myself.

As a young actor in New York, with a big ego and a certain amount of talent, I let my Catholic faith slide. However, after twenty-one years of setting my hair on fire and trying to put it out with a hammer, I found myself venturing back into the fold. Mother Teresa drove me back to Catholicism, but Daniel Berrigan keeps me there. My reunion with the Catholic Church was not made in heaven; on the contrary, I joined the church of Vatican II, Thomas Merton, Dorothy Day and the Catholic Worker communities; the church of Cesar Chavez, Archbishop Romero, Dom Hilda Carma, and Father Aristide. It was the church that celebrated the poor and the marginalized and followed the nonviolent Jesus. I would no longer be inspired by the idea of immortality, but rather by the promise of resurrection. As a result, the past fourteen years have been the most difficult, but equally, the most meaningful and by far the happiest of my life.

The Reverend Martin Luther King, Jr., said the church is a place from which to go forth and I could not go forth without an identification for this new adventure. I believe all of us need to identify ourselves no matter who we are.

For my own part, I've prepared a personal ID, should I ever lose sight of my true self. It goes as follows: I am Ramon, called Martin your brother, a private citizen with a public image who tries to confront the vital issues of peace, the environment, and social justice through a loving commitment to nonviolent witness in an effort to unite the will of the spirit to the work of the flesh.

We are not God. For most of us, that's a great relief: for some of us, it's a big problem. *We are of God,* and I believe that no matter where we are, what we're doing, or who we are, we are in search of God. But we are free to be ourselves. Our lives are wonderful gifts, exciting mysteries to be joyfully explored. Our lives are not problems to be solved.

An honest life is not easy; it's not supposed to be. If it were easy, it wouldn't be life, and it certainly wouldn't be honest.

We are each of us here for each other. But if we become ego-centered and selfish, focusing only on ourselves with no care or service to others, fear and anger will dominate our lives. We'll be like the man standing on the corner on the coldest day of the year who wets his pants. He gets a very warm feeling for a little while, but that's about it.

What I do for peace and social justice is what I do to stay alive. During a recent interview, I was asked if my activism had hurt my career, and without hesitation I responded, "I hope so; I'd hate to think it was because of bad acting." No matter what I am called to do, I am never asked to be successful; I am only asked to be faithful and the only person I can ever change may be myself.

Homelessness on our streets is a reflection of who we are inside. We're spiritually homeless. We are so governed by fear. I see it in the faces of people all over this country. People are afraid to be themselves; people are afraid to express their hearts and expose their souls to anything that is not acceptable. The problem with our culture, towards the end of this millennium, is silence. All I'm trying to do with my life, my work, and my appearance publicly or privately wherever I go is to put words on the heart, put words on what we're really thinking and feeling, and to alleviate some of this awful fear.

There is nothing to be afraid of. Express your heart and soul and let the spirit in and be pushed towards real freedom. I don't think you can get off the hook without having some measure of spirituality, whether you call it that or not.

—*Martin Sheen*

∾

There are incalculable resources in the human spirit, once it has been set free.

—HUBERT H. HUMPHREY

A few years ago, I compiled a book called *Are You Happy?* So threatening was its title that at the eleventh hour the publishing house strongly suggested the title be changed to *What It Takes to Be Happy.*

I was so invested in the original title—I think they call that ego—I was incapable of making the change, rejected their suggestions, and adamantly insisted on my title. I was wrong. My own pride, self-righteousness, and inability to accept change gracefully may have cost the book some of the success I feel it deserved.

I'm sure my life is filled with thousands of similar incidents that have caused me unhappiness over the years. My life is usually motivated by my perception of what is best for me. So is yours. It's human, so let's not beat up on ourselves. We think that our way is the right way and that what we want should be the way life is. The ongoing battle between fantasy (what I want) and reality (what is) is one of our greatest challenges. *To believe that we are the center of the universe is grandiose at worst and naive at best.*

∾

Psychologist **Wayne Dyer** is convinced that we're in the midst of a great spiritual revolution and people are looking upward and turning inward in their search for peace and contentment:

THE SPIRITUAL REVOLUTION

MY BOOK *Your Sacred Self* is about the triumph of the higher self over the ego. My last three books have all had a spiritual flavor.

It's been happening in my own life too. Everywhere I travel I find myself talking to spiritually minded people—what I call "fringe dwellers." These people are in the world but not really of it. They know there's a deeper, richer experience of life and they're after it.

We're in a spiritual revolution. It's a natural outgrowth of the changes that have taken place on the planet over the last three or four hundred years. There has been movement from a feudal system to an agricultural system, to an industrial revolution, to an urban revolution, and now to the technological revolution. We have become blasé to the changes that have been taking place in the world. Imagine a few years ago predicting there would be no USSR, that a black president of South Africa would be elected democratically, that the president of Czechoslovakia and ex-president of Poland would be former prisoners of conscience, that dictatorships would be failing, that communism would be a thing of the past. Massive changes have been taking place in the political structures and they're also taking place within each one of us. As Victor Hugo said in *Les Misérables,* "There is nothing more powerful than an idea whose time has come." This is going to be called the God decade. It's a decade of higher awareness.

Enlightened spiritual people don't experience fear. When someone told Maharaj Nisargadatta, a great teacher of mine in Bombay, they had troubles, he said, "In my world, nothing ever goes wrong." What a great affirmation. He just watches and sees that it's all in the divine order. Some people are born and some die. Some get sick and some don't. He's not indifferent to that, but he's not attached to something that should or shouldn't be happening; he just notices. You have to practice getting rid of doubt and cultivate a witness mind-set. You have to shut down the inner dialogue and get quiet. You have to meditate on a regular basis. You have to tame your ego. You have to get rid of your false self and understand that who you are is not your ego.

YOU ARE YOUR SACRED SELF

In *A Course in Miracles,* it says if you knew—it doesn't say if you believed—who walked beside you at all times on the path that you have chosen, you could never experience fear again. It's as if there are two of you at all times. There's the observer and the one whom you are observing. Most people believe they are their body, their career, their money. Well, there's also somebody observing all of that. That's what your sacred self is about.

Once you're the noticer you notice everything. You're not attached and you're not afraid.

Security is one of those things we think we need because we identify ourselves with the ego. We think we are our body. We think we are all of the things that come to us in the world. We think that we are more secure when we have things. I ask my audiences all the time, "How would you feel if you won the lottery?" "What would you experience in your inner world?" The answers always are, "I would feel secure," "I would feel safe," "I would feel happy," "I would feel marvelous," "I'd feel content," "I'd feel thrilled," "I'd feel blissful." Then I tell them, "The myth is that you have to win a lottery in order to have those things.

"You can have everything that you all said," I tell them. "You don't have to have one more thing in your life. It's a matter of how you choose to process your world." Get rid of the idea that something has to happen outside of you in order for you to feel blissful, secure, and content. You are not a human being having a spiritual experience, you are really a spiritual being having a human experience.

THE WITNESS INSIDE

Your primary identification is not with your ego, your lower identity. Who you really are is the noticer, the observer, the witness. That part of you is changeless and eternal.

Everything in the world is in a constant state of change, but the noticer, the observer, the witness inside, remains the same. I'm fifty-four years old, and there is a part of me—a five-year-old witness—that hasn't changed at all. It hasn't aged, isn't sick. It isn't wrinkled, it isn't losing its hair.

The part of you that never changed is where love resides. That's the part of you that is within. Once you have your primary identification there—instead of on that which is changing—all your fears, anxieties, and stress dissipate and you begin to have what I call a "knowing."

What I'm suggesting goes beyond the thinking and understanding that not only are you not your body, your accomplishments, and all your accumulations, but you're also not your thoughts. You are the thinker of the thoughts. So you don't want to focus on what you are thinking, you want to watch thoughts come and go. That's what meditation does. It teaches you to watch your thoughts.

We have approximately sixty thousand different thoughts every single day. The problem is that we have the same sixty thousand we had yesterday and the same ones we had the day before. However, if you go beyond that consciousness and watch them, you'll begin to notice the thoughts that are going to work for you and you're going to place your attention there. The thoughts that don't work for you are the ones that are going to produce negativity, illness, or scarcity. You let those subside. All the time you are detached. You're just the observer. It's a very, very peaceful place to be.

OBSERVE, DON'T IDENTIFY

Years ago, when I had a therapy practice, I had a client who was chronically depressed. I would ask her, "Is there any part of you that is not depressed?" And she would say, "No I'm always depressed. I sleep depressed, I wake up depressed, I'm a clinically depressed person." I asked, "Have you been noticing the depression more lately?" She said, "Yes, I have." Then I asked her the key question. "Is whoever it is that is noticing this also depressed?" That was our entry point—because there was no depression there.

You teach people who have chronic pain to observe the pain and not identify with it—to notice when it appears. "How big is it? What does it look like? How frequently does it come? When does it leave? Is it possible for you to move it?" They begin to detach themselves from all of their suffering.

Ram Dass was training people to handle emergency hotline calls. He got a frantic call from someone who was going to commit suicide. The person was totally out of control. Finally, Ram Dass said, "Stop right there. Whoever the person was that made a decision to pick up the phone and dial this number, put that person on the line."

THE HIGHER SELF

There are two people living within you at all times: one is the ego, which is demanding, which is garrulous and is insane because it would have you convince yourself that you are something that you're not—which is what insanity is; then there is the hidden higher self who's rarely heard or attended to. That is the piece of you that allows you to observe. That's your sacred self. All the sacred part wants is for you to be at peace. The question is, "Does whatever is going on in my life promote peace in me?" If it doesn't, it's your ego; if it does, it's your higher self and you have to listen to it more and more. Blaise Pascal, the French philosopher and scientist, said, "All of man's troubles stem from his inability to sit quietly in a room alone." Most people can't do that.

THE MIND IS LIKE A POND

I use the metaphor of a pond. The pond is not the surface. The surface is only a tiny fragment of the total thing called "pond-ness." Yet all of the disturbances are on the surface. The waves, the freezing and thawing, the dirt, and the churning all take place on the surface. I call this the chatter level. Chatter, chatter, chatter.

If you want to know what the pond really is, you've got to get below the surface and just below the mind surface is a level I call *analysis*. Instead of chatter, chatter, chatter, you analyze: "Why did I do this?" "Why did she do that?" When you go *below* that level, you stop trying to pick things apart to figure out why and you come to a level that is even deeper in the mind, called *synthesis*. Instead of tearing things apart there, you begin to see how things are held together. You begin to see the connectedness with all of this: "When I did this, that happened," or "If I stop doing this, it would probably impact on that."

THE UNIFIED FIELD OF ALL POSSIBILITIES

By going deeper still you begin to quiet the mind. You let in fewer and fewer thoughts. You come to a place where you empty the mind, where you have no thought and rest at a place called *the unified field of all possibilities,* which is really the difference between knowing about God and knowing God. Knowing about God is a belief that other people have given you, but when you get to the unified field, you have the blissful experience that **with God, all things are possible.** God is that divine organizing intelligence that is all things. God and His divine energy are who we are. Every one of us is an extension of God. You can only know that by going there. A "knowing" isn't something that comes from outside yourself; a knowing is something that comes from within.

CHANGE YOUR LIFE THROUGH MEDITATION

If you would meditate twenty minutes, twice a day, morning and night, I would guarantee you a lot less stress in your life. You would start looking younger. Your blood pressure would go down. I would guarantee relief from a whole lot of physical symptoms including fatigue, skin problems, and arthritis. Daily meditation would guarantee you'd feel more peaceful and would probably improve your relationships dramatically. Meditation challenges the assumption of your being separate from others. Meditation really brings you into a sense of unity where you feel yourself to be a part of all things. It also shatters the illusion that you are separate from God. Meditation teaches you to go to the part of you that is changeless. It is that part of you that is eternal.

FALLING UPWARD

Usually when you see people make giant strides in their lives it is almost always preceded by a fall. The alcoholic who comes to grips with his alcoholism or the drug addict who wakes up in his own vomit have fallen very far. When they got to the bottom, they had an awareness. The bottom is really important for spiritual development.

The ego doesn't want you to experience a fall, because when you have a fall, you find your higher self, the spiritual part of you, or God. The ego is terrified of that, so it promotes a steady little river of misery and helps you to avoid a fall.

The Kabala teaches us that in order to be able to move from the physical level to the spiritual level, you have to generate an incredible amount of energy and the only way you can generate this energy is through a fall.

THE COURAGE TO TURN INWARD

The opening line of *Your Sacred Self* is, "You have been facing the wrong way." You don't find the courage to change by facing outward and looking for it anyplace outside. When we're born the door opens just for a split second and we enter a room called daily awareness. It's all of the things we have learned about who we are, what we can do, what we can accomplish, what our goals and limitations are. However, it's only one room in this house of potential human awareness.

The only way 99 percent of the people know how to get out of the room of daily awareness is to die. At death the door opens again, just for a split second, and out you go. We call this your life.

GOING BEYOND FEAR

There are a few who really explore. Most people spend their life pushing on the walls looking for a door that opens outward. A few people have an awareness, an instant awakening, an epiphany, and realize that the door to higher awareness, to other rooms in the house, opens inward.

You've got to step back and pull the door inward. You have to metaphorically turn yourself in such a way that you can face inward instead of outward. That's where you'll find the courage to change. Instead of having to die in order to experience heightened levels of awareness, you can learn new ways of going outside the room of daily awareness and explore all the other rooms in the house of potential awareness that go beyond fear and beyond all limitations.

—*Wayne Dyer, Ph.D.*

∾

I mean it's very hard to meditate and live a spiritual life in America. People think you're a freak if you try to.

—J. D. SALINGER

A former mentor of mine used to say that the purpose of life was to "Know yourself, accept yourself, love yourself, and forget about yourself by loving others unconditionally and being of service to them." He also said that the journey of life was a spiritual one and that our ultimate goal was to develop our relationship with God.

I'm not exactly sure when I finally accepted that we were all traveling a common life-journey; but at some time I did. There is something very exciting in knowing we are all on the identical path even though we may be at different points along the way. I grew up as an Irish Catholic boy hearing from the nuns, "Everybody has his or her cross to bear." While the image may not be very inviting, the concept is true. That cross is our humanness. While our struggles take many forms, we all have them.

Accepting that we are all the same—from Bill Clinton to Michael Jordan, from Roseanne to Princess Diana—gets mucked up when we have to sort out the beautiful people from the average, the rich from the poor, the worldly successful from the apparent failures, the healthy from the sick, the popular from the shy, the happy from the sad. Birthplace, citizenship, nationality, race, sex, age, job, and titles all get tossed into the mix. We focus on the differences and miss our similarities. We all have shortcomings, character defects, and "bad" habits. We all make mistakes of judgment, hurt others, and do inappropriate things. We all experience disappointments, rejections, and losses and we all battle our self-will and the seven deadly sins: pride, anger, lust, gluttony, envy, sloth, and greed. We are also capable of giving and receiving love and facing life with courage. What an incredibly contradictory package we are and what an exciting journey we travel!

From the day we are born, our growth experiences are leading toward God. A relationship with God does not happen overnight. That deep bond, that "partnership with God" that Father Girzone speaks about, takes a long time to build. A life of the spirit requires desire, commitment, action, and humility.

ↄ

Humility is teachability and the willingness to kneel. **Susan B.** relates her struggles and her success:

I Was Shown the Real Me

I HAD ALWAYS THOUGHT OF MYSELF AS OPEN, EASYGOING, and flexible. Until I sobered up. It was after a mighty struggle with pride that I began to see the real me for the first time. The flexibility of which I was so proud was only skin deep. I could change for you on the outside, but never for me on the inside. Honestly, I didn't think that it was me who should make changes anyway. On top of all that, I certainly didn't know how to change. In my estimation, if there were any changes that needed to be made, it was people, places, and things that needed to change, not me.

My first experience with my own need to change came as a shock to me. It also proved to be the beginning of my real recovery—even though I had been sober in AA for eighteen months.

I had just begun to listen to other experienced recovering AA members. I had always heard them, but hardly tried to practice what they suggested. After a year and a half of being nothing more than sober, I was still quite miserable. I was actually thinking of not attending meetings anymore when the hearing started to become listening. My sponsor suggested I get on my knees to say "thanks" and ask for help.

Kneeling to say any sort of prayer was alien to me. I found the concept threatening. I still don't know why I felt that way. Kneeling to ask for help was even more foreign to me. My pride—an aspect of which I was unaware—wouldn't allow me to bow down to anyone, Higher Power or no Higher Power.

106

I found it nearly impossible to bend my legs, much less get on my knees. At times I felt as though there were a hand on the top of my head gently pushing me down into a kneeling position. Naturally, I fought the fight. Sometimes I would bend one knee and sort of squat. Other times I would only bend from the waist. It took me about three months finally to be able to bend both knees, get down, and say a quick "thank you," often feeling that someone was watching and laughing at me. How self-centered! I lived alone. There was no one around to watch me!

One day, after one of my quick "thanks," I was shown the real me. That flash of insight was a gift from my Higher Power. I hadn't known anything about my pride, my goal of total independence, my arrogance, or my fear. These deeply imbedded aspects of my personality became very clear to me as I fought to finally humble myself in the presence of my Higher Power.

Kneeling was the beginning of my growing up in AA. Kneeling was the surrender I had not experienced when I stopped drinking. To this day I am grateful for the gift of humility and pray that I remember to remain grateful.

—Susan B.

∽

Betty J. Eadie reported her own amazing spiritual experience in her phenomenal best-selling book, *Embraced by the Light*. "There is no death," she says. "It's leaving one state of being and graduating to another level of being. We're just here for a season. If you could see your timeline compared to eternity's, this is just a drop in the ocean":

GIVE YOUR DAY TO GOD

ON NOVEMBER 18, 1973, I HAD MY NEAR-DEATH EXPERIENCE and was shown into heaven. I was in the presence of my guardian angels and in the presence of God.

I miss the time I spent with Jesus. It's the most incredible feeling I've ever experienced in my entire life. I had never felt that way before and haven't since. I love Him and to be without Him, to be away from His presence, is like hell. I long for Him. I yearn for that return. I've learned that this is not home. I'm an alien to this place.

On earth we do material things, and forget about why we are here. We're here to learn to love. We're here to grow. We're here to use our free will to learn to be creators like God.

My experience changed me totally and completely. I love unconditionally now and it's very difficult to be around people who have a hard time being loved unconditionally. I don't even have to know you to love you. No matter what you say or do, you can't hurt me, I love you. That's uncomfortable to people who do not feel that they are worthy of love.

I see God differently from how I did when I was a child. God is like someone you bow down to and yet He isn't that way at all. He is very much available, reachable, touchable, tangible. He wants us to feel closer to Him, more like He's our Father. When I pray today I don't say, "Dear God," or "God," I just say, "Father, today I messed up. I know that You know my heart and You know that my desire is to always do Your will. Help me to remain humble."

Even though I've had this experience, I've come back and I'm still human. I err but I know I can talk to Him. The communication is two way. It's not just me talking to God. He actually responds. It's not an audible thing: answers come into my mind.

Each morning when we get up, we create our day. In the first five minutes of the morning we actually seal our day by our thoughts. So as you get up, create a day. Give it to God and say, "This is a day that I want to be beneficial for others." Do it for others and let it come back to you like a ripple. We are developing as God wants us to develop. Learn to be a creator like He is.

—*Betty J. Eadie*

∾

MEDITATION

One night I dreamed a dream.
I was walking along the beach with my Lord.
Across the dark sky flashed scenes from my life.
For each scene, I noticed two sets
of footprints in the sand,
one belonging to me
and one to my Lord.
When the last scene of my life shot before me
I looked back at the footprints in the sand.
There was only one set of footprints.
I realized that this was at the lowest
and saddest times of my life.
This always bothered me
and I questioned the Lord
about my dilemma.
"Lord, you told me when I decided to follow You,
You would walk and talk with me all the way.
But I'm aware that during the most troublesome
times of my life there is only one set of footprints.
I just don't understand why, when I needed You most,
You leave me."
He whispered, "My precious child,
I love you and will never leave you
never, ever, during your trials and testings.
When you saw only one set of footprints
it was then that I carried you."

—"FOOTPRINTS," BY MARGARET FISHBACK POWERS

PRAYER

My Lord God,
I have no idea where I am going.
I do not see the road ahead of me.
I cannot know for certain where it will end.
Nor do I really know myself, and the fact that I think that I
am following Your will does not mean that I am actually
doing so.

But I believe that the desire to please You does in fact please You.
And I hope I have that desire in all that I am doing.
I hope that I will never do anything apart from that desire.
And I know that if I do this, You will lead me by the right road though I may know nothing about it.
Therefore will I trust You always though I may seem to be lost and in the shadow of death.
I will not fear, for You are ever with me, and You will never leave me to face my perils alone.

—THOMAS MERTON

The spiritual life is not a theory. We have to live it.

—ANONYMOUS

6. FEAR

Fear is a darkroom for developing negatives.

—A.Word.A.Day, Internet

Overcome fear, behold wonder.

—Richard Bach

HUMAN BEINGS ARE VULNERABLE. WE SEEK SECURITY. IT'S the normal thing to do. We like our comfort zones so we try to protect what is predictable and dependable. Unfortunately, we often call our security "happiness" and believe that what we have is as good as life gets. So we don't change. We stay. We settle.

Our daily lives become our universe and we are bound to it. Change threatens not only our security but our sense of self as well. Most of us don't like change, and even those who do, welcome it with care. Consequently, we stay in jobs we hate, houses we dislike, and relationships that are harmful. We permit bosses to take advantage of us, tolerate the unacceptable behavior of others, keep our "bad" habits, and we work, eat, smoke, and spend ourselves into frenzy or depression.

These are all very real situations in which we can and should initiate positive action to improve our circumstances and enhance our self-esteem and sense of well-being. However, even if our status quo produces unhappiness and pain, at least we know it; and when contemplating change, we often predict failure based on imagined evidence. So we stay stuck in our present circumstances even though we know change is called for.

Another edge to change that keeps us locked into the status quo is the fear that surrounds the sense of being out of control. Divorce, moving, changing jobs, the loss of unfulfilled dreams, sickness, injury, or aging can leave us feeling overwhelmed by powerlessness.

CHALLENGING THE POWER OF FEAR

Many major life transitions produce hopefulness, pleasure, and happiness. Getting married, having children, receiving a promotion, buying a new car, moving to a new city, joining a gym, vacationing in Europe, or renting a house at the beach are some of the very best things life has to offer. However, all change creates anxiety and even good changes can produce fear.

I spent a lot of my life looking at the downside of change. A major transformation in my life has been the ability to set aside predictable negative thinking in the face of change. Slowly over the years, I've increasingly gotten to trust that when I "lose" something or someone, at least the potential is also there that something better or someone special in a different way will come into my life. The biggest fears I've had to face are the fear of the unknown, the fear of making a mistake, and the fear of failing. I've made some major attitude adjustments in these areas as well.

∽

My past inability to change in some situations was probably tied up with a belief that pain was my punishment, suffering was noble, or that life was supposed to be difficult. I'm not embarrassed to admit to being human in this regard. Today, this anchor of masochism no longer keeps me mired in destructive and self-defeating situations. Do these ideas by psychiatrist **Natalie Shainess** resonate with you as much as they did with me?

FIGHTING THE NEED TO SUFFER

A MASOCHIST IS SOMEONE WHO LIVES A LIFE OF SUFFERING. Freud's famous remark, "A masochist will always hold out his cheek when there is an expectation of a blow," really says it very well. Why people feel they have to suffer is rooted in early experience. There probably was a parental figure involved and there probably were conflicts involving power and cruelty.

Masochists feel like a cipher, a nothing; and even if they have the intellectual ability, they dare not think further. They are always very apologetic. "I'm not going to do anything to make you be angry with me, I am so inadequate." They also hold the belief that if they confess that enough, life will be all right. Of course, life doesn't work that way. Self-destruction, self-punishment, and self-defeat are all part of the modus operandi of the masochist. It is the opposite of power. It's a denial of power. "I'll hurt myself before you hurt me. I'll punish myself. I'll defeat myself. I will be no threat to you, so don't hurt me."

The masochistic person, out of fear, has not developed social skills. The masochist is afraid of everyone and therefore doesn't know how to develop an alliance with a friend. Fear of others is a big part of the whole masochistic picture, which gets more extreme as the person goes through life. The masochist doesn't see that there are any possibilities in life other than suffering. That is the imprint on them of what life is: to suffer.

—*Natalie Shainess, M.D.*

∽

Since starting my own television production company a few years ago, I've put a lot of time, energy, and personal money into it. My stubborn Irish nature, my willingness to go the extra mile, even fear kept me going at times when the future looked grim. I dug deep into myself—and my pocket—to keep the ship afloat. However, a saying caused me to change the way I was trying to raise money, a difficult task in today's competitive media marketplace, and literally may have saved the show:

**You're getting what you're getting
Because you're doing what you're doing.
If you don't like what you're getting,
Change what you're doing.**

About the same time I was dwelling on this advice, a friend reminded me of a classic definition of insanity: "Repeating the same behavior and expecting different results." I wasn't producing results I wanted and needed, so I made a decision to radically change my modus operandi and do things differently.

I began to network—a difficult assignment for someone who wrongly thinks he has to do things alone. I sought the help of experienced fund-raising professionals and got them involved in the search. A successful conclusion—some very generous sponsorship support—was the happy outcome. In retrospect, I kept putting one foot in front of the other and let my fear push in a positive way. With a lot of prayer, hard work, and support from others, it did.

We must travel in the direction of our fear.

—JOHN BERRYMAN

∾

In each lifetime there will be real fears to experience as we face life's most predictable changes. Actress **Betty White** covers some of the major ones she's faced: getting older, the death of her husband Allen, and career ups and downs. Betty's positive attitude is tremendously inspirational. Her message: Gratitude and acceptance are keys to successfully dealing with change:

DON'T BE AFRAID TO BE HAPPY

IF I WERE ON A GAME SHOW, AND SOMEBODY THREW OUT the word *change,* my free association would be "uprooting," or on a personal level, "adaptation." Age is a good example.

Dinah was a retired guide dog that I took from my friend Tom Sullivan when Dinah couldn't handle his new guide dog taking over her job. I had Dinah from the time she was eleven to the time she was fifteen. I learned a great deal about accommodation from her. Tom always said Dinah taught him to grow up and me to grow old. She took everything in stride. It happened about the time I was going from wishing I could hide my age to "Hey, I'm pretty proud of the fact that I'm still functioning at this age." It's a very comfortable transition if you don't fight it. Now I find myself bragging about how old I am instead of saying, "Well, let's get off the subject." It's a passage that we all have to go through. I'm seventy-three. It was painful for me to say that for a long time. In my business the minute you pass twenty you're over the hill; you're middle-aged at twenty-one.

My husband Allen Ludden went through a long, long illness before he died. Four years later I went through the same thing with my mother. Both of them were of the philosophy that if I allowed their illness to rub off on me, I would be letting them down terribly.

I've always believed in making the most of every day and every year. We don't know if tomorrow some horrendous thing will happen to us. When it does, we ask, "Why did I waste all that time?" You can't afford to waste any time, mentally. Relax, sure, but don't pick away any of that good time by worrying it to death. I am blessed with good health and believe me, that's the bottom line. If you feel good every day, you love every day. If you feel lousy, it's no fun to get up in the morning.

When I said "adaptation" was my free association to the word "change," I think "acceptance" was the word I was fishing for. Acceptance without fear, rejection, or apprehension. If things are going badly or if there's someone close to you in trouble, you're going to suffer, you're going to go through hell on wheels. But in day-to-day, normal circumstances you can't sit around saying, "Oh my God, I'm seventy years old, what am I going to do?" Pretty soon you get to be seventy-three.

When I was a child, my mother and father and I were very close. The three of us were great friends. I grew up with looking on the lighter side of things. Even if something was terribly tragic, you couldn't let it grind you into the floor. As my parents both grew older the lines in their faces were "up" lines. If you look at some people, you see that all their lines are down because they don't smile very much and everything is a worry.

There are ups and downs in my business too, and that's when all the good philosophy goes to hell in a handbasket. Each time I do a show I know that it's not going to go on forever. Each time a series ends I go through that terrible feeling of separation, because by that time I've gotten fond of the people I work with. It goes with the territory. There is a down period. It's somewhat of a comfort to know that it's happened before (and it'll probably happen again), but it doesn't alleviate that feeling of "Oh, it's the end of the world." But you have to rise above it. Something new will come along tomorrow.

That's why writing is such a saving grace for me. If things get hard, I write. It doesn't always work because the creative juices sometimes dry up; but I find the time to write and that's how my four books came about.

The happiest change in my life was when I married Allen. It was a wonderful change. That's not to say that adjusting to a marriage later in life is easy. There are times when you think "What am I doing?" but certainly in the overall picture, I knew at the time that this was something very worthwhile.

There's a difference between love and being in love. I had never felt about anybody the way I felt about Allen. It took me a year to get smart and realize it. He actually campaigned. He could have given courtship lessons. We missed being together for eighteen years by just three days.

It's an easy thing to blame everything on the fact that nothing's the same. Nothing ever will be the same. It won't. Face it, it's going to be different. You don't get better, you get different. If you let yourself get into that little eddy of a downward whirlpool, it's awful tough to pull yourself out of it. You just have to stay terribly still and not grind yourself into the ground. I get so many letters from new widows and I always answer them as fast as I can because I know what they're going through.

Yet you find some women who thrive on that grief. "I'm so miserable." "Look what happened." "Why me?" You've got to roll with that body blow, that punch.

Being down can be an addictive thing. It's habit-forming. I really worked, fought against it so much. I would look forward to those rest times. Maybe five minutes would go by that I didn't think of Allen, then maybe a half hour, and then maybe half a day. Maybe a week would go by when I was able to put my focus on other things.

I know too many people who are afraid to be happy. They're ashamed if they laugh. That can go on longer and longer until it becomes a habit.

—Betty White

∽

Is it really possible that many of us actually fear happiness even though we say it's our primary goal? Therapist **Dennis O'Grady** says it's the "fear of success" that prevents us from achieving it:

THE FEAR OF SUCCESS

PROBABLY ONLY 20 PERCENT OF PEOPLE ARE HAPPY. IT'S amazing to say, but people actually fight to block pleasure. I like the word *pleasure* more than *happiness* or *feeling good,* although they're all interchangeable. The challenge in our society today is how can we feel pleasure. Fear is a big part of the problem.

We've been raised to believe if you feel too much pleasure it's a bad thing. You may become immoral; you may lose your bearings; you may become mean; or you may lose your friends. The message: It's lonely at the top. I think people have been scripted in our culture to think that tragedy follows success; and religiously, we've been indoctrinated with the idea that pleasure is sinful.

When I'm doing workshops I write on the blackboard: SUCCESS = PLEASURE. Then I take that one step further and say that the ability to embrace change or risk positive change extends the equation to CHANGE = SUCCESS = PLEASURE.

There are five fears of change:

Fear of the unknown
Fear of failure
Fear of commitment

Fear of disapproval
Fear of success

Any one or all of these can rear their ugly heads when we are faced with change.

Sometimes people get a horrible feeling that if they try to do something positive, they'll be rejected. Other times they are simply afraid to fall flat on their faces. Fear of commitment certainly gets in the way of partners enjoying each other or parents loving their children.

In addition, adults think they ought to know all the answers—that they ought to know what's going to unfold next. It takes strong self-esteem to admit that you don't have a lot of control over life. In the end, so much of it boils down to a fear of success—which is really the fear of pleasure.

Symptoms that tell you something in your life needs to be changed are:

Boredom
Resentment
Excessive complaining
Falling asleep at the wheel of life
Any continuing addictive behavior

A person called me recently and said that his group wanted a workshop on how to get beyond change. I told him his concept was a contradiction in terms. If you're alive, you don't get beyond change. Too many people have the attitude: "Let me get beyond this. I don't want to be here. I want to be there." Well, when they get there, they find another there.

Change is always part of our lives. Some people are very stirred spiritually by change. Their souls are breathed into by change.

Change is what makes us tick. It's what makes us able to live.

I give exercises in my workshops to help people get accustomed to change. I suggest that they park in a different spot each day, eat at a new restaurant, get out of the office and walk around their building, go to a support group meeting in a new place, travel where they normally don't go, or visit a college campus. The exercise is saying, "Relax, there's nothing wrong with change."

—*Dennis O'Grady, Psy.D.*

∾

Psychiatrist **Lonnie MacDonald** has been an important person in my life. Lonnie and I have been involved in a twenty-five-year conversation about how important childhood experiences may dictate the ease or difficulty with which we handle loss and change as adults:

HEALING OLD WOUNDS

HUMANS COME INTO THE WORLD EXTREMELY DEPENDENT upon others for their care, nurture, safety, and development. As infants we have needs for affection, attention, nurturing, and love. Our feelings of self-esteem, security, comfort, and safety are influenced by the crucible of early growth and development.

Consequently, when an infant meets situations in which his or her needs can not be immediately met, such as hunger, the discomfort of soiled diapers, the pain of a pin stick, or even a cold, there is frustration. If the frustration is not dealt with successfully at the time, or if there develops a pattern of dealing with that frustration in ways that cause even more discomfort, deep feelings of helplessness, hopelessness, and powerlessness are produced.

Sometimes the fear associated with those unmet infant needs can be extremely strong and carry with it such a sense of danger that major emotional wounds or traumas result. The infant's need to protect self from distress will result in various kinds of self-protective defenses that block off sensations.

At times the attempts at relief are miscarried in so much as they do not open up a path to resolution but only block off emotions in the service of survival. Consequently, at times there can be such an accumulation of feelings of discomfort and distress that the threshold is assaulted: no more is tolerable and defenses are activated against the further experiencing of pain.

SEPARATION ANXIETY

Let me use my own experiences of separation anxiety. When I was a child I was severely burned; while I was in the hospital I was separated from my mother. During that time I was exposed to the profound fear of being left alone and of being helpless and powerless. Situations came about later in my life that reactivated those old wounds.

I was a product of an era when there was a lot less information and understanding about the power of emotions shaping and influencing us. When I was ten and my sister died, it was not talked about. Therefore, opportunities to express how I felt and get from others the kind of responses that would enable me to grieve and heal were not available to me. Consequently I blocked off those painful feelings.

Two years later when my brother was murdered, there was a reactivation of the old wounds—again not dealt with in a healing manner. That trauma further compounded the old, blocked-off, festering pain pocket. Later in my life as a young male teenager, a relationship would break up and it would again trigger the reactivation of those old feelings.

I would deal with them by blocking out the feelings and behaving in ways in which I would be "acting out," but not helping myself to heal. These would be miscarried attempts at helping me to feel better. I distracted myself by getting involved in some other relationship or in situations where my ego would feel better—such as in sports or scholastic achievements.

COURAGE IS FACING FEAR

The attempt to retreat from pain as the consequence of rehashing old wounds is incredibly strong. The pull is what I refer to as the emotional undertow. Often we relieve it by detachment, but that, of course, does not heal either. Other miscarried attempts at healing are even more evident in the case of alcohol and drug use and abuse—in that they modify feelings.

It is critical for a therapist to really understand through history-taking what an individual's earlier experiences with losses have been. *Any significant loss can threaten feelings of inner security, self-confidence, and self-worth and bring about feelings of deep insecurity, self-loathing, self-hatred, and inferiority in the face of fantasized or real danger.*

Facing fear is what courage is all about. It is crucial for most of us to have the external support that encourages us to move through the pain when we confront those feelings of helplessness, hopelessness, and powerlessness. We can't do it alone.

When you get to the point when you feel you can't go without a drink any longer, or you've got to pick up a cigarette even though you made the resolve not to—that is where I as a therapist would identify the vulnerability to reconnecting with extremely painful feelings of the past. This is the crucial turning point—when a person will either withdraw and retreat or when I can say, "Let me give you my hand; everything is going to be okay. I know it's painful and it doesn't feel like healing. It feels terrible and you want to run away, but trust me, let's go ahead."

Therapists, friends, support groups, family, and clergy can all be helpful. It's so important that we have those sanctuaries where we can expose our wounds and get the support to keep going. Depending upon how deep those wounds are and how sensitive people are constitutionally, it can be very difficult for individuals to overcome the kind of intense fears, terror, and panicky feelings that they experience when they attempt to change, especially to change in giving up the old self-protective defenses.

In childhood all of us are wounded to some degree by the very nature of being human. However, sometimes the emotional undertow, the negative energy, is so strong that change is not only very difficult, but sometimes cannot be accomplished at all. So we leave this planet without having been able to move beyond a certain point in our journey of change. We see that everyday. For example, the majority of alcoholics and addicts don't make it.

I know of a man who had ninety days of sobriety and took a

drink, then over the next two weeks desperately tried to get sober. He went to recovery meetings drunk; at least he was in a sanctuary. But then, he tragically overdosed on alcohol and died. It's not because he was not bright or because he didn't have the desire. He was addicted to alcohol. The predictable consequences for a drinking alcoholic—or using drug addict—are quitting, wet brain, or death.

On the other hand, I've just talked with someone who was working in a most debasing job with a very abusive boss. He was constantly berated and called names. With encouragement, this individual was able to quit the job. Then immense, nightmarish feelings rushed in and told him he was wrong and that something was wrong with him and he shouldn't have quit. He couldn't sleep at night because he had stepped beyond the point of perpetuating the abuse. He was able to get up the courage— he'd been in this job for over a year—to say, "I quit." What was reactivated were the projected consequences of the defiance of authority going back to childhood. Feeling so alone, he believed the consequences of quitting were going to destroy him. With help, however, he was able to reexperience his feelings, talk about them and move through them successfully rather than run away by going back and asking for the job again.

—*Lonnie MacDonald, M.D.*

∾

Over the years I have run into variations on the following list of stress-producing events. I once saw a list like this in a magazine; a point value was assigned to each change absorbed in the previous year. I recall that my stress score was astronomical. I'm not sure when that was, but I lived, so there is hope. It may be a comment on how much stress we can handle—or at least how much I could and did at the time.

In descending order, here are the changes that produce the most stress:

Death of a spouse
Divorce

Separation
Jail
Death of a family member
Serious illness
Getting married
Being fired
Marital reconciliation
Retirement
Change in health of a family member
Pregnancy
Sexual problems
Birth or adoption
Major change in business
Major change in finances
Death of an intimate friend
Change in career
Change in number of arguments with spouse
Getting a mortgage
Foreclosure or bankruptcy
Getting a promotion
Child leaving home
In-law trouble
Personal achievement

∾

The greater the change, or the greater the number of changes experienced at one time, the more serious the stress and the deeper the fear. No one can better help us understand what is going on when we are under the influence of change-related stress than holistic physician and author **Dr. Andrew Weil:**

THE ESSENCE OF EXPERIENCE

WHEN WE LOOK AT THE RELATIONSHIP BETWEEN STRESS and how it affects the body and mind, there's a tremendous amount of research and evidence that shows ways in which those interactions can occur. It shouldn't be any surprise that stress can produce major disease or aggravate disease of all sorts; nor should it be a surprise that a dramatic change in a person's state of consciousness or emotions can produce healing. Although I've written about cases in which I've seen the disappearance of long-standing diseases when people fell in love, I can't always arrange for that to happen. (It's important, however, to know that potential is there and maybe there are other ways to release it.)

When I'm working with patients, I take a careful history. I ask about people's lives in great detail. I'm interested in their work, their relationships, and their sex lives. A lot of my evaluation is based on intuition; however, in terms of looking for physical symptoms that signal a need for change, there are certain categories that are most likely to be associated with stress:

Digestive symptoms of all sorts
Headaches
Chronic pain
Muscular pain
Skin problems
Insomnia
Anxiety
Depression
Frequent infections

I've had only one episode of debilating back pain in my life. It happened about seven years ago. I've never had anything wrong with my back before or since. This was something that was initiated by slipping on a rock. It was a kind of a harmless little twist; however, it sent my back into a period of spasms that lasted for three weeks. At one point the pain was so bad I was unable to dress myself. It was very clear to me that this was emotional in origin.

The source involved two things that happened at the same time: one was the realization that I had to break off a very tumultuous relationship and the other one was the death of a very close friend and colleague. It had to do with emotional loss in one instance and there was nothing I could do about that. As for the other, it was clear to me that it was a relationship that I had to end.

In my own case, the reason I stayed in the relationship was there was some sort of security in being in it, even though it was obviously destructive. To not be in a relationship—to give that up—was scary. When I came out of the relationship, it led to a change in my life in which I got married—a marriage which I'm happily in now. I don't think I could be in this marriage if I hadn't had that other relationship. Being in that relationship made it possible for me to enter this one.

CULTIVATE THE ABILITY TO CHANGE

Sometimes when I work with patients and I have a sense that their problem is their job, their spouse, or their kids, I may point that out to them gently. Often with these things, for various reasons people are unwilling to make changes. On the other hand, sometimes I've worked with patients over a period of time and they have come to see that they had to change and some of them were able to do it.

For the ones who can't, one thing I can do is try to give them stress reduction strategies to neutralize the stress or protect their bodies from the effects of it. At least, I keep reminding them where the stress is coming from, what the real cause is. If they utilize the strategies, accept the situation, and alter their attitude about it, they may be able to come to a better equilibrium.

TAKING POSITIVE ACTION

When you are going to take some action, what is required is hope that where you're going to end up is going to be better than what you've got and faith that if you leap into the void, the universe will catch you. It's a belief that there's some kind of safety net out there to save you.

That faith might resonate with your own past experience or with other people's experiences. The great fear is that you're leaping and you don't know what comes next.

The essence of experience is change, and the ultimate certainty of life is that there is change and change is uncomfortable. Finding the courage to change may be one of life's greatest lessons.

—Andrew Weil, M.D.

∾

He has not learned the lesson of life who does not every day surmount a fear.

—RALPH WALDO EMERSON

Sometimes the fear associated with change causes such panic it paralyzes us from taking the action necessary to protect ourselves. On the other hand, that same fear can also be converted into a powerful force that helps us to create change or move though change we are facing.

∾

It is courage—our inner strength—that enables us to act in spite of our gravest fears. Dancer and choreographer **Bill T. Jones** refuses to be controlled by fear:

I AM ON FIRE

I BECAME PUBLICLY KNOWN AS HIV POSITIVE THROUGH A cover story in *The Advocate* magazine. I must have mentioned I was positive very casually in my interview with their writer because I was shocked when I saw it in the first paragraph of his article. I was really worried about it because it suddenly got a lot of national exposure.

I called the writer, somewhat perturbed, and he said, "Well, I'm sorry. I gave it to my editors and they didn't edit it. They didn't ask me to fact check on it. They just printed it." He said, "And besides, you did say it." And I did say it. I guess I could have asked for a retraction, but that would have been hypocritical. I decided there was no reason for me to hide it.

It was printed everywhere and because there's such a shortage of people in my field who are open about being HIV positive, I took on all the attention. That had an effect on my work, how my work was perceived, how I was written about, and how people framed an image of me. It took a lot of soul searching and sleepless nights to understand how to deal with it.

When the article came out, there was terror and a deep feeling of violation that I had betrayed myself. I said to myself, "No one is going to support a choreographer who they feel is dying." I thought that not only was I being affected by this, but everything that Arnie, my late partner and lover, and I had built—that the company itself would suffer.

Professionally, I feel as if I changed in the public eye a great deal. As a person I was forced to change as well. I became more self-conscious about what I did and said in some ways and in other ways more brash and bold. I was constantly upping the ante, trying to contextualize this new me who had become "the other," trying to understand how this other fit into the world. In doing that I made mistakes and, in some ways, I made some good moves too. Sometimes there was a lot of anger in my work, but the world, because of the newness of knowing a public person who was HIV positive, could see only the personal side of it. They were not able to distance me from the anger and the fear.

The audience is not only the theater audience, but it's your family, the people in your bank, the people in your supermarket. If you are a public person like I am and it's printed that you are HIV positive, then everyone with whom you come in contact who might have read it knows that intimate thing about you. Suddenly, you're not a "normal" person anymore. When do you lose your membership as part of the anonymous group of "well people"? Everyone holds on to that. The great fear about illness is that suddenly I am set apart. So there's not only the fear of disapproval or criticism, but the fear of exclusion as well.

That article certainly cut through any denial I still may have had about being HIV positive but it was all happening while I was still grieving over Arnie's death, so everything was like having a hangover.

OVERCOMING DAILY FEARS

Let's talk about Bill's fear, my fear. I come from a large family with a very strong mother figure. I was raised in a very macho male environment. Fear was something that you were supposed to hide. Yet in our house we all had our fear. I was known as the too sensitive one, maybe the sissy one. I wasn't allowed to watch horror movies after a while because I had nightmares. I remember saying to my brothers, "Wait until I grow up, I won't be afraid anymore." We thought that as soon as you became a man, something happened and men just weren't afraid.

Now, something did happen to me and I don't know if it had to do with race. My father decided to be a black Yankee and move us all to a predominantly German/Italian fruit-and-vegetable growing community in upstate New York where we worked and where I grew up. The first day on the bus going to kindergarten I was surrounded by white kids. I had never met a white child in my life. I had to make friends with new kids, K through 12. Every day from the age of five to when I graduated at eighteen, these were my comrades. I had been told by my mother that these were the people that ran her father off—that you couldn't trust them, yet I was expected to bond with them on the most intimate level—and I did. So I had to overcome fear daily. My fear was that I was not going to be able to cut it academically, that I was going to be rejected out of hand. I was always waiting to be rejected and I could smell it a mile away. But it was the same smell that gets the blood pumping and it turns into a good healthy head of anger and resolve to go through whatever you're facing.

My mother used to say that when you get scared in a fight you've got to connect with that part of you that will go through a person. It's a very violent image: "You mess with me and I'm going to go through you." You're talking about fear being an engine. Fear turns into a good head of anger and you just go. Later you might be trembling at what you did to get over that hurdle, but you did get over it, using whatever resources you had.

Now, when the world offers you a situation where you say

to yourself, "Oh my God, Bill, now you have been outed as 'the other.'" You say, well, I'll be damned if I'll be ruled by it. In the words of the traditional spiritual, "Before I'll be a slave, I'll be buried in my grave." I'll be damned if this world, this society's ideas about my sexual orientation and my life, are going to keep me from reaching what I have envisioned as success—the glory of what art means to me. That kicked in. It doesn't mean there wasn't a lot of sadness, uncertainty, and distrust in the face of looking constantly for rejection in people's eyes.

THE POSITIVE EFFECTS OF COURAGE AND COMPASSION

What kept me going was something akin to anger, a steely resolve. I'm not quite sure what it is. I think it is courage, but it's also "I'll be damned if I let this thing set the course of my life, if I succumb to it." Even as I speak, I feel something similar to tears and bile. It's something I inherited from my parents. It has an historical and a social component to it. I know I have it and that's what helped me live once I decided I was gay and Arnie and I were starting our relationship.

I went to a gay dance at the university. No one knew about my sexuality. The black kids crashed the party. While holding Arnie in my arms and slow dancing, I saw them gathering around the periphery of the floor, gawking at "the queers." I did not look at them; nor did I stop dancing or move off into the shadows. I said, "Let come what comes." I was scared to death. There were girls there I had been flirting with, and suddenly I was revealed, but I stood my ground. I didn't know what else to do at that moment. *Don't run,* something said, *don't run.* I don't know what it's called. I call it a survival instinct. Sometimes it just means standing your ground and looking in the eyes of your accuser.

"He's already lived a nontraditional life, but now he's HIV"—there's another kind of fear that's going to come from family and from moralists who say that people who get AIDS are guilty. Can you look that in the eye? Can you look an accusing brother or sister in the eye? Can you deal with gossip? This is different from someone lynching you in a racist act; this is more subtle.

There are a couple of Bill T. Joneses. One is the person who comforts the other in the morning while I'm brushing my teeth. When I haven't been able to sleep that night because of the latest horrible things written about me, that other person says, "You know, you're all right." It's compassion—friendship with myself—which says, "You're all right, William, you are okay and it's okay if you're frightened right now." What I'm learning about life is that it takes a hell of a lot of compassion to live, and that compassion coupled with humility starts with yourself. That's something I have been cultivating every day. It's all right to be afraid. If you're afraid, you're human. But to be controlled by fear is something I will not accept.

I am on fire. I am in flames constantly with the repercussions of trying to live the life that I live. Going through the fire I've been talking about, I am constantly in doubt and fear, yet I have never felt so alive as I do now. I feel strong. Of course, I have a wonderful partner, Bjorn Amelan. I decided that I had to find a person I could respect and who has the same take on fear and courage as I do. We can go through it together. That's one reason I'm able to do this. Although I think I'd be able to do it without him, I don't know if I'd be able to do it as gracefully, and the quality of life wouldn't be as good.

Yes, I have made a lot of wild choices, sometimes to illustrate the irrationality of fear, but somehow also to outline what it means to be "the other." I have to acknowledge both and this has sometimes been misunderstood. Yet even this misunderstanding is part of building something. I don't think the edifice will be complete until I'm dead.

What I'm building—my company, the body of my work, my personal legacy—will only be understood historically. If you ask me if there are repercussions and side effects, let's talk in fifty years.

—*Bill T. Jones*

John K. tells about battling his fear with the successful coping strategies of therapy, positive thinking, and prayer:

FACE YOUR DEMONS

WE ARE BORN WITH TWO SIMPLE BUT DEFINITE ABSOLUTES in our lives. The first is that we are going to live for a time here on earth and the second is that we are going to die at some point in the future. Neither of these is negotiable.

We have the least amount of control over dying. We can eat nutritious foods, exercise, and develop a healthy way of living, but this does not guarantee longevity, only a better quality of life.

The quality of life we have on planet Earth is really up to us through the choices we make. Many outside factors present us with good fortune or challenges, but as life progresses, we hope to learn to deal with our choices in positive, life-enriching ways. As adults, how we choose to react to outside circumstances is entirely up to us, especially if we are awake to the human and spiritual dimensions of life.

I found myself at a juncture in life filled with incredibly painful physical symptoms caused by an addiction to fear. I gave up alcohol and drugs only to take on a new addiction to fear and worry. So even with nine years of sobriety, I chose to go back into therapy and look at the monsters that were under my bed. Therapy is not a fast process, but it has brought the most relief.

FEAR IS AN INVENTION OF THE MIND

Fear has been one of my greatest challenges. Fear of failure, fear of not being liked or accepted, fear of not having enough, fear of dying. The list goes on and on. Fear is one of the most powerful feelings that any human can experience. But 90 percent of the fears we experience hold no water in the reality of life. They are horror stories we make up and project in our mind. Most of the time, the body does not know the difference between what is real and that which we create so vividly in our imaginations. The body reacts in defensive ways even though there is no actual threat. Adrenaline is pumped throughout the system, which only makes us more hypervigilant. This causes more stress. Stress in turn has many physical ways of expressing itself: headaches, ulcers, fatigue, insomnia.

As a society, we self-medicate, treat the symptoms, and rarely get to the underlying causes. Those remedies may work for a while, but the root cause usually pops up in another manner. The symptoms are a wake-up call that something is out of balance and needs to be looked at. Fear is not a bad feeling. It helps us in times of challenge by alerting us to danger and giving a boost of energy to activate the "fight or flight" response.

I cannot tell you how many times I have lain awake in bed playing out my fear scenarios over and over again only to wake in the morning exhausted. Those scenarios I created never happened, but my body felt as if they had, and my life reflected turmoil and disease.

"Face your demons or they will bite your butt" was some advice I got a number of years ago. There are still fear scenarios that I invent that make me sick; but I try not to play the "What if this horrible thing happens" game.

Fear-based living is an addictive lifestyle. The price of playing with imaginary fear scenarios is too costly for me. I start my day with prayer and use positive thoughts to keep me centered in reality. At bedtime I thank God for the day and its lessons and consciously choose uplifting thoughts before going to sleep. A fearful thought may pop into my mind, but I do not entertain it. I cannot stop someone from knocking on my door, but I do not have to let him into my home.

—*John K.*

❧

No passion so effectively robs the mind of all its powers of acting and reasoning as fear.

—EDMUND BURKE

❧

Some years ago, **Dr. Lonnie MacDonald** introduced me to a painting called "The Circle of Fear." Since that time the painting's powerful message has been in my mind whenever I am knee deep in change. Dr. MacDonald's description will allow you to get the picture. *If there is a graphic representation that illustrates what goes on when we confront major change, this is it:*

THE CIRCLE OF FEAR

I WORKED WITH A FEMALE PATIENT FOR MORE THAN A YEAR. We discussed and explored various kinds of experiences and patterns she had as an adult relating to a succession of men in her life. The kinds of fears she experienced in those relationships were similar to fears she experienced when she was growing up. The negative results of her defiance of authority as a child manifested themselves in the present as submitting to and pleasing adults.

This woman created a painting that epitomized the concept we had been discussing in therapy, which we referred to as "the circle of fear." It is a large painting, measuring almost three feet by four or five feet, and it is very dramatic. At the center of the drawing is an almost angelic little girl kneeling in a rather pliant posture against a peaceful blue background and holding a single rose. Surrounding her is a large circle. Beyond the perimeter of the circle in all parts of the rest of the painting are monsters, dragons, and animals with knives and daggers. They are all horrible and threatening. In the circle are the words *Good* and *Yes*. The implication: If the young girl obeys and does what she has been told to do by the adults—if she is a good little girl—then everything will be okay.

Outside the circle is a black background. In addition to the monsters are the words, *No* and *Don't*. The power of the painting is the further implication that if the patient, as the little girl, were to step beyond the border of the circle (that blocked her from becoming a woman and maintained her as a little girl in a woman's body—living and relating to people more as a child than as an adult), she would be in danger of being attacked by monsters and of being annihilated.

It was a wonderful thing for the two of us that she had presented such a concrete depiction of the process. It also became a centerpiece of my being able to explain to subsequent patients, in the course of their therapy, the conflict between fear and growth.

STEPPING OVER THE LINE

Anytime someone steps over the line—outside "the circle of fear," so to speak—that person will reopen the old emotional wounds that contain those feelings of fear, helplessness, terror, and panic. Once a person has stepped over the line, and is faced with such anxiety, the individual will have two choices: The person can absorb, experience, and deal with the anxious feelings, and thereby enlarge the circle, or the person can be so consumed with fear he or she jumps back inside the circle. When the individual has gained sufficient courage to step beyond the limiting perimeter—to make dramatic change— this is the time when encouraging the patient to persist is so crucial. Allies are essential because the undertow—the pull, the force to go back, to get away from the pain, to retreat—is so powerful.

In the process of change we endeavor to transform feelings of self-doubt, self-loathing, self-hatred, inadequacy, and inferiority into an increasing sense of self-worth, self-confidence, security, and self-acceptance. Through the process of reentering the old emotional pain pockets we have a chance to correct the programming that has left us with a diminished, distorted, and deformed sense of self. As we grow we are increasing our capacity to realize, "Oh, that was what I was led to believe, but that's not really true of me."

IDENTIFY YOUR OWN CIRCLE OF FEAR

In my own case, I was deeply affected as a by-product of blacks brought up in an era of intense Jim Crowism. I was told that I was a second-class citizen, that I was not fully human. In addition, in terms of my own personal circle of fear, if I did not observe the boundaries set—such as don't sit in this section of the bus, or don't sit in that section of the movie house, or don't go in this door, or don't go into that neighborhood—the consequences, the dangers of punishment, were very great indeed. Back at that time there were lynchings.

Over the years I've come to identify the perimeter of my own circle of fear. I couldn't tolerate the amount of anxiety that was stirred up when I moved from the all-black school system over to the high school, which was predominantly white. I blocked it out. I could not be aware that I was in enemy territory and had to be so anxious about stepping over boundaries.

My defense was to become a superachiever.

—*Lonnie MacDonald, M.D.*

∾

Supersalesman **Zig Ziglar** says that change begins with small steps—and gives specific examples to support that belief:

THE COURAGE TO TAKE ACTION

FEAR HAS AN ACROSTIC: FALSE EVIDENCE APPEARING REAL. It's fear that the unknown is going to be worse than the known even though the known is considerably less than desirable. People have an image, a picture of themselves, and that picture will not permit them to move higher.

For twenty-four years of my adult life I weighed well over two hundred pounds. During those years, I must have lost a couple thousand pounds. It's easy to lose weight. You take it off, you put it on. You take it off, you put it on. Of course, the real problem was not what I was eating. When my youngest daughter, who's now grown, was a little girl, I taught her to call me "fat boy." I had pictures of me lying on the diving board of my swimming pool. At least part of me was on the diving board. I could look in the mirror and see I was a fat boy. Every time my daughter called me "fat boy"—and she obviously did not know what she was doing—I laughed outside, but I cried inside. Until that picture changed and I saw myself as being slim and healthy, I could lose all the weight but I always gained it back.

The real breakthrough had to do with my faith. I started reading the Bible very carefully and I discovered the great truths of life are all there. As I studied the principles, I came to the conclusion that I did have real worth, I did have real value, I was here for a purpose. I knew I could do things more effectively if I were active physically, if I were healthy and energetic. Then the weight came off and stayed off.

I was in the midst of writing a book. In the book I said, "You can go where you want to go, do what you want to do, and be what you want to be." When I looked at those words and then looked at my waistline, I knew I either had to take those words out of the book or I had to take something off me. I made the commitment that I was going to do it. It took me ten months. To lose thirty-seven pounds all I had to lose on average was one and nine-tenths ounces a day for ten months.

One of the books I wrote has now sold well over a million and half copies. Three hundred and eighty-four pages. All I had to do was write one and a quarter pages a day, on average, every day for ten months. When you break it down, it's like the old saying, "By the mile it's a trial, by the inch it's a cinch." It's not just a phrase, it's a reality. Greatness or success is not achieved in one big leap: life is not a sprint, it's an endurance race.

Change starts with very small steps. Goals become more of a commitment when you write them down. Otherwise, they're just a resolution. A resolution is generally just a confession that you ought to do something. So if you put your goals in writing, that means your commitment is more likely to grow. You can review it daily; it's there in front of you.

One of my favorite little sayings is "When you discipline yourself to do the things you need to do when you need to do them, the day is going to come when you can do the things you want to do when you want to do them." One hundred seventy-five of the CEOs of the Fortune 500 companies are former Marines. In the military they teach discipline, commitment, responsibility, and decisive action. These things are all part of the package.

Life is not easy, it's tough. What qualities do people have to possess in order to be successful? If you build upon honesty, character, and integrity, you can develop the other qualities. It takes courage to take action, to do the right thing. You have to accept responsibility for your behavior and the responsibilities you have on the job or at home.

Patience and persistence are important lessons to learn. In 1952 I decided I wanted to be a speaker. It took me sixteen years before I was able to speak on a full-time basis. Three weeks ago I signed a seven-year contract to do a daily newspaper column. I've been working on that one for twenty years. Persistence paid off and I'm excited about it.

The primary ingredient for having a good night's sleep is a clear conscience. People with integrity have nothing to fear because they have nothing to hide. It also has to do with security: you can sleep more comfortably if you're confident and competent in what you do. In my own particular case, my faith has been a great sustaining force in my life. It changed the course of my life dramatically.

—Zig Ziglar

MEDITATION

There are two days in the week about which I never worry— two carefree days kept sacredly free from fear and apprehension. One of these is Yesterday. Yesterday, with its cares and frets and pains and aches, all its faults, its mistakes and blunders, has passed forever beyond my recall. It was mine; now it is God's.

The other day I do not worry about is Tomorrow. Tomorrow, with all its possible adversities, its burdens and mistakes, is as far beyond my mastery as its dead sister, Yesterday. Tomorrow is God's day; it will be mine.

There is left, then, for myself, one day in the week, Today. Any man or woman can fight the battles of today. Anyone can carry the burdens of just one day; anyone can resist the temptation of today. It is only when we willfully add the burdens of these two awful eternities, Yesterday and Tomorrow—such burdens as only the Mighty God can sustain—that we break down.

It isn't the experience of Today that drives men mad. It is the remorse of what happened Yesterday and fear of what Tomorrow might bring. These are God's days—leave them to Him.

—"THE GOLDEN DAY," BY ROGER JONES BURDETTE

THE PRAYER FOR PROTECTION

The light of God surrounds you;
The love of God enfolds you;
The power of God protects you,
The presence of God watches over you.
Wherever you are, God is,
 And all is well.

      —UNITY PRAYER

Where fear is, happiness is not.

      —SENECA

7. COURAGE

Courage comes and goes. Hold on for the next supply.

—THOMAS MERTON

Courage is almost a contradiction in terms. It means a strong desire to live taking the form of a readiness to die.

—G. K. CHESTERTON

A FRIEND OF MINE RESCUED TWO PEOPLE AT THE BEACH A couple of summers ago.

The surf at the Delaware shore was as rough as I've ever seen it. While the water was fun to play in at times, huge waves often knocked swimmers down and, to be honest, fighting the waves and the undertow often left me out of breath. Some days it was incredibly dangerous; there were times when it was too much for me. According to the local newspapers, lifeguards made thousands of rescues during that summer; yet, some lives were lost.

I was just arriving at the beach and from a far distance I saw my friend playing in the crashing surf. When I saw him start to swim out toward two others, well past a point of safety, I remember thinking, "Why the hell is he going out there?" A crowd was gathering on the beach watching what was happening and I quickly put it together: he was swimming toward a couple of guys who had gotten themselves out too far in the heavy surf and couldn't get back to shore. My friend grabbed one of them, and fighting the waves, pulled him in to safety. He swam out again—another swimmer joined him this time—and together they rescued the second person. By this time, lifeguards were involved and helped get both men out of the water.

By any definition, my friend performed an act of great courage, taking action in the face of fear or danger. My friend's rescue was an outstanding demonstration of physical and emotional bravery. It was a situation of life or death and what he did entailed great risk.

After his adrenaline slowed down, I asked him what had happened. He said he heard the two people yelling for help, and when he looked around he realized he was the only person in the water and nobody else was noticing what was going on. "I've never been as scared in my life," he said. "It was fast, intense, and scattered. I just prayed and swam to them."

I have witnessed other examples of magnificent courage with friends who have lived and died with AIDS. Very recently I have also watched another friend, who—after a heroic battle of several years to save his ailing foot—made the medically necessary decision to have a below-the-knee amputation.

What strikes me in talking with them is that none thinks of what he did as particularly courageous. I do. In conversations for this book, others also have downplayed their own courage—which I and others clearly see—in regard to something remarkable they have done.

People tell us, "Don't sweat the small stuff." The truth is: "Almost everything in life is the small stuff."

The bigger stuff—the Big Challenges—require courage. That's a quality we all possess, and sooner or later, we'll all discover we have it. Life has a way of showing us we have courage. Circumstances bring it out of us to help us meet serious challenges. Major life transitions are a part of life, and our hidden reserve of strength keeps us going. It's courage that sees us through when we create change ourselves and when we are forced to accept the unacceptable.

You may be wrestling right now with whether or not to make a major change in your life. That decision may be producing great stress. In order to move to where you want to go, you must tap into your available supply of courage. It requires faith and hope to do so. Prayer helps: "Please God, give me the strength to do this." Affirmation helps: "What I am trying to do is hard, but I know I can do it." Support from others helps: "You can do it!"

While fear may conspire to keep us from changing, courageous people listen to their feelings and acknowledge their fears. They ask for help, set upon a course of action, stay with it, and achieve the results they want. They also get rewarded for their efforts.

∾

Jack Valenti, president of the Motion Picture Association of America, recalls a tragic day in our country's recent history—a time of great courage for all of the principals involved—and for everyone in America:

CHANGE IS A WAY OF LIFE

I WAS ABOUT SIX OR SEVEN CARS BACK IN THE MOTORCADE. The vice president had asked me, because I had an advertising and political consulting agency, to manage the press and logistics of the trip by President Kennedy and the vice president to San Antonio, Houston, Fort Worth, Dallas, and then supposedly on to Austin for the climatic event on the night of November 22, 1963. My agency was deployed around the state and I traveled with the vice-president from Houston and Fort Worth and then on to Dallas. So I was in the motorcade when the president was slain in the streets of Dallas. It was a mindless, senseless act.

I was ordered by a Secret Service agent to go to a room where the vice-president was sequestered. When we arrived, it was empty but another Secret Service man was there who said, "The vice-president wants me to take you to Air Force One." When I got aboard the plane, the new president beckoned to me and said without any ceremony, "I want you on my staff and you're going to fly back to Washington with me." He didn't ask, "Would you like to come?" And so I learned then that when the president of the United States, no matter who, asks you to do something, your answer is "Yes sir," or 'Yes ma'am," as the case may be.

During World War II I flew fifty-one combat missions with the Twelfth Air Force in Italy. I guess the fact that I survived allowed them to give me the Distinguished Flying Cross. Somebody once asked me, "What did you learn from the war?" and I had a ready answer. "I learned to live with fear." I learned to do my job as a professional even when I was absolutely frightened to death. That's a good lesson to learn. Men and women can do all sorts of things under the most harrowing of circumstances, if they're trained and they're professionals, and do their job.

LBJ was the coolest man on the airplane. He'd spent twenty-four years in Washington at the pinnacle of power. He understood the art of governing and the political minefields one must journey through. He was determined to show the country that while the light at the White House may flicker, it never, never goes out. He summoned Mrs. Kennedy to his side to be in the swearing-in picture to show that while President Kennedy was dead, the legacy he left to this land would carry on. He was trying to soothe the fevered brow of his country and I think he did that with remarkable skill. The rest of us aboard that plane were in varying states of hysteria.

I was absolutely captured with emotion. I couldn't believe that this had happened. I thought that at any moment I'd wake up as I did when I was a small boy and find out those odious dreams were nightmares and that wonderful soft reality would come back. It didn't. It was real and grotesque. All the way back to Washington I felt the tremors of total disbelief. The aides of President Kennedy, Larry O'Brien and Kenny O'Donnell, were catatonic. One day they're in power following their prince, the next day he's struck down in a millisecond. They couldn't believe it.

On the trip back President Johnson was talking about assembling the government when he arrived. He was on the phone a lot to Bobby Kennedy, Bob McNamara, and to McGeorge Bundy to make sure that when he landed he could begin the art, and it was and is an art, of telling the country, "Don't worry. Everything will be all right. The Constitution is intact."

There's an old phrase that dates back to Machiavelli's day about an Italian prince about whom they said, "He was never better than when water was up to his neck," meaning that when a crisis was on, he responded. What the country needs are formidable leaders who, when the dagger is at the nation's belly, respond with decisive, courageous action.

In the twinkling of an eye, LBJ was ready to assume command. Almost anything you can say about Lyndon Johnson, good or bad, has a tinge of truth, except that you could never call him dull. His greatest asset was his ability to play the political game like a chess master, five moves in advance of the board. The thing Johnson loathed the worst was to be surprised and one of his greatest flaws was that he always felt his education was more barren than it ought to be. Ironically, John Gardner, the great academic and scholar who later became Secretary of Health, Education and Welfare, once said that Lyndon Johnson was the single most intelligent man he had ever known, and I share that view. He was a man of the land and he did a lot of things that assaulted my senses: I thought they were sometimes not polite. He could be a bully. He could be mean. But when he determined to do something, nothing would keep him from it. He was the most formidable political leader that I have ever known in the last thirty years, and I've known them all. Vietnam was the fungus on the face of his great ambitions to lift the quality of life in this country.

All you have to utter are the three magic words "The President wants," and brave men cower before you. I said to some of the new people in the Clinton administration a few years ago, "Beware of hubris, the onrush of arrogance." I told them, "When you leave the White House some years from now and you look back on the experience, it will be the summertime of your life."

Society has changed. The Congress has changed. Those of us who resist change are doomed to vast disappointment. I welcome it. Change is good, though not all change is progress any more than all movement is necessarily forward: but change is endemic; it is a way of life.

—*Jack Valenti*

෮

Courage is resistance to fear, mastery of fear—not absence of fear.

—MARK TWAIN

When I used to think of courage, I most often thought of the physically heroic action of soldiers on the battlefield. That unique kind of fearlessness is indeed inspiring. However, as I have grown to understand what makes people tick, I have become even more impressed by a different kind of courage—the courage to be a human being. While some extraordinary situations are very dramatic, I think it takes a quieter kind of courage and heroism to live, to be a friend, to get married, to raise a family, to grow, to change, to get older, to retire, to face illness, to die. I see that kind of courage around me every day.

∽

The books by psychotherapist **Thomas Moore** have consistently been on the best-seller lists for the past several years. His writings have touched people who are seeking human and spiritual guidance. He gives us a unique perspective on courage in daily life:

DIVINE FOOLISHNESS

MY LIFE HAS BEEN ONE OF ALMOST CONSTANT CHANGE, from the time I left home at thirteen to enter a Catholic seminary to watching my daughter being born in my fifty-first year. I've been chastised by teachers for not following a straight career path, and I feel remorse and some embarrassment over crooks and twists in my personal life. Yet in the midst of these changes I have never felt particularly courageous, but rather profoundly and inescapably foolish.

For me, it takes courage to rise up from mistakes, to be ignorant and uncertain about the right moves to make in life, and to risk falling on my face. As I look at my past, it appears that each time I've done a dumb thing or acted from naïveté, I've entered one small notch further into the paradoxical wisdom of the fool. I see nobility in a certain kind of foolishness, the kind depicted in the many wonderful traditional stories of the Holy Fool, the one who forsakes worldly prudence for a different, humbler kind of truth.

These days we are all expected to be knowing and clever. We have experts telling us how to eat, drink, sleep, love, work, and relate, but all this expertise is in some measure a defense against the possibility of doing something foolish.

As a therapist who has worked with many people, I know

very well that most of us are not as smart about daily living as we pretend to be, and I think we suffer from carrying the burden of appearing clever and capable. Yet I believe there is liberation and lightness in letting the fool have his place. We don't always have to understand ourselves, know the world in which we live, or relate to each other properly and effectively. We don't have to be growing all the time. The Holy Fool portrays the deep mystery by which ineffectiveness and cloudy ignorance are prerequisites for a full, if not terribly intelligent, life.

The courage that I prefer, then, is the kind that allows me to live in divine foolishness—to fail, to misunderstand, to say the wrong thing, to make the same mistakes over and over. I realize I could be misinterpreted, because there is a fine line between masochistic wallowing in one's weaknesses and finding liberation in the full reception of one's incapacity. I'm not advocating wallowing, but rather an active, courageous owning of one's foolishness, speaking from it and for it, avoiding the temptation to cover it over with a false face of confidence. I'm not glorifying human stupidity, but rather seeking a deep form of unknowing.

Many things look like courage that are not the genuine article. Real courage doesn't puff up the ego, save face, or even give the sensation of accomplishment. At best, courage stems from the allowance of a will beyond our own and an acquiescence to fate and necessity. People who are forced to face serious illness and yet can affirm the beauty and joy of life, even after the disease has step by step made them feel foolish in their incapacities, know courage. Those who have been abandoned by a lover or a spouse and who resist the temptation to chase away the feeling of being made a fool know courage. Anyone whose motives and actions spring from the heart rather than from the face knows what it is to be initiated into holy foolishness, and therefore is acquainted with deep courage.

I expect a future in my life of more radical and serious foolishness. I hope I can get to the point where I can convert passing notions of awareness and intelligence into the deepest possible ignorance and incapacitation. Then I know my life will have been fabricated by forces beyond my mere intentions and finite understanding, and I will have found the brand of courage that is small but life-shaping, empty of bravado but full of heart.

—Thomas Moore

❧

Courage is the foundation that underlies and gives reality to all other virtues and personal values.

—ROLLO MAY

❧

Change is part of the fabric of humanity; and if we have already navigated some major life changes, we have probably already exhibited some courage of our own. Perhaps we have not given our courage a name or perhaps we have misidentified it. Perhaps we did not give ourselves credit for having courage and we are embarrassed to "own" our virtue. We may see courage only in physical terms. To the contrary, standing up for your beliefs, doing the right thing, and being loyal to yourself all require a different kind of courage, according to broadcaster **Armstrong Williams:**

MORAL COURAGE

THERE IS A NATURAL CONNECTION BETWEEN COURAGE AND change, because change propels us into the unknown, the foremost natural object of human fear.

Change is perhaps the most relentless and constant element of human existence. Time is inexorable; we cannot stop its processes. Our bodies mature and then begin to decay. Our relationships form, grow, and sometimes end as we lose loved ones or grow apart. In the dizzying pace of modern living, our tools and environments are constantly changing with technology and metamorphosing economies. We change occupations and often change locations. We encounter new situations and problems and have to adapt to them continually.

But while we must face the ravages of time and endure the changes that come with them, we are not passive to the changes in our lives. We have to grow up as well as grow old, and growing means facing the inevitable changes while making the necessary ones. It takes courage to do both.

Courage has to do with action. We must act despite the discomfort and fear of change to better ourselves and our surroundings. It takes courage to always try to insure that the changes we make are for the good, and that we take what is good from changes beyond our control. Courage is especially necessary to initiate needed changes in ourselves. We have to take steps, sometimes painful ones, to make ourselves into what we want to and ought to be. It does not just happen. Just as it takes discipline to keep our bodies fit, it takes courage and discipline to keep our spirits so. We have to be willing to face pain to achieve our goals for both body and soul.

TO THINE OWN SELF BE TRUE

Most acts of courage will not be physical ones like those of a television action hero. Most courageous acts are moral ones. They aren't glamorous or often even appreciated, which makes them all the more courageous. Moral courage entails resisting the little daily pressures and enticements of the world. It sometimes means taking an unpopular stand. It means subtle things like resisting peer pressure, or refusing to take the easy way out. It ultimately means facing up to your duties and obligations, taking responsibility for yourself and your actions, and what results from them. It means doing right even—especially—when it is not easy.

Moral courage is the most important kind of courage, particularly in a society or a world that has lost its moral compass. It is also the most difficult. It takes a great amount of courage to do the right thing when the world does not respect the right thing. While physical courage can make you a hero, moral courage can be unpopular. The Old Testament prophets were made outcasts for proclaiming the Word of God to a people with a heart of stone. The world does not want to be reminded of its duties. The world often does not want to hear the truth when the truth conflicts with its desires. Real courage can even get you persecuted unto death, as it did Christians from the Roman catacombs to the

Soviet gulags to Martin Luther King, Jr., here in the United States.

I have often personally seen people rejected rather than respected for sticking to their principles, for refusing to go along with the crowd. The idea of taking responsibility is not popular in this age of victimization. It is far easier—and cowardly—to look first to find fault in the rest of the world for our own problems. This is not to discount real victims. It is the mind-set of victimization that detracts from real victims by failing to make the distinction between our failures and disappointments and real injury.

I used to take abuse for promoting the virtues of self-help and principles of racial equality with which I was raised. By insisting on moral living as well as charging black Americans with taking full responsibility for their lives, I often ruffle feathers. When I first began on the radio on a black-format station in Washington, D.C., I was under constant attack, often of a virulent and personal sort. It hurt me deeply for a time, but I was convinced that I was speaking the truth, so I continued. And that perseverance in the face of adversity eventually led to success.

Courage and perseverance do not necessarily insure success in the worldly sense. Christ was despised and murdered by the world. But they are absolute prerequisites to real success in anything—success cannot be had without them. And courage gets results. It helps us make changes in ourselves and accomplish our higher duties. The results of acting with courage are what make life worth living.

—*Armstrong Williams*

❧

Sometimes even to live is an act of courage.

—SENECA

❧

It takes a lifetime to grow. On our journey we travel through predictable stages of development. Dependency rules childhood, independence and the search for identity motivate adolescence and early adulthood, and love and purpose push us toward maturity. Time and experiences assist us as we change. **Dr. Natalie Shainess** reflects on her own life and growth:

TAKE THE FIRST STEP

IT WAS SHAKESPEARE WHO SAID, "SWEET ARE THE USES OF adversity." Adversity can work two ways. It can make some people sink into being terribly defeated and help others develop the ability to conquer the worst. The latter become extraordinary people out of being tried. There are numerous examples of those victories. What makes for the capacity to be able to do that? It may be genetic; it may be a matter of experience. It may be a combination of many things. It's really very hard to say.

There are some children who have suffered emotionally. They've been abused, they've been mistreated. Whatever it is, they don't have the fortitude in them, or it's been rubbed out of them, to overcome or to try to make something of themselves. "Sweet are the uses of adversity" speaks to the other type of person, who, somehow, in spite of the most terrible things that happen, becomes worthwhile.

I can speak of myself and say that I had some great trials in my life. I was a very timid person. It amazes me that I was able to become more assertive and become the person I am. There were certain things I wanted to do.

I entered medical school in 1935. It was still almost unheard of for a woman to do that back then. I was frightened yet I dared to go on interviews. I had two things against me from the very start: I was a woman and I was Jewish. Wherever I went to apply, they let me know that. They also said, "Oh, you'll quit and have children." Well, I did have children, but I didn't quit. I am also proud of the fact that I wouldn't give in, not only because of the lack of support, but also in the face of unbelievable hazing in both medical school and during my internship.

I have asked myself over and over again, "What did it?" I did have backing from my parents to go to medical school, which was a tremendous help. At the same time it confounds me that I persisted and I don't know even myself what it was, except to say that I was very determined even at an early age.

What is it that makes one persevere? In the course of analysis or therapy some people give up. Others won't give up no matter what. Being tested by adversity, however, is in some way very important. It can predict to some extent what's going to happen to a person when faced with problems.

We never know what courage we have until the moment comes. People who are frightened can try thinking, "Other people have done it; if I try hard enough, I can too. I don't have to give up." Now, of course, that's an intellectual thing, whereas the real situation is emotional. However, the people who read this book will probably have something inside them that impels them to want to change. That's a very significant first step.

What would make me feel that I could put up with all the nonsense I did with those medical schools when I was scared to death? It appears that the challenge brought out in me a characteristic I didn't know I had—a will to fight back.

I think the greatest joy comes from achievement. It comes from doing and appreciating something that's been especially meaningful. I have become a different person than I was initially, which surprises me.

People have unknown resources and it's important that they don't doubt them before they try to use them. The question is: Shall they get into the race or not? Once into it, they can do it, but very often many people are afraid even to try. The first step is the hardest, but life has its surprises. Sometimes people who you never think could overcome do—because they have taken that first step.

—Natalie Shainess, M.D.

THE SERENITY PRAYER

God grant me the serenity
To accept the things I cannot change;
Courage to change the things I can;
And the wisdom to know the difference.

Living one day at a time;
Enjoying one moment at a time:
Accepting hardships as the pathway to peace;
Taking as He did this sinful world as it is,
Not as I would have it;
Trusting that He will make all things right
If I surrender to His will;
That I may be reasonably happy in this life
And supremely happy with Him forever in the next.
Amen.

—REINHOLD NIEBUHR

༄

Most people are familiar with only the first few lines of the Serenity Prayer, which emphasizes acceptance, faith, and hope. **Hamilton B.** reflects on the wonder of the prayer and talks about how to find courage:

WE HAVE TO DO THE FOOTWORK

THE SERENITY PRAYER BEAUTIFULLY CAPTURES THE OP-tions we have regarding the things in life we do not like: accept them or change them. Growing older, the death of a loved one, and the loss of a job are painful. So is growing up, loving another human being, and finding that financial success is not quite enough. All of these events involve some kind of change, and all involve acceptance. Acceptance is, itself, change; it is coming to terms with our inability to change some outside factor—and changing ourselves instead.

The courage to change comes from within ourselves as well as from outside through Divine assistance. We have to do the footwork of change. When we do, somehow we are given the courage we need. Prayer and contemplation are crucial, but so is action that speaks to the desired result—action that assumes a courage that is sometimes yet to be.

Often, it seems, courage is given to us in the very act that requires it rather than in anticipation of that act. For me, courage has not so often preceded the fearful changes I have made as much as it has coincided with them. Paradoxically, courage is itself a reward of the courage to change.

Finding courage takes effort, honesty, discipline, and faith. It is generally not accomplished alone. We find courage in prayer and meditation, through the examples and encouragement of others, by acts of love and grace. Courage may come quickly like a summer storm or slowly like a change of season. But come it will in the moment when it is required of us. Although it is earned by our effort, courage is also a gift. It is a gift of faith. When we step out in faith to do the fearful or the seemingly impossible, we will always find what we need: the courage to change.

—Hamilton B.

∽

Life only demands from you the strength you possess. Only one feat is possible—not to have run away.

—DAG HAMMARSKJÖLD

∽

Dr. Dennis Kimbro, who lectures for the Napoleon Hill Foundation, challenges us to have the courage to be ourselves— and be successful:

I CAN

BOOKER T. WASHINGTON SAID YEARS AGO, "THE CIRCUM- stances that surround a man or woman's life are not important. It is how that individual responds to those circumstances that is the number one determining factor in whether they will fail or succeed."

Success is a progressive realization of a worthy goal or ideal. An individual who says, "I want to become a schoolteacher," and sets out on a path to become one is just as successful as the wealthiest person in America.

I've interviewed scores of achievers from all walks of life. They had four common characteristics: Number one, they were inner directed versus outer directed. They weren't so quick to believe well-meaning friends or family who said, "You can't do that." Number two, they had a passionate desire for something they wanted desperately to attain or accomplish in their lives. Number three, these individuals committed themselves to personal excellence. They refused to be average. And last but not least, they flat out refused to fail. I'm not saying they didn't fail. Many of them actually failed their way to success, but failure did not stop them.

The Census Bureau can tell you there are 2 million millionaires in America. There's a brand new millionaire created in the United States every fifty-eight hours. The average millionaire goes bankrupt 3.2 times, dibs and dabbles in seventeen different ideas or companies, doesn't hit it big until the eighteenth try, gets his or her dream at age forty-seven, and becomes a millionaire at age fifty-four.

Everybody has a shot, if they have desire, if they have a dream. You have to ask yourself, "What is my area of excellence?" and in defining your area of excellence, you must ask yourself these critical questions. What is it that you love to do? What do you have a passion for? What can you throw your whole heart and soul into? What would you do without financial reward? When you're doing what you love to do and would do it for free, your work is your play. If your work is your play, you'll never work a day in your life. Ask yourself, "What comes easy to me but difficult to someone else?" In other words, find your area of unfair competitive advantage. Last, ask the people who know you best, your friends and family: "What do you see me as?" "What do you think I would be good doing?" When you answer these questions honestly, you will have identified your area of excellence. The key in this hypercompetitive economy: The market pays superior rewards for superior performance.

We don't live in a society that's divided between rich and poor, black and white, haves and have-nots. We live in a society that is divided between dreamer and nondreamer. People get in trouble in life not because they want too much; they get in trouble because they settle for too little. Don't settle for. Make it your goal to find a goal. Somebody better get excited about your life and you better pray it's you.

Through countless interviews I've had with successful individuals, the question was, "What are the words, the pictures, and the images that successful people think about?" They think about dreams, they think about visions, they think about productivity, they think about going places and doing things. They think about the two words, *I can*.

What are the words, pictures, and images that go through the minds of unsuccessful people? They think lack, they think about scarcity, they think "Woe is me," they think about the words *I can't*. The thing that a person needs to do is exchange the data on the diskettes because we walk toward the dominant impulse in our mind. Mind is everything.

When I interviewed John H. Johnson, founder of Johnson Publishing Co., I said, "Come on, Mr. Johnson, give me the real deal, give me the 411, the real information, of how you built *Ebony* magazine." He said: "Number one, I never looked at the distance between where I was and where I wanted to go. And Number two, which was so important, I relinquished everything for the dream." When I talked with Henry Parks of Parks Sausage, I asked, "Mr. Parks, what is greatness? What is success?" He said, "In the one hand you have a dream. In the other hand you have an obstacle. Which one grabs your attention?"

Success is never a question of Can you succeed? It's a question of Will you succeed? Will you have the self-discipline? Will you pay the price? Will you persevere?

—*Dennis Kimbro, Ph.D.*

∾

Courage is not simply one of the virtues, but the form of every virtue at the testing point.

—C. S. LEWIS

We could never learn to be brave and patient, if there were only joy in the world.

—HELEN KELLER

8. FAITH

Faith consists in believing not what seems true, but what seems false to our understanding.

—VOLTAIRE

God, through all failure, weariness, and disappointment with ourselves, is working out his harmonies for the future. We can only shut our eyes and do what lies in us and trust him.

—JANET ERSKINE STUART, RSCJ

IN HIGH SCHOOL, LaSALLE ACADEMY IN PROVIDENCE, Rhode Island, I decided I wanted to become a Christian Brother—a teacher in the religious order that ran our school. I never wanted to be a priest. "Brother Dennis" would make it, I guess I decided; "Father Wholey" was too much to say with a straight face.

I brought home the papers for my parents to sign, and made some declaration to them about leaving home to join the religious life. My mother cried and my father suggested that perhaps it might be wiser if I waited a few more years or weeks or days before making such an important decision. I was probably thirteen or fourteen at the time. You may have noticed that the religious life was not the path I followed.

With some present-day fondness for my father's ability to understate the obvious in that case and maneuver me in the direction of his thinking—he was a lawyer and probate judge—I remember with even more clarity and affection his cleverness in getting me to go away to college, which he unselfishly thought was best for me.

I wanted to go to Providence College after graduating from high school because a number of my friends were going there. My father thought differently, as fathers often do. He offered me the following choice, "You can go to PC, but with no car and no money, or you can go to CU and we'll give you a hand." I, of course, chose Catholic University, where my oldest brother was a senior. Much to my surprise, there was no car and very little money—at least for the first year.

During my four years of college I always had one or two jobs. However, my father—true to his word—did come through with help to buy a car in my sophomore year; and although I was probably as broke as other students, I never starved. My father's decision was the right one on all counts. He never made a great deal of money; and later on, to help out financially and use her own talents, my mother went back to school, got a masters degree, and became a librarian in a middle school. At one point all five of us children were in "paying" school. How my parents pulled that off is beyond me. I appreciate their sacrifice. The cost of putting kids though college today must be downright frightening for parents.

I ended up as a freshmen, just turned seventeen, away from home for the first time. As a math major I could take chemistry as opposed to biology, French and not German, and Latin instead of Greek. You can see how very carefully thought out my decisions were in those days. My life as a math major lasted less than two months.

My brother Joe (Skef to us in the family) was the CU student council president, and he asked me to host the crowning of the homecoming queen at the big Friday night dance of my first homecoming weekend. It was fun to dress up in white tie and tails and I was told I did a good job. I celebrated by getting drunk (after the crowning), and made another important life-changing decision in the shower while trying to sober up and stop the world from spinning. I decided to take an F in the midsemester math exam scheduled hours away at eight A.M. on Saturday morning and change my major.

A couple of decades later I regret saying that I returned to the scene of the crime—yet another homecoming weekend dance—and, after a number of scotches, took to the dance floor dressed as a nun in a rented habit, Sister Mary Band of Angles, begging "money for missions." That bad performance—there's more to it but it hurts to tell it—wrecked the weekend for my friends and was one of several incidents that fall that finally led me to seek help for my alcoholism.

However, I have digressed. Back to a younger time. Have you

noticed that math classes and other courses that collect people who can think logically are always scheduled at eight A.M.? It was not a pretty thought to entertain that those early morning classes were going to be my lot in life for the next four years. So, I went back to my room, got out the catalogue, and selected a new major—speech and drama—based solely on the fact that it had all afternoon classes. And it is true, there is no business like show business!

In college I developed a close friendship with a priest who—observing the emotional roller coaster on which I was living—suggested I see a psychiatrist. He offered to pay for a couple of sessions out of his own pocket. The diagnosis was that I might be headed for some very serious trouble if I didn't get into therapy immediately.

For the next couple of school years—and for two years after I graduated from college and taught high school—I saw a psychiatrist. I would just disappear: my classmates and teachers never knew. Somehow my parents found the money to pay for it until I could. The therapy probably saved my life.

Over the years, psychology and psychiatry have been very much a part of my life. I have had excellent therapists. Much of my journey has to do with self-discovery and self-acceptance. Using skilled and professional assistance in getting to know who I am and helping me to get to where I want to go has been the right choice for me.

While at college—away from the watchful eye of my parents—I started skipping Sunday Mass. Although I kept going when I was home on vacations, I drifted away from God and religion. Since my priest friends seemed to play a big part in my life, perhaps their presence was a trade-off for protection. I wandered further and further away from God: He didn't exist in my life at all. I prayed for help when I was in a jam; but I called on God only when the chips were down. I've learned from others that the route I traveled wasn't so unusual. A lot of us drift away but God is very patient. He waits for us to call Him into our lives. He's like the veteran quarterback—watching from the sidelines—ready to come in and get things moving in the right direction when called upon to do so.

The spiritual dimension of my life began to take shape at the time my recovery started. I remember hearing someone define faith as the belief in the experiences of other people. That was something I could understand. Translated, it meant that other people with bigger problems than mine had quit drinking and were doing just fine. So I believed in them. Later on I believed in a couple of individual members of the recovery circle with whom I hung out. Finally, a piece of me believed in God.

I began going back to church regularly when I moved to Washington because of a friendship with another priest. I decided that if he could attend my TV shows, which he did, I could attend his Masses.

There is an old saying that goes, "Bring the body and the mind will follow." I did, it did, and the spirit was not far behind. Within a couple of years, I was going to church—not for my priest friend anymore, but for me. Somewhere along the way, I began to develop a relationship with God. When I finally learned to pray and trust God, life seemed to get easier and gain some substance. The more I connect with God, the more I can leave aside my old self-appointed responsibilities as GENERAL MAN-AGER OF THE UNIVERSE. I try to get out of my own way. I've stopped trying to control the events of my life, the lives of other people, and their responses to me.

God had been playing a major role in my life all along and I didn't know it. I had thought that whatever good happened in my life was my own doing and whatever bad happened was rotten luck or God's punishment. Today I try to run my life with faith squarely at the center.

∽

Actor **Michael J. Fox** asks the key question: "What's courage but having faith instead of fear?"

KNOWING WHO'S THERE

THERE'S SO MUCH CHANGE IN MY LIFE RIGHT NOW THAT not to change would be a change. However, to me, the idea of not changing is frightening. Stagnation is unacceptable. I look forward to change the way other people might want something set in concrete. "I don't know what's next" brings about a certain amount of excitement for me.

As a kid I moved a lot because my father was in the military. When I was six years old I traveled three thousand miles across Canada and then three years later moved back again. Yet I saw that there was a real consistency in my life. I've been asked, "How could you cope as a kid with being torn from one place and then another?" I never thought of it that way because I was with my family. I had three sisters, a brother, mother and father. I had seen us weather all kinds of ups and downs. Through my own eyes as a child, I saw that in this group you made it; and if you really really screwed up, you might hear it from my father, but he would always be there.

The character of Alex Keaton, which I played in *Family Ties*, is not very much like me at all. However, I was interested in the fact that the reason Alex had the courage to do things that he did—the ability to think of himself as being so great he could accomplish anything—was that somewhere in his unconscious he knew that if he fell backward, he'd be caught. I had that confidence growing up and I related to that in him.

Tracy and I got married eight years ago. When our son, Sam, was eight months old, my father died. I had both a close and tumultuous relationship with my father. Ultimately, he was someone I loved very much and he was there for me even though the way fathers do that for you is not necessarily the way you want it done. They do it their own way. Up to the point when I became a father myself there was some ambivalence for me about what exactly a father did and what a father was. But when my son was born I realized, "Oh I get it, I get why my father's there. He's there so I can call him and ask, 'How do I do this?'" By the time I realized how much I would need my father to be able to fill the new role of being a father myself, and how much I misunderstood that the role wasn't just a disciplinarian, rule maker, or beast of burden, but actually a living participant in the process of raising a child, my father was gone. This all relates to the concept of falling backward and knowing who's there to catch you.

There's an exercise we do in acting class in which someone stands up, actually falls backward, and trusts that someone is going to be there to catch him. My son loves doing that with me because he absolutely knows I'll be there. He'll say, "Don't catch me so soon. Catch me closer to the ground." He loves the idea that he can almost feel himself hit and he knows I'll catch him.

There's a church I go by every day. There's always a saying or aphorism on the bulletin board out front. One day when I was in particularly troubled times the sign read, "When you pray, don't ask God for a lighter load, ask for broader shoulders." I think that's what my family did for me. There were a lot of times when I was really angry that they didn't carry the load for me; what they were doing was creating broader shoulders.

If I fall backward now, there doesn't have to be anybody there to actually catch me because I have a spiritual faith. That came out as the courage to have faith in a family. The decisions I make today are hugely influenced by them.

To be married and have a family has not meant giving up freedom. If I were by myself I'd set my agenda. In my family, I've got three children and a wife who are creating agendas for me. They're opening vistas for me and I get the privilege of seeing the world through their eyes. Their experiences are creating experiences for me I wouldn't have if I were still on my own. I thank God everyday I don't have the so-called freedom I used to have.

If you live in such a way that you have faith and you try to do unto others as you would have them do unto you, you'll find that no matter what kind of wish list you've made for yourself, you'll get to a point in life and see you've undersold yourself.

If you say *without limitation,* "I'm going to go out into the world and have faith," you'll get all kinds of things. Don't be limited by any vision. I took the road less traveled and that has made all the difference in the world.

RICH, FAMOUS, AND LOST

When I decided I was going to move to the States, I used to sit around with my buddies drinking beers. They would give me a hard time saying, "You're going to move to the States, become rich and famous, and be on the cover of *People* magazine." And I'd say, "How could I become rich and famous and be on the cover of *People* magazine? Look at me, I'm a little short fat Canadian kid. I just want to have a career as a character actor, work with interesting directors, and do the best work that I can do no matter how big the part is."

Cut to five years later: I was rich and famous and on the cover of *People* magazine—and I was lost. Then I got married, started my family, and went through some changes. I got to a point in my career where I looked at it and said, "What am I doing? Why am I doing these goofy movies in which I don't really have much invested?" I stepped back and said to my agent, "I don't want to do these big things." And so I did a Woody Allen TV movie and I did a small part in an improvisational film with Wayne Wang. I did a secondary role in *The American President* and went to New Zealand and worked with a filmmaker named Peter Jackson. In other words, I became a character actor who worked with interesting directors, doing parts I really liked, no matter what size they were.

With fame and fortune I found myself in a place that I didn't really know, that didn't feel right, but had been characterized as the big enchilada. I thought, "I've won the grand prize; who am I to question it?" Finally I was able to say, "It's just not me." I would say to my wife, "I'm going to spend four months working on a movie, they're going to pay me a pile of money, and I don't think people are going to like it." She said, "Don't do that. Go spend two weeks with Woody Allen. Go do something improvisational." So I started to do what I wanted to do back in 1979 and interesting things began to happen.

I was killing myself because I thought I was an ungrateful schmuck, but it didn't fit me. It took my family and the kind of support I get at home from my wife Tracy, my son Sam, and now my two daughters, Aquinnah and Schuyler, to force me into a new way of looking at me, my life, and my work.

I've come to know it's okay to do something for me. That's balanced because on a daily basis, as a parent and husband, I do things regularly for them. Whatever those individual acts are, they build up a reservoir of trust that I can use when I have to make my decisions.

What's courage but having faith instead of fear? I used to say

that I lived with fear that one day there was going to be a knock
on the door and someone was going to come and take it all away
from me. I think the reason I used to say that was because I
didn't want it. What I have now, I know that no army can take
from me. I have myself.

—*Michael J. Fox*

❧

*Faith is to believe what you do not see; the reward for this
faith is to see what you believe.*

—ST. AUGUSTINE

❧

Political activist and columnist **Arianna Huffington** talks
about her belief in God with even more passion and conviction
than when she's discussing politics, the media, or the arts:

ACCEPTING GOD'S TIMING

WHEN I THINK OF CHANGE THE WORD THAT IMMEDIATELY
jumps into my mind is *risk*. So often what stops us from
initiating change, whether it's in our careers or in relationships
that don't work, is fear—fear that we're going to fail. There is
also a human predilection towards inertia. However bad things
are, at least we know what we're handling. For me a spiritual
faith is the only way to overcome that fear of change and of
taking risks.

Growing up in Greece I learned about Pericles, who said,
"Courage is the knowledge of what is not to be feared."

What has made my life possible, not just to accept but to
grow in quantum leaps through hardships, through things that
did not go my way, through losing our first child, through major
losses as well as trivial daily disappointments, is a sense, an
absolute conviction, that there is meaning to everything, even
when I don't see it.

DISCOVERING THE REAL PURPOSE OF LIFE

The purpose of life is not the success of our projects, or even the success of our relationships, but is really our growing connection with God and how we manifest that in our daily lives. Knowing that our projects, our relationships, and our successes are not our ultimate goals takes away tremendous pressure. I'm much more effective when I operate from that awareness. I can't say I'm in that place all the time, but what matters for me more than anything else is being there. The Bible talks about "the peace that passes all understanding." It is a tremendously powerful place to be. It's not a kind of "sitting in a warm bath doing nothing" place. It's a place from which we can change the world. It goes along with the trust, courage, and fearlessness about taking risks, and also the clarity that comes when we are connected with a higher source.

I don't struggle with faith. The world is not a place of God. We work to make it more of a place of God, but it's Caesar's place. Those who underestimate the struggle are giving us false hope; it takes constant vigilance. I have never doubted the existence of God. I feel very blessed that when I was three years old I remember kneeling and praying, unprompted, to the Virgin Mary. What I struggle with is making faith part of my life every moment. I don't struggle with knowing it, I struggle with being it, and with allowing it to dominate my life.

My husband Michael's loss in the U.S. Senate race in California was a most profound spiritual experience for us. It was so liberating. Suddenly, I saw how freeing it can be when you lose something for which we both worked very hard and which we both thought was so important. In the end, I realized that all the really important things in my life were strengthened—my family, my faith, my friendships, and what my life was about.

What I believed in and what I wanted to work for were clarified. The haziness went. It was remarkably effortless. It sprang from the sense that this loss was not an accident, especially when Michael lost the race by under 2 points, having started 30 points behind. It would have been so easy to get into the "if only's" and "what if's." But there was no scenario under which he would have won it because what was best for him—and for us—was clearly to lose it.

What is best for Michael goes much beyond a career. I see the incredible changes in him and I know that if he had won, there would not have been the room that it takes for these changes to occur, because he would have been totally in a worldly mode. He would have been creating an office, working sixteen hours a day, and not seeing his children.

The worst thing about life's losses is thinking that they're accidental. We think this happened or did not happen because of some trivial thing we did wrong. That's not to take away from the fact that obviously our Senate campaign made mistakes. But the truth is there is nothing that just happens.

Colette wrote in her memoirs, "I had such a wonderful life, I wish I had realized sooner." So many of us are programmed to wake up every morning and focus on what's not working in our lives. The self-talk that goes on inside us constantly is the most trivial of all: "Oh, I look awful," "I have more wrinkles," "I put on ten pounds," "I haven't exercised"—or whatever we say to ourselves. I wish one day soon some great American company would invent a device that we could attach to our head to transcribe what we say to ourselves about ourselves in the course of a day. Our worst enemies don't talk about us as we do.

I was recently reading to my children a Hans Christian Andersen fairytale called "The Snow Queen," in which a remarkable goblin produced a mirror in which everything that was beautiful was reduced to almost nothing and everything that was ugly was magnified. I feel our world has become like that. In our own lives we tend to look at our world and magnify the darkness and reduce to almost nothing the beauty, the heroism, and what is noble.

GRATITUDE AND FAITH GO HAND IN HAND

Gratitude is like a muscle that we have to exercise. It helps us to cope with a great deal. If we're grateful for what we have, we're strengthened by that and we can deal with a lot more hardship. We can deal with a lot more change, which we know, even when it's positive, has its own stresses. I have a tangible and concrete sense of gratitude about my children.

Not a moment goes by, whether they're with me or whether they're at school—even when I tease them about running me off my feet—when I don't feel so incredibly grateful for them. It may have to do with the fact that I lost my first child. The baby was stillborn at five months. What made it particularly painful for me was that I was already thirty-six and I'd never had children. The doctors didn't know why it happened, so I didn't know if I could have a child and having children had been extremely important to me. I had always wanted them in a vague sort of way. However, by the time I was twenty-six I was saying, "I wish I had a child." I was thirty-eight when I finally had a baby.

So often, whether it's a child or a job, we know we want it and therefore we feel we have to have it now. Accepting God's timing, not giving up, and persevering are what divides people who succeed at what they want from those who fail— the ones who get discouraged too soon. That's where gratitude, trust, and faith are such tremendous sources of strength.

—Arianna Huffington

∾

Not truth, but faith, it is
that keeps the world alive.

—EDNA ST. VINCENT MILLAY

∾

In a lifetime each of us will be asked to accept major losses. I've had my share and I'm sure you've had yours. Yet, after the anger and tears, all we can do in the end is feel the pain and have faith that there will be a future for us. We muddle—sometimes for a long time. That is the human way. Times of adversity require great courage. To put one foot in front of the other day after day and walk through the woods until we come out the other side requires the support of friends and family. Equally important, as beautifully presented by broadcaster **Tim Russert,** are acceptance and faith:

THIS IS GOD'S DESIGN

MICHAEL GARTNER, THE FORMER PRESIDENT OF NBC News, had a son named Christopher who used to come to visit him. The family resided in Iowa, but his dad worked in New York. He was a big bear of a kid, likable and lovable. I would always banter with him in the hallways when he visited.

A couple of years ago I took *Meet the Press* to the Super Bowl out in California and my son Luke, who is ten, sat with Christopher and cheered for the Buffalo Bills to no avail. We had that kind of relationship, and my son Luke looked up to Christopher.

Five months later, I got a call from Michael's former secretary saying that Christopher had died of acute juvenile diabetes; she said Michael was in very rough shape.

I didn't quite know what to do, but the next day I called him and said, "Michael, I'm so sorry and I want you to know that." He really was hurting and said, "I don't understand this, I don't know how to deal with it. I had a wonderful, robust healthy boy on Tuesday, he got sick on Wednesday, and he died on Thursday. I am just having a very difficult time. No matter what people say, nothing seems to help."

So I answered, "Let's talk about this a little bit," and since Christopher was adopted, it may have made it a little bit easier for Michael to focus on what I had to offer. "Think of it this way," I said. "If God came to you and told you, 'Michael, here's our understanding: I am going to give you this beautiful, wonderful, happy, healthy, and lovable son Christopher for seventeen years, but then it will be time for him to come home,' you'd make that deal in a second." Michael replied quickly, "You know, you're right; I wouldn't even have to think about it."

Michael called me later and said that he didn't know if that was the deal but my words had helped him. "Rather than thinking of what has been taken away, I should be thinking about what God has given me." So I told Michael, "That's where you draw the strength. It's not your decision; this is not any retribution against you. This is God's design, God's plan. He blessed you with Christopher for seventeen years."

Michael wrote a column that appeared in *USA Today* and he got more than a hundred letters. I got several myself. They said, "I too lost a child and I want you to know that I found strength in your words." I felt a little uneasy because I did not know Michael was going to publish what I had to say. My words were spontaneous. I had not thought them out. I had not checked them with my parish priest. However, I received a letter from Monsignor Holding from Des Moines, who wrote, "Your theology and compassion are right on target."

I talked to Michael several times during the year. He told me that people saved his column and made mention of my words. What was particularly helpful to Michael was a person who had written, "Mr. Gartner, after reading your column I want you to know something else. If God went to Christopher and said, 'Here is our arrangement: You will go and be with Michael and his wife and the Gartner family in Iowa for seventeen years,' Christopher would have taken that deal too because you are a helluva father."

Michael drew even more strength from that and said, "So I understand, both Christopher and I are part of God's design and we are both happy and content because we had a chance to do exactly what we wanted to do—and that was to be with each other for seventeen years."

In terms of faith, you really do realize that there is a design of which we are all a part. I had called Michael that day because he was my friend, he had lost his son, and he was grieving. What inspired me to say what I did, I don't know to this day. It's not something that I had said before, but it is something I believe deeply as a Catholic and as a Christian. It was something Michael found healing and it was based on faith, theology, and belief. I can't say the Holy Spirit descended upon me, but clearly, my role was to try to point out to Michael the importance of faith, the importance of coping, and the importance of accepting and even celebrating God's plan in order that he might be content and happy with the seventeen blessed years that he had with Christopher.

HELP THOSE WHO ARE HURTING

We can't withstand major crises and the huge changes they bring about alone. We are not strong enough. We really aren't. When people are confronted with a crisis, particularly with the death of a loved one, the most important thing is to reach out to them. Help them, because they can't go through their loss alone. It is inexplicable in their lives at that time. You have to be there for them and help them to understand, "There is something here to accept. This is out of your control; this is a power far beyond yours."

It is at its core a message of faith and a message of acceptance. It's also a recognition of another side to this mystery of life. In order to accept faith, we have to resign ourselves as mortals to the fact that we are a small part of a grand design. To accept that is very difficult; but either you accept faith or you wallow in pity.

Sometimes, however, it's a lot easier to teach acceptance than to accept, and to talk about faith rather than accept in faith. I pray daily, "God give me the strength to be able to deal with loss myself—the way I am asking, suggesting, and helping other people to do." I am the first to say and weak enough to know that, God forbid, anything like this ever happens in my own family—to my own son—I don't know how I would cope. I would in the end, I know that. But I also know that I would need other people to remind me of this lesson of strength, this lesson of acceptance, and this lesson of faith.

—Tim Russert

∽

In matters large and small—from putting additional effort into bad relationships to not giving myself enough time to do what I want to do, I have frequently caused myself anxiety and heartache. After years of this crazy-making, stress-producing, and self-defeating behavior, I now realize there is a more adult and mature way of doing things. Sometimes we just have to admit defeat, quit, and give whatever we are struggling with to God.

The short form is: I can't, He can, let Him.

∾

Many of us think we know what's best for someone else and we have to constantly remind ourselves—or be reminded— that others have the right (and the need) to find their own way. As much as we think we have all of life's answers, they're usually not wanted and probably we don't anyway. Out of necessity, newspaper columnist **Cal Thomas** changed the way he was relating to his children. His decision to do so required faith:

FROM HOLDING ON TO LETTING GO

FEW YEARS OF MY LIFE HAVE BROUGHT ME AS MUCH personal anguish as those in which I reared the children my wife and I helped to create. I believed that if I did the "right" things, took them to church, taught them right from wrong, and lived by the standards I set for them as best I could, that they too would choose the way I had chosen. Parents should do these things, but not with the idea that if they do them their children will automatically share similar views and values.

The problem with the "cookie cutter" view is that I had left out free will. If environment and the proper father figure were enough to cause children to choose wisely, we would still be in the Garden of Eden with Adam and Eve, for they would never have sinned.

After three of our four children openly rebelled, I was forced to accept the courage God offered me to change my way of relating to them. I was so frustrated by my own inability to maneuver and manipulate their lives, there was nothing left to do but submit them to God and let Him handle their lives.

Everybody rebels. Adolescence itself leads most children to

believe that they are somehow gifted with a sense of wisdom that has eluded their parents. I'm often reminded of Mark Twain's famous line, "When I was eighteen I thought my father was an idiot, and when I became twenty-one I was amazed at how much he had learned in three years."

My children didn't get into a lot of trouble, nothing illegal, nothing with the law. The kind of rebellion I'm talking about is rebelling against the standards, the moral code.

Going from trying to control them to putting them in God's hands was an excruciating process for me. You don't want to see your children hurt. That's why we tell people, "If you drive down that road, look out for the pothole; I was just down there and it ruined my tire." If your children are going down a road that has brought pain and suffering into your life, you don't want them to experience it because you love them. However, you realize sometimes that it is necessary.

When our youngest daughter said, "Gee, I wish I'd listened," that did not bring joy or comfort to me. I'm not high-fiving my wife saying, "Yes, vindication!" It's a bittersweet thing. It's bitter because you wish she didn't have to learn the hard way, but it's sweet that she's learned.

Parents play the blame game better than anybody. I've relived my life in my own mind hundreds of times. If I had done this another way, would this have happened differently or not happened at all? There were feelings of guilt, lack of worth, and wondering "Where did I go wrong?" I had to admit I never got serious about the things of God until I was about twenty-seven or twenty-eight, right about the time this reawakening started in our youngest daughter.

I actually went from holding on to letting go with my kids. When I made my decision I didn't notice any behavior change in them, but it produced a discernible change in me. I think the pressure was off all of us. It was off them to do something to please Dad, and the pressure was off me to try to conform them to what I thought they ought to be.

Since this change within me, I have been given peace and assurance about my children. I am aware that the ultimate responsibility for them is not mine. It is God's. I am also aware that His power is far greater than mine and that His ways (and motives) also differ greatly from my mine.

Already He has begun the task of reclamation. Last Christmas, I received a framed poem from our youngest daughter, which ends with these lines:

Always know my heart fills with joy
as I marvel at the dad you are,
For I know you love me no matter the distance
How great or far. . . .
I love you Dad, with all my heart.

My two sons and I went to Promise Keepers this weekend. It's a phenomenon unlike anything I have ever seen, and is focused on bringing men back into a right relationship with God, their wives, and children. I've never experienced anything like it: sixty thousand men singing in one voice in RFK stadium; it was unbelievable. Both of my sons hugged me spontaneously, which has not happened in I can't tell you how long.

—*Cal Thomas*

∾

Prayer has been called "talking to God" and meditation described as "listening for the answers." When we wrestle with what we are supposed to do in any given situation, God can touch us in many ways. Some people are fond of saying that "God talks to us through people." **Natalie C.** elaborates on many ways we can receive the answers we are seeking:

ANGELS DISGUISED AS STRANGERS

I AM A STORYTELLER AT HEART, SO PLEASE LET ME BEGIN with a story to illustrate how life's experiences can be dramatic sources of inspiration for change. It's about an encounter with a dazzling stranger driving a powerful and expensive car and wearing a glittering diamond bracelet. Her message was *freedom*. And freedom requires a brave heart. The place was near the two-mile Oregon Inlet bridge connecting Hatteras Island with Bodie Island at the legendary Outer Banks on the coast of North Carolina. This beautiful woman passed me at a high speed but I caught up with her at a red light on the bridge. Immediately, young bridge workers, doing repairs, gathered around her car to strike up conversations.

When the light turned green, her left hand shot up through the open sunroof as she waved good-bye to her many instant admirers. The brilliance of her bracelet was blinding. Once on the other side of the bridge, this angel in disguise made a quick turn around and headed straight for me. She was wearing a large stylish hat, a fur coat, and big dark glasses, Jackie Kennedy style. As she neared, she slowly lifted her left hand through the sunroof, dazzling bracelet sparkling, and waved, smiled a knowing smile, then disappeared back over the bridge.

Wasn't a bridge the perfect setting for the message? "Natalie, whatever happened to that free spirit and playfulness you used to take with you everywhere?" "You've lost it . . . with your choices," the wee small voice within whispered. Here was the catalyst for change—to recapture peace of mind and release my creative spirit from the bondage of a destructive relationship. I bought a large rhinestone freedom bracelet as an ongoing reminder of that extraordinary encounter.

Later, I overheard a conversation about "stars and bars." Something about stars representing possibilities and bars being constraints. Of course, I was looking through the bars to the stars and it was my responsibility to begin the long journey to freedom beginning with a single step, one day at a time. Isn't change about the only state of existence that's permanent? An oxymoron for certain.

The only way I can talk about change is to link it with fear and courage—paralyzing fear and overpowering courage. Major changes or shifts in my life's experience bring to mind three dramatic decisions: courage to stop drinking and face cataclysmic changes; courage to leave a secure, high-paying professional career to strike out and pioneer a new business; courage to flee from a spirit-killing relationship while in my sixties. With every decision, I've discovered, there are two elements: risk and promise. I have come to see life at two levels simultaneously: the world's view, reality; and the spiritual view with its mystical approaches to change.

Clear thinking, practical advisers, and mentors help up to see realistic, and sometimes negative, aspects of anticipated change. And spiritual counselors go with ethical approaches reminding us of a commitment to do the next right thing. No short cuts. No soft and easy ways. They are both right, and often contradictory. Fact versus intuitive validity. Then it's up to us to consider reasonable advice and weigh other sources of information that appear, often magically (synchronicity), to summon the "courage to change" things.

Answers often come unexpectedly through conversations, the Internet, E-mail, books, television, radio, mail, meditation, and thought. Or angels disguised as strangers?

It's about following your bliss, losing it, and finding it again—pursuit . . . setbacks . . . determination . . . ultimate realization. The task before us is never as great as the Power behind us.

—Natalie C.

∞

MEDITATION

Faith is complete confidence and belief in something we cannot see or prove.

Throughout history, man has believed in a Supreme Power or Being who has not only created the world and humankind but who cares about us individually and collectively.

We struggle with our faith and that faith is tested when we are battling for our health, security, and happiness. Yet faith that God loves us, cares for us, and will see us through is what we fall back on when the chips are down.

Those who have faith take the good with the bad and often can find meaning and purpose in their suffering as well as their joy. We marvel at their belief and envy their sense of peace. Perhaps suffering exists to force us to reach out to God. We come to not only believe in Him, but trust Him. That trust in turn makes our lives easier in the end.

—RABBI JOSEPH TELUSHKIN, AUTHOR OF *JEWISH LITERACY*

PRAYER

The Lord is my shepherd;
   there is nothing I lack.
In green pastures You let me graze;
   to safe waters You lead me;
   You restore my strength.
You guide me along the right path
   for the sake of Your name.
Even when I walk through a dark valley,
   I fear no harm for You are at my side;
   Your rod and staff give me courage.
You set a table before me
   as my enemies watch;
You anoint my head with oil;
   my cup overflows.
Only goodness and love will pursue me
   all the days of my life;
I will dwell in the house of the Lord
   for years to come.

—PSALM 23

Faith is the substance of things hoped for, the evidence of things not seen.

—HEBREWS 11:1

9. HOPE

If winter comes, can spring be far behind?

—PERCY BYSSHE SHELLEY

It still holds true that man is most uniquely human when he turns obstacles into opportunities.

—ERIC HOFFER

As I've already confessed, I'm not going to win any awards when it comes to voluntarily initiating change. Reality—mixed vigorously with equal doses of pain and fear—usually moves me in new directions.

However, when I review what motivates me to change, I usually don't give enough credit to hope as the primary force that has helped me on any number of occasions. Hope has been my inspiration many times when I've made decisions to change a behavior, break a habit, or try something new. Of course, I often stop, start again, and stumble because I'm human; but I continue to hope. In days past, I'd beat up on myself for not succeeding perfectly the very first time. I don't do that anymore. Nobody should.

Hope certainly influenced me when I quit smoking and when I started exercising. In both (separate) cases the "hope" was for a better quality of physical health and a more positive total lifestyle. In the case of smoking, I tried to quit many times. I can assure you, it's easy to quit smoking; it's staying quit that's difficult.

Finally, with the help of a gifted psychologist, Tom Strange of Takoma Park, Maryland, who's had some terrific success helping folks quit, I stopped smoking for good. It is not part of who I am anymore.

I'm totally committed to getting exercise. I try to get to the gym—that's city living—or at least walk several miles every day. It's hope that led me to believe that exercise would help me get rid of stress, stay in shape, maintain my weight, exercise my heart, and have some fun. From being a nonexercise person for much of my adult life (I was busy drinking, remember?) to becoming someone who ranks exercise as one of his hobbies is a pretty huge change!

Change is doing something new or different, and it's the hope of reward that drives the engine of our actions. So it's easy to see the role hope plays in getting married, having a baby, taking a class, going on a vacation, starting a new job, beginning therapy, buying a bicycle, or signing up for an aerobics class. We all want to improve personally: we all want a better life. Desire and the expectation of success move us forward as we pursue our goals. It's impossible to live without hope. Hope keeps us going.

There are some thoughts in this chapter that can change your life. Some of these ideas focus on daily living, and because of them, you may be influenced to make new or different choices. In a more significant way, you may even discover a totally new vision of who you are that may set you moving in an entirely new direction.

∾

Shad Helmstetter rejoins us to get you thinking about where you are right now and where you may be going:

WIRING A NEW ROAD

A LOT OF LIFE IS "TO BE OR NOT TO BE." WE'RE ALWAYS contemplating either staying in the same place or changing things. To change or not to change? Promoting more happiness is a very good yardstick in making decisions. One of the healthiest things a person can do is to give himself permission to make a change, and permission even to stumble, get back up, and keep moving forward.

There's a space in which all of us live that asks, "What's this all about?" "What am I really doing here?" "What am I going to do with the rest of my life?" Those questions can create marvelously worthwhile and healthy crossroads for people if they allow themselves to move ahead.

I only have so many years left to live. What am I going to do with them? Do I want to live out my life in the greatest possible way or should I just work with what I've got now? Perhaps you can summon up the self-belief to say, "Wait a minute, I think it's time to be, instead of to not be." The next step would be to say, "And I'm going to give myself permission to do this. It's time, I deserve it, let's go for it." That takes a certain broad perspective that looks at life a bit differently than a lot of people do because they're busy paying the rent, getting the kids to school, and getting to work on time.

SEEK ADVENTURE

I remember telling my sons many, many years ago as they were growing up that when they could, they should get on the first ship leaving the harbor and seek adventure in the most positive, worthwhile, healthy, and happy way. If they did that, I told them, they'd not only find adventure, they would find themselves and they would find a much broader, wonderful future in front of them. One of my sons recently climbed to the top of Machu Picchu and right now he's in Russia. My other son has climbed to the top of a figurative mountain, breaking new ground—in computer technology. When I talk to them today, I don't think they have the notion that life is difficult or things are impossible. They simply look for the next ship that's leaving the harbor. It's wonderful now to see their own children growing up the same way.

There are many times in my own life when I have no idea what's going to happen next. Do I walk across the street or don't I? I can't imagine stopping and saying, "Well I'm afraid, I'm not going to do this." Of course we're cautious, we try to figure things out, and we try to reduce risks. But when it comes down to it, we don't know what the future is going to hold. I think that when you say, "Yes, I'm going to go for this and why not?" and "Yes, I'm going to do everything I can to keep myself and my family happy and healthy," and "How many lives can I touch along the way?" then you step forward and you feel good about yourself. It creates momentum. That's the opposite of sitting still and going nowhere.

SUCCESS IS CONTAGIOUS

If you read a lot of books about successful people or you spend a lot of time with successful people, you see that other people with greater problems or fewer possibilities than you got through a change successfully. Then at a point when you think, "Gee, I just can't do this," or "It's not going to work for me," or "I'm not cut out for this," you've got a lot of examples of successful people who got through the same kind of thing, and that adds a lot of positive reinforcement.

You should associate as much as you can with people who are achieving their goals as opposed to those who are losing their struggle. If you spend your time with more positive people, your chances of success are much greater. If you can boost your own belief by recognizing the success of others, you then have something that you can actually picture in your mind.

Somebody just telling you to change or get better doesn't create very many clear pictures. In fact, it probably opens file cabinets in your mind that have a lot of pictures of "But I can't, I've seen myself fail before, so I know what failing looks like." But when you see people who are doing it and have done it, you actually get to picture those things. Those are very strong programs. You're chemically and electrically changing the input into your brain.

CREATING A NEW CIRCUIT

Interestingly, these programs are actual pathways in the brain. We become "wired" and it's very physical. All of the latest neurological research suggests something very profound and that is, if you stop using the old circuitry, the old program, long enough, it actually begins to break down chemically. It begins to lose its strength. They've discovered that every time you think the same thought or repeat the same habit you are actually sending food to those circuits in the brain. In very simple terms, when you stop using those programs, you stop feeding them. Since they're organic, when you stop feeding them, in time, they begin to break down.

Those studies have come out of the research that's being done looking for the causes and cures for Alzheimer's and similar kinds of brain dysfunction. What they're finding is something that looks like a complex neurological phenomenon, yet has a very practical play in our everyday life. It suggests that if you can find a way to practice not using the old program long enough, the new program becomes stronger, and the old program begins to die out. When people find alternative ways that are simple, easy to follow, and pleasant, what they're actually doing isn't merely giving themselves a new habit, they're literally creating a new circuit. Once the new circuit gets put into place, the old one gets fed less and less and less. The challenge is to find some way to rewire these programs. If something isn't working and it repeats itself, it's bad wiring. If you ask, "Is this hard for me?" and the answer two or three times in a row is yes, it's wiring.

CHANGE IS CREATING A NEW HIGHWAY

Fortunately, that doesn't put any guilt or fault on the individual. We got wired and repeat programs. One of the reasons there is such change in therapy these days is because the field of molecular biology seems to be overtaking the field of general psychology. More and more people who are studying the sciences are suggesting—and I agree with them—that it may be a questionable practice to spend too much time going back and trying to dig up what the old programs are. It's better to deduce that there might be something you want to do and then spend time and effort constructing a "new highway." Get off an old road and watch what happens when nobody drives on it for a year. The old highway cracks, gets weeds in it, and breaks. It's a pretty good picture. There is enough similarity between that picture and what's actually taking place in the brain so that people can comfortably say, "I know exactly what happens when we stop using an old road. Now if I follow new suggestions, maybe I can get off the road long enough for a new road to get built."

—*Shad Helmstetter*

~

The conflict between maintaining the status quo and moving toward something new will always present us with an emotional tug of war. Our own inner voices—and the voices of others—will create a debate worthy of prime-time television. However, as CNN anchor **Judy Woodruff** tells us, it's the hope that what's to come will be more meaningful and pleasurable and produce more happiness than what we presently have that motivates us to change:

I WANT TO BE A PART OF IT

WHEN I THINK OF COURAGE, GUTS AND TENACITY COME TO mind. But it's more than that. It's a willingness to put yourself into a difficult situation. The big professional changes I've made—moving from NBC to PBS and moving from *MacNeil/Lehrer* to CNN, required some courage. In both cases it was entering unknown and unchartered territory, as far as I was concerned. In the case of the move to *MacNeil/Lehrer* almost everyone said, "That's crazy. Why in the world would you do that? Why would you give up NBC to go to public broadcasting?"

The idea of what Jim and Robin were putting together appealed to me strongly. I really identified with their attempt to create an hour of television journalism that was serious, that was purposeful, that was going to take people beyond the headlines. I thought, "This is a wonderful thing and I want to be a part of it." It was hard to explain that to other people because they looked at it as a known quantity versus an unknown quantity. They saw it as giving up the security of working for a network where I could presumably stay forever. When I went I thought, "Well, I'll try it, I'll see what happens and if in a few years it hasn't worked, I can always figure out what I'm going to do next in my life." I certainly never dreamed that it would be the huge success that it turned out to be.

I was at *MacNeil/Lehrer* ten years when the CNN opportunity came along. When Tom Johnson of CNN first asked, "Would you ever think about leaving *MacNeil/Lehrer?*" I said, "No, I'm very happy." He came up to me at a dinner in Washington and said, "Why don't you think about it because we're looking for someone to play a very important role in Washington anchoring and in all of our political coverage. Just think about it for a few days and call me if you're interested, or I'll call you."

CNN was created in 1980 and I thought that Ted Turner was whistling in the wind when he said he was going to create a twenty-four hour, international all-news network. I thought, "Good grief, there's no way they can do that." Then lo and behold it turned out to be the only place doing consistently sound international coverage and the place that people knew they could turn to for breaking news. I thought, "It's a whole new venture in journalism," which was what *MacNeil/Lehrer* had represented to me ten years earlier. It was another place to break new ground. That's what appealed to me back then and that's what CNN appeared to be ten years later.

THE INFLUENCE OF CHILDHOOD LESSONS

When I was turning five my family moved to Mannheim, Germany. We lived there for three years. Then we moved back to the United States and lived in Fort Leonard Wood, Missouri, for exactly a year. Then we were at Fort Monmouth, New Jersey—actually, we lived in Red Bank for less than a year—and then my father was transferred to Taiwan. My mother, my sister, and I moved back to Oklahoma to live in Tulsa while my father got settled. After six or seven months he sent for us. I finished the sixth grade back in the United States in North Carolina, living with my grandmother, while my parents got settled in Georgia. Then I moved to Georgia in the seventh grade; and after the eighth grade, my father decided he was going to retire from the Army.

Moving around so much at a very young age must have taught me that I could land on my feet in a totally new situation and survive, and not fall apart, wilt away, or disappear. It must have been what gave me the courage when I worked for a local station in Atlanta back in 1974 to go knocking on the doors of the NBC and CBS networks in New York to see if they would hire me as a correspondent.

The changes I had to make as a child were very tough. Those moves, however, were much harder than I even like to admit as an adult now. It was really hard to give up good friends and to go into totally strange situations, make friends, become comfortable and fit in. I don't think you can overestimate how difficult it is for any kid who's moving a lot like that, whether it's a military, civilian, or diplomatic family or whatever the reasons are.

The changes I've made as an adult have been by choice. It takes a certain amount of courage every time you change a job, because you're plunking yourself down into a completely different environment, trusting that you're going to establish good working and personal relationships with new people.

I had no desire to move somewhere where I thought I couldn't make a go of it. If it didn't work out, however, I was prepared for the consequences and prepared to do something else. You never go back; you go somewhere else.

—*Judy Woodruff*

࿇

Strong hope is a much greater stimulant of life than any single realized joy could be.

—NIETZSCHE

Weddings are about big change and big hopes. Two years ago I attended a marvelous wedding of two special people, Allison and Jackson. At the back of the church, I picked up a little pamphlet titled "When You're Faced with a Big Decision," by Linus Mundy. It's part of the Care Notes series, published by Abbey Press of St. Meinrad, Indiana. This is how Mr. Mundy, the author, begins his terrific essay on decision making:

I lay awake at night, heart racing, hurling questions at the darkness: "Will my life be better or worse—if I decide to do this? What if I fail miserably? How can this be right when it seems so hard to do? Am I following my heart or am I selling my soul? Am I being fair to my family? Is this worth the hurt that might result?" But the darkness didn't answer back.

∾

I've had more than a few sleepless nights myself wrestling with big changes—haven't you? It's our nature. Change is scary and we worry. We probably are in conflict because we like some of what we have and want to keep it. However, change requires taking risks and giving up what we have with the hope that what we are choosing and moving toward will be much better in the long run. It's normal to doubt our decisions—and ourselves. Psychoanalyst **Theodore Isaac Rubin** presents some challenging thoughts on decisions and why we have difficulties making them:

MAKING DECISIONS

DECISIONS SHOULD BE GUIDED BY HAPPINESS AND SELF-realization, which is a road to happiness. Decisions should be made relative to the extent that you can make use of your assets, your resources. If a man is very talented in music and ignores it completely, he isn't going to be happy. People end up in jobs they hate. It's a tremendous source of unhappiness. The reason they hate their job is because either the job does not have the potential for them to be self-realizing, or for whatever reason, they themselves have so deprecated the job, that even if the potential to do something worthwhile was there, they have destroyed it for themselves.

THE FALSE SECURITY OF SUFFERING

Staying stuck in a painful situation is a particular form of self-hate. It is resignation, it's giving up, it's feeling hopeless and saying, "Well, the hell with all of this, there is nothing I can do about it so here I am."

Glory through martyrdom or glory through suffering is a

very powerful instrument. It produces guilt in people; it manipulates people. There is self-glorification that is not at once apparent in suffering. It's a kind of self-idealization. Suffering people are very often more powerful than people who are having a good time in terms of getting recognition. However, the cost is enormous because they're deprived of any kind of happiness or joy. They're caught in a security blanket. It gives them a sense of safety. The feeling is, "I'm suffering and therefore you will not hurt me or pick on me. Since I have suffered so much, you owe me, the world owes me." There are people who feel they're owed because three generations ago their ancestors were abused. It's a very common kind of psychodynamic. People will not give up their abused reaction because they have based so much on it. "I've been abused and I shouldn't have to do what other people do."

SURRENDERING OPTIONS

To the extent that you are self-accepting, to the extent that you know yourself, to the extent that you know what the human condition is about, you can make better decisions. However, if you are an individual who really thinks that given five options regarding a particular situation, you can succeed in getting all five options, you're going to be miserable. You've not learned to surrender anything. You don't know what it is to be human. You haven't bothered to really assess your own limitations and assets. The biggest part of making a decision is giving up options. It's not that it's so hard to pick one, it's hard to give up the ones you don't pick. The reason people can't give up the ones they don't pick is because they really feel they can have it all. We're taught in our country that if you're really clever, you don't really have to make a decision because you can have it five different ways.

People believe on a relationship level they can work it out so that they can enjoy a committed relationship—and all the joys that a committed relationship brings—and at the same time be free to have a hundred relationships. You can't do that. You can be married, but that relationship would hardly be a committed relationship—and you're not going to get a

lot more out of it than you do with the ninety-nine others. The
surrender of options becomes crucial. To the extent that you
know yourself, you also know what is meaningful to you. You
know what your priorities are. You have a hierarchy of priorities,
you know the human condition so that you understand you
must give something up. Then you're in a lot better position to
make a decision that's reasonable. And remember a decision is
not a decision if you don't stick with it. If you make a decision
today and tomorrow you say, "Oh, I'll do something else," you
haven't made a decision. Of course, you can change your mind if
there's a reason to change your mind, but most people never
make a decision in their lives.

ACHIEVING A SENSE OF CONFIDENCE

As you make decisions and really commit to decisions in your
life, there is a greater feeling of self. It's empowering. It gives
you a sense of confidence that nothing else can. It's therapeutic
but not easy. On the other hand, if you wait for something to
happen, you're going to wait all your life. It doesn't happen.
Some people are waiting for a bolt of lightning.

INVOLVEMENT IS FIRST

Everybody thinks that interest comes first and involvement
comes second. It doesn't work that way. You have to involve
yourself to at least a certain extent in order to get interested in
whatever it is you are going to do. You have to take the chance,
get sufficiently involved so you will get interested. For example,
you can't know who a person is until you're involved with him
or her. When you're involved sufficiently, then you'll know
whether you're interested or not. If you're waiting to be knocked
off your feet by anything or anybody, you'll wait all your life. I'm
advocating making a decision, stepping forward, getting involved.

Often you want your decision to be so perfect you're afraid
to make it. Unconsciously we're terrified of what we will inflict
upon ourselves if it doesn't turn out the way we want. Usually
our standards are so high that it won't turn out the way we want
anyway. What people expect is impossible!

CHOOSING AGAINST SELF-HATE

In having freedom to choose you must stand up against self-hate. That means no matter what you choose there will not be repercussions afterwards. If it turns out to be a bad decision, you will not chastise yourself. What keeps people from making decisions and what inhibits them enormously is the terror that if they turn out to be wrong they will hate themselves. If you can be loyal to yourself no matter what, that already is an incredibly freeing experience. No matter how it turns out, "I'm still going to like myself." Harry Truman said, "Once I made a decision I never looked back."

—*Theodore Isaac Rubin, M.D.*

꩜

There is a tide in the affairs of men
Which taken at the flood leads on to fortune;
Omitted, all the voyage of their life
Is bound in shallows and in miseries.

—WILLIAM SHAKESPEARE

Hope is a risk that must be run.

—GEORGES BERNANOS

Hopes and dreams—I'm fortunate; I've gotten to live many of mine. I'm a "country boy" from Stillwater, Rhode Island, and a C college student. But I've followed my dreams and put in what had to be done in order to get to where I wanted to go. Early on, I dreamed of hosting a late-night, telephone talk show on network television. I got it. The show was called *LateNight America* and was broadcast nationwide on 146 PBS stations.

So many people do what they think they're supposed to do, what someone else told them they should do, what they think will make them money, what they fell into or was easy. With an investment of time, some success, and the acquisition of personal and financial obligations, the die is cast and too many people are trapped in a lifetime of unhappiness. They are the right people in the wrong place.

**What did you want to be when you were young and used
to dream?**
What are your special talents?
Do you use them?
**What could you be doing today to celebrate your
uniqueness?**
What would be fun to do?
**What benefits would that work bring to you and
others?**

❧

These questions are central in determining your level of
happiness. Entrepreneur **Rebecca Maddox** reflects on hopes
and dreams. Perhaps her ideas will help you to answer these
important questions:

ORDINARY PEOPLE DO

EXTRAORDINARY THINGS

I ALWAYS WANTED TO WRITE A BOOK AND THEN, ALL OF A
sudden, I was writing one. People asked, "How'd you do that?"
And I said, "I just decided I wanted to do it, and I did it."

A lot of successes I see aren't by people who had major
business contacts or were Rhodes scholars. They believed they
could "do it" and they succeeded—sometimes against incredible odds. I believe in the power of believing. (I never let negative
thoughts remain in my mind. If they stay there too long, they'll
cause what I'm thinking to happen.)

We've all sat at the breakfast table and talked about a great
idea. Six months later we say, "Damn, they stole my idea." It's
fun to dream; it's fun to create. However, there is a huge, huge
difference between ideas and dreaming and actually taking an
idea and doing something with it.

So often the successful idea is relatively simple. It doesn't
have to be the invention of the Weedwacker. I remember
meeting a man who made zippers. Everybody needs them and he
was fabulously successful. He knew everything there was to

know about zippers, even though you may not think there's much to know. Success involves the person behind the idea. (Many failures are due to falling in love with an idea and doing a business plan on our idea. Unfortunately, we never do a business plan, which I call a "lifescape," on ourselves.)

WHAT DO YOU WANT OUT OF LIFE?

When I start working with new people, I always ask them what they want out of life and how they will know when they get it. I ask them to write me a letter that addresses these two questions. Writing clarifies thought. It also requires a skill, a discipline. When you write, you have to select words and it requires a different level of specificity. Most people never achieve their dreams and goals because they never put any specificity to it. Right now I have twenty-five hundred "Dear Rebecca" letters. Almost every letter either starts or ends with "Thank you so much for making me do this. I feel better already." It's kind of coming face to face with what you really want. Some people go on for pages. It's forcing someone into the discipline of answering the question, "Okay, you're miserable, so what do you want?"

I don't want you to tell me you want to be rich, thin, and happy, because we all want that. What you write gives you a launching pad. If you can be even more specific on how you'll know what it is when you get there, it gives you direction in terms of how to take the first step.

I find it interesting that so many write in their letters to me, "Thank you for making me—with 'making me' underlined—do this." People are looking for someone to make them do things, as opposed to having the total freedom—a huge responsibility—to do things themselves.

I send the letter back in six months so the writers can see if that is still what they want. If it is, then their action plan should focus on achieving specifics as opposed to dreaming. We can only take action on specifics.

DO YOU REALLY KNOW WHO YOU ARE?

It's important to know yourself and spend the initial effort in getting a handle on who you are when you're contemplating making changes in your life. If the external and the internal don't have congruency, you're going to make another change and another change and another change. Sometimes I think the entire world is going through a midlife crisis because we let external events, trends, and opportunities dictate which way our lives go. What we inevitably find out is that our lives don't match who we are as individuals.

I think it was Norman Mailer who said Americans look for the two-minute answer to everything and if they don't find it, they're off to something else. Most people spend most of their lives trying to avoid finding out who they are and what it is they want out of life. For whatever reason, that seems like really hard work, and it presents choices that we don't want to make.

How many of us say, "Gee, I've been in engineering for twenty-two years. I never really wanted to be an engineer. I just sort of ended up there." We have a very difficult time starting and building our life from the inside out. It's scary to most of us. Knowing yourself is not an activity you can measure so it's not seen as a valuable investment of time. However, most people who are successful tend to have spent more time on themselves than those who are not.

The notion that you can combine earning a living with your fantasy, whatever it is, has become totally foreign to our society. You can't think of one thing someone could love that they couldn't earn a living doing or that someone's not earning a living doing already.

How do people get to know themselves? There are a number of ways. You get to know yourself by being with yourself. Most of us will do whatever we can not to be with ourselves. My Dad told me a very long time ago, "If you can't go into a room with nothing in it except you and be happy, keep looking." I probably thought he was nuts when he said it, but we should be able to be with ourselves, and if we can't, we need to practice.

TAKE A PERSONAL INVENTORY

I also think people see us differently than we see ourselves. You can learn a lot about yourself if you'll listen to what other people say, so ask for feedback. The best way to get to know who you are is to spend time with yourself, and keeping a journal is a great way to do that.

You should know what your resources are and look at your daily activities, your personal relationships, and your relationship to money, your physical being, and your key beliefs.

Make lists of things: the magazines you read, the books you buy, and the signs and slogans you have posted around the house and on the refrigerator. Make lists of the important things you like and what you dislike. Women are notorious for clipping things, saving them, and putting them in files. Just seeing the clippings people keep tells a lot about who they are—even if they don't realize it.

We're always running, doing, and acting. Everything's so thin in our lives. If you can pull together where your depth is—and you can't always see it without really doing the work—it can be very startling.

Probably, only 5 percent of us live up to our potential, and I'm being optimistic. When Albert Einstein died, scientists took his brain and studied it for years. Finally they held a press conference to unveil what they had discovered that was different about Albert Einstein's brain. Everybody was looking forward to great news. The findings were 100 percent conclusive. The scientists reported there was absolutely nothing different about the brain of Albert Einstein. He was able to use an incredible amount of his potential because he spent his time doing what he really loved to do. When we don't enjoy what we do, we only nick the surface of our potential.

Ordinary people do extraordinary things.

SUCCESS COMES ONE STEP AT A TIME

Dreams don't just come true. Being what we want to be and doing what we want to do with our lives doesn't just happen. Dreams are made real one step at a time over the proverbial long haul. Dreams take long-term commitments. From the first to the last, we need focus, discipline, persistence, and the ability to keep in sight the vision of what we are slowly creating.

The reason I encourage the "Dear Rebecca" letters is to encourage people to take dreams and make them concrete. Then I say, "Okay, if that's really what you want, the reality is one step at a time, the overnight success of seven years." Too many people spend their whole lives dreaming about their dreams. That's just a diversion. Unless you can start to carve out some reality, they'll always be dreams.

The poet May Sarton has a wonderful quote about people who are afraid of dying. She said, "The fear of death is because people aren't ready. They haven't had their lives."

—*Rebecca Maddox*

∾

When written in Chinese, the word crisis *is composed of two characters. One represents danger and the other represents opportunity.*

—John F. Kennedy

∾

Jeff N. tells a beautiful story of many changes filled with hope—from the exciting expectations involved in moving his family across country to begin a new job to the frightening and pain-filled days and nights of his battle with cancer:

Very Few Things Can Disturb Me Now

My family and I came to California as the result of a promotion and transfer. I found much of California to be like the Midwest I grew up in. We assimilated rather quickly. Then the corporate downsizing and consolidation of the early nineties took their toll on our new office. My company decided to centralize operations back in Michigan, and I was offered the option of relocation again. Instead, I took a severance and stayed in California. My wife had just gotten a job she enjoyed and my children had grown to love California and didn't want to leave friends behind again.

It was a very tight time in the commercial finance business— my specialty. Banks were merging, consolidating, and altogether closing, leaving many qualified people looking for work. I was among them. I tried a number of different types of work. Luckily, my wife's employment as a substance abuse counselor was able to help us maintain some stability to our home environment.

Being of service to others appealed to me and I sought human services employment. I began working at a psychiatric hospital as a mental health worker and went back to school taking nursing prerequisite classes. After some months, my wife's employer decided to add a psych unit to the hospital and I was offered a job in it.

However, the company moved out of state, the facility closed, and my wife and I were both out of work. I was able to return to my first hospital as an on-call employee. To keep the family afloat I had to drop out of school. I was a good mental health worker and after a few months I was offered full-time status. We had been without benefits for so long; I was sure I had "arrived." Two days later, I hurt my back lifting a patient onto an exam table, rupturing a disc and herniating another.

My wife began working at yet another job and I had back surgery, after which I felt worse. I began using a cane because my legs were numb. My doctor said it was the result of extensive nerve damage. A few months later I developed bladder trouble and had pain in my kidneys. At the same time my wife was diagnosed with depression and had to take a leave of absence from her job. I was begging my worker's comp carrier for another back X-ray. I thought that possibly they had missed something or more could be done.

This went on for five months. Finally, they sent me to a doctor and he ordered an MRI. They found a tumor the size of my fist on my spine, just above the area where I had surgery. My worker's comp benefits were discontinued as the cancer was not a result of my injury. We applied for and got state disability and Medi-Cal.

The biopsy showed that my cancer was a malignant seminoma. The tumor on my spine was a secondary tumor; the cancer had begun in my testicle. The necessary surgery followed, but the spinal tumor could be treated only with chemotherapy.

Treatments lasted four months and I was hospitalized four times, each time for a week. I lost weight and my hair. I had to avoid crowds, fresh fruits and vegetables, or anything else that could make me sicker. It was all worth it, because the cancer is gone today. The tumor that had been the size of my fist is now a small string of scar tissue the size of my pinkie finger. The bladder and kidney trouble went away after the first doses of chemo. This whole process was very hard on my family, but my wife's depression was successfully treated at the same time and we have our life back now.

I'm back to work in commercial finance and my wife is a substance abuse counselor again. I still walk with a cane, but I can walk. My fortieth birthday is soon and you've never seen someone so excited to be turning forty. I know I made it through all of this by the grace of God and with the help of some very wonderful people. My children did without so many things and helped in ways beyond their years. Love and caring came from so many people; frequently we were supported not only emotionally, but financially as well. The "miracle" was in the healing and in the love received.

In the darkest moments, hope remained. My friend Ed defined hope as "the time and energy devoted to the not yet certain future." I kept holding on through some pretty grim times. My potassium was depleted at one time and I became toxic on the chemo drugs at another. However, I was at peace with my Creator and dwelled in love. I wasn't afraid of dying; but I wanted to live and be there for my family.

Ironically, I believe if I hadn't hurt my back in the first place, I may not have found out about my cancer in time. To me, this is evidence that all things work out for the greater good. The labels I attach to good and bad things are more often determined by my reaction to them. Frequently, I have been able to see in hindsight that I have attached the wrong labels to events, after holding on long enough to see the good outcome.

Very few things can disturb me now. I take life with so much more gratitude. My associations are with people who enhance my life. I am available to offer love and assistance to them and they offer theirs to me. I enjoy sitting on our back porch watching our dogs play, spending time with my children, and being anywhere with my wife. I enjoy my work, the challenges it brings, and the rewards it has to offer.

The benefits to all this extend far beyond any surface one. I enjoy many people with whom I come in contact daily and my closest contact with God is through people. The changes that took place on the outside were obvious. The changes that have taken place on the inside have been the result of the manner in which I responded to those events. What has taken place inside me has lasting value.

—Jeff N.

&

The motivational experts tell us to write out our goals. As a writer, I can assure you that the writing process itself—transferring a thought from brain to paper (or computer screen)—forces me to organize and select very specific words to define what I want to say. While thoughts seem to drift or float in an undefined way, written goals are the very first step in transforming dreams into reality. "How does it work?" we ask. "It works fine," the experts say. **Shad Helmstetter** tells about a goal-setting exercise he uses himself:

TURNING GOALS INTO REALITY

A MAN GETS TO THE OFFICE AND HIS SECRETARY SAYS, "There's an important meeting at five after nine and they're expecting you in the boardroom." He says, "Okay, what do I need to take to the meeting?" And the secretary says, "Apparently just your notebook, a pen, and your calendar." He grabs them and goes to the meeting. At the meeting, the group makes some decisions about what they're going to do about a marketing or manufacturing challenge. Before the group leaves, they've written down some ideas. Now even if those notes aren't ever read again, they have written them and they've gotten very specific about what action steps they are going to take because of what they want to have happen.

Now if a couple having a relationship problem got out

notebooks and a calendar, went out to dinner, talked things over, and wrote some things down, their chances of making it would be much greater—almost by the number of pages they've written on. It's amazing what happens if you talk about it, write it down, and ask, "What do we want to have happen?"

In moving to Virginia Beach, my wife Bonnie and I went on a retreat and we spent three or four days talking about the outcome we wanted. We said, "We know where we are now; what do we want to happen, and what do we have to do to achieve the outcome we want?" So we wrote our goals down.

When you find somebody who's done that for a long time and they go back ten years later and look at their old notes, it's astonishing to find out how many of those old goals turned into reality.

—*Shad Helmstetter*

❦

Rebecca Maddox encourages the use of dreams and imaging as pathways to success and change:

EXERCISE: DREAMS AND IMAGING

JACK NICKLAUS, PROBABLY THE BEST GOLFER WHO'S EVER lived, goes through a mental rehearsal before every shot. Just the thought that he has the discipline to see success before he executes his shots is a very powerful lesson. We may think he just gets up there and hits. Actually, he's made a skill out of seeing the trajectory of the ball, seeing how it is going to bounce, seeing the white against the green. He's imaged it in minute detail. He never hits a shot without seeing the success of that shot. Nicklaus does something more than just wishing and hoping. He uses a skill of seeing where the ball is going before he ever swings the club.

The thing I like about dreams and imaging is that we already do it. If we don't give it a name, we're really comfortable doing it. If we have to give a presentation at work, the night before we'll toss and turn, and we "hear" a tape of what we're going to say playing in our mind. By the time we give the presentation, we feel we've already done it, because we have. The whole notion of living through and feeling *as if* is a skill. Athletes use it all the time to see themselves going through the motions. There's a great difference between this and the sort of amorphous dreaming of "I'd like to be rich," "I'd like to be thin," "I wish I didn't have to work everyday."

Use dreams as a preparation by seeing yourself actually doing something in minute detail, and play that over and over again to the point that when you start to do it you feel as if you've already done it. People who are successful play events over in their mind many, many times before they do it. It's usually no accident that they're successful.

—*Rebecca Maddox*

∾

<u>PRAYER</u>

One who gives breath, we acknowledge you exist!
You created all things.
When we are afraid, we pray.
Our voices sing with joy.
You have taught us your ways,
Your words you gave us,
All of these things are true.
Our hearts fill with joy.

—OKLAHOMA CREEK INDIAN SONG, CIRCA 1895

Hope is the feeling you have that the feeling you have isn't permanent.

—JEAN KERR

10. SELF-DISCOVERY

Everyone has in him something precious that is in no one else.

—MARTIN BUBER

IN THE 1970S, I RAN MYSELF INTO DEBT TOTALING $50,000—no small amount in any decade, but really a lot of money at my age back then. I painted myself into a corner with an approach to living that had no basis in reality. It wasn't a case of spending more than my income, I spent everything I had saved and more and had no income. A balanced budget meant nothing to me. Obviously, the federal government was watching me and learning because Washington has managed to dig itself into a pretty deep hole too.

At the time of my slide to the bottom, I was living in a great apartment in New York City with a terrace that wrapped around the entire apartment with sensational views of the city in all directions. However, I was also drinking myself into disaster, borrowing money from friends and family to stay afloat, and staying only a half step ahead of the bill collectors. I can remember coming home some nights, totaling up my most pressing bills, and promising myself not to drink until I had gotten on the phone and raised that amount of money.

I would then call as many people as necessary to borrow the money I needed. Sometimes it took hours. To celebrate the completed job well done, I would drink myself to sleep. The next day, with an incredible hangover, I would meet people all over town—usually at lunchtime—to pick up their checks to deposit in my bank before it closed at three P.M. so I could go home and pay my bills. It pains me to remember the scenes of those nightmare days and nights.

I voluntarily left that terrific apartment owing three months' back rent, returned all my credit cards, and wrote to all my creditors, at the suggestion of an attorney who advised against bankruptcy, explaining my situation with the promise to repay my debt—which I did, a few years later, every dime, every penny.

In those days I was represented by an agent and a manager who heard about a job possibility in Detroit to be the guest host of a morning television talk show. I told them both, "Absolutely not!" However, they—and others close to me—made it clear that there was nothing to lose by going out there, taking the money, and running back home to New York.

Station WXYZ-TV was looking for a permanent host for its *AM Detroit* show. Many people had been auditioned for the coveted spot, many wanted the job, and I certainly did not. In the end, I hosted the show for two weeks, did some of my best work, and the job was offered to me. It was almost over my dead body.

I decided to fly back to New York at the end of my first successful week and began my celebration of another job well done by taking the staff out to lunch. Well, a few drinks there, a few at the airport, more on the plane, some with dinner, and then a bunch more at my Friday night card game added up to my arrest at about three A.M. Saturday morning for being drunk and disorderly and disturbing the peace. A lawyer bailed me out around breakfast time and I can remember him asking me, "Why do you do this to yourself?" I didn't know.

Here I was—desperately needing a job to jumpstart my stalled career and put a dent in the financial mess I had created, and I had screwed up royally. I can't even begin to imagine how I physically, mentally, and emotionally recovered, made it back to Detroit, and pulled myself together in time to go on the air Monday morning at seven A.M.—less than forty-eight hours later. I was so scared by what had happened I didn't drink for months. But drink again I did, and it was another seven years and some more very sad adventures before I finally found my own courage to change.

Moving to Detroit and later quitting alcohol and Valium— "I'm having difficulty sleeping, doctor"—were two of the biggest changes I've ever made in my life. The rewards? Let me count the ways.

A SECOND SHOT AT LIFE

I'm alive; that's for openers. I no longer have the need, the compulsion, or the desire to drink and use pills. I have a successful career and many good friends. During my Detroit days, I revived my sagging career, learned the craft of interviewing, and was blessed with wonderful people who came into my life. While I didn't want both of these mega-changes—Detroit and sobriety—the rewards of each turned out better than I could ever imagine. With the help of others, I got sober in Detroit and some of the most important people in my life are there today.

Benefits? I don't smoke. I exercise. My peers respect my work. I have a spiritual life and peace of mind. I'm not tripping over myself to get somewhere else and most days I'm a pretty good family member, friend, and boss. My books are my way of passing along to you and others some of the things I've learned.

A hard-learned guiding principle for me is: Wear the world as a loose garment. What a change that's been! Not too much happens nowadays that concerns me greatly.

∽

Former Texas governor **Ann Richards** has been learning about life, too. She frequently talks with young people, and when she does, she shares her own rules for living:

NOW LET'S MOVE ON

WHEN YOU SAY *change,* I think *good.* There is no doubt that change improves the product. I think positively about change because I think that with it I'll be a better person, my life will be better, or my grasp of living will be stronger. Maybe there is something in me that thinks that who I am and what I am is not enough and that change may produce it.

In my commencement addresses or when I'm talking to young people, I always tell them that I've got several rules in life, and one of them is: Do not be afraid of failure.

When everything is positive, you think it was an accident and that you didn't cause it to happen. But when you fail, you're pretty sure that you were responsible. You learn far more from failures than you do from all of your successes put together. I've learned far more from my negative experiences than I did from my positive ones.

The most dramatic and difficult changes for me were the acceptance of my alcoholism and going into treatment; and right up there on a par with that was my divorce. Recovery from alcoholism was the most strengthening, the most building, and wonderful experience in my life. I wouldn't trade it for anything. From my divorce I learned an acceptance of myself that I had never known. I learned to enjoy my own company and an independence of style and operation. I discovered that it was okay to do what I wanted to do instead of what I thought I had to do. It was a huge thing.

People say, "You must have been so brave to make the big changes you have made." It always comes as a surprise to me that anyone would think that courage was involved. Perhaps the fact that we are not afraid to act is interpreted as courage when it really is nothing more than the fact that you're not afraid. I think fear of change sets in when you feel you have something to lose. A lot of us who are alcoholics have been there, done that. I don't think we're as fearful about what we have to lose.

I would be less than truthful if I told you that when I lost the governor's race my reaction was anything more than, "Well, so be it. Now let's move on." I felt tremendously honored to have the opportunity to do that job. I had the chance to do a lot of things. But it was a job.

It is very hard for a lot of people to differentiate who they are from what they do. Being governor was what I did. It wasn't who I was. So that loss or that change in occupation was simply a shift in what I do. It didn't change the core of who I am. My divorce and my treatment for alcoholism affected my core because they dealt with who I am, not what I did.

Humor is a lifesaver for me. If I can't see the amusement and the silliness of the human condition in everything I do, I lose my perspective. I suddenly get to thinking what I'm doing is truly important. When you get to that point, you really are in trouble; then you really can't change. You turn to stone. I had a friend last night tell me she needed to set down what she wanted at her funeral. And I said, "Oh, get real. Let me share a little surprise with you. When you're dead, you're not in charge. Why don't you save everyone a lot of trouble and let them do whatever it is that they've got to do to deal with your death. If you make some long, exotic list of who's going to sing, who's going to dance, and who's going to march, all you're doing is creating a lot of trouble for everybody. Get your legal affairs in order, put them in a locked box somewhere, and quit all this trying to control what happens after you're dead."

If you think you're important or what you're doing or what you have to say is so important, well, obviously you believe you have to hang on to it. Letting go is the key to all of life.

—Ann Richards

∾

Learn what you are and be such.

—PINDAR

"Who am I?," "What am I doing here?," and "Where am I going?" are questions we ask ourselves now and again as we travel through life. To be who we are is one of the main reasons we are alive. If we don't do the job God gave us to do, who will do it? Chances are it won't get done. The rewards of matching your talents with your life's work are high self-worth, freedom to be yourself, making a difference in the lives of others, and happiness.

∾

When you're miserable at your job, banging your head against life's wall, a good question to ask yourself is: **Would I rather be rich or would I rather be happy?** If you are pursuing financial reward and are unhappy, you may be interested in the dramatic decision made by former millionaire and Habitat for Humanity founder **Millard Fuller:**

CHOOSING LIFE

WE HAD A BOOMING BUSINESS AND A VERY AFFLUENT lifestyle. I drove a Lincoln Continental and we had a maid. My wife Linda had so many clothes she couldn't get them all in the closet. We had a cabin on the lake, two speed boats, and two thousand acres of land. With my business partner, we had hundreds and hundreds of cattle, fifteen riding horses, and six or seven fishing lakes. We had everything money could buy. *The Birmingham News* ran a Sunday magazine piece with our picture on the front page. "Outstanding Young Men Making a Success in Business" was the theme of the article. We were the whiz kids of Montgomery, Alabama. It was a very exciting life. We were doing one promotion right after the other and almost all of them worked. We were making tremendous sums of money.

I had ensconced Linda in a big house and pretty much abandoned her in terms of my own personal attention. Linda was like a dream come true for me. My own mother died when I was three. I was raised by a stepmother who was a fine woman but I never got along with her. I was not a happy child. My daddy loved me dearly but he was torn. He was trying to make his marriage work with his second wife and here he had this little kid who couldn't get along with her. It was a battle in our house from the time he married when I was six until I left home at eighteen.

I really wanted a loving family. When I was a kid growing up, I dreamed about having a home where there would be peace and tranquility, love and harmony. I married Linda and we had a child, a boy. A little girl was born a couple of years later. It was a beautiful, picture-perfect, textbook situation. I was twenty-eight years old with a beautiful wife, a beautiful house, a little boy and a little girl. We were the epitome of the American success story.

NEVER TOO LATE

But one night I came home from work and Linda sat on the edge of our king-size bed and told me she didn't love me anymore. It was a total shock to me. Since I've been a little kid, I've been in charge of whatever I've been involved in. That's true from the time I was president of my little Junior Achievement company, raising chickens and rabbits and selling firecrackers. As a young person, I became president of the youth organization for the Southeastern part of the United States for the Congregational Christian Church. I'd just formed the company with my business partner and I was president. I had a lifetime of being in charge. But here was this woman, sitting on the edge of our bed with tears in her eyes, saying she didn't love me anymore and was thinking about leaving. I couldn't believe it.

There are certain events in life that are riveting. No matter what happens, you always remember them. I remember sitting there saying, "How can you say you're going to leave? I got you a Lincoln, a maid, and house, and all this stuff. How can you say you don't love me? That's ridiculous." That's how I thought, but her eyes and her tears told me that there was a lot missing. So she left. She went to New York.

I was a shaken person. It was like a death to me. It brought back those horrible memories of my mother dying. Here was this other special woman in my life and she was on the brink of taking off. She had taken off. The only thing I didn't know was whether she would come back or not.

I did a lot of soul searching and questioning of what I was doing with my life, and Linda eventually let me come to see her in New York to talk. We hadn't been talking to each other. I was too busy to talk. I would come home tired, go to bed, get up, eat breakfast, go to work—ten, twelve, fourteen, sixteen, eighteen hours a day. Some nights I'd spend in the office. So in New York we talked and we shared very deeply and it was very painful.

One night we went to Radio City Music Hall and saw the Rockettes and a movie, *Never Too Late*. We started back to the Wellington Hotel and like a sensation of light in the taxi, it became very clear to me that we should leave the business, give our wealth away, make ourselves poor again, and start over. I turned to Linda and told her what I felt. She was in total agreement.

So we went back home and set in motion the process of selling the business to my partner. When you try to give away a lot of money, obviously you can't do it quickly, so over the next several weeks, and months, many people said, "You need to change your mind! Don't you need to hold some back? You've got these kids to educate when they grow up. Is it fair to them? You're giving away their inheritance." I said I'm doing what I think God wants us to do and I didn't waver.

A NEW BEGINNING

We set off on a different path in life. We said we want to seek God first and quit chasing money, which had brought us a certain amount of happiness but had almost torn us apart. Our own relationship was very special to us. We ended up at a small Christian community near Americus and I met Clarence Jordan. He was a Greek scholar and he thought like Jesus. He said, "You made the right decision. Any amount of wealth you have on earth, you're going to die and leave, but if you have spiritual riches, they're forever." He became my mentor.

Somebody once said, when the student is ready to learn, the teacher appears. Clarence was the most incredible human being I've ever met and I've had the privilege of meeting a lot of wonderful folks, including a lot of world leaders. He was an awesome human being.

Looking back, I knew instinctively deep within my soul that I was literally choosing between life and death—and I chose life. It was my family, it was love, it was meaning, it was purpose. When I told Linda that I would give away everything, that touched her deeply and she saw how much I loved her. We've been married now for thirty-six years and we're like two honeymooners. We go everywhere together and we work together. Before I left the business, she had nothing to do with my life outside the home and my life in the home was negligent. Today her life is my life and we have two more children born out of our reconciliation.

The rewards that came out of that decision were many. For me, it's a heart that's at peace—for Linda, a husband and a peaceful heart within her too. We got the gift of a beautiful marriage which had been falling apart, a family of four children, and now three grandchildren. In terms of what it meant for the world? The most physical thing is Habitat for Humanity, which is now building homes in eighteen hundred cities in forty-eight countries. A typical Habitat house has six or seven people in it, so we've housed a quarter of a million people. We continue to house somewhere between 180 and 200 people a day, seven days a week. It keeps growing in a geometric way.

In 1996, our twentieth anniversary, we built around ten thousand homes and our fifty-thousandth house. What sum of money would you pay to be involved with this kind of blessing to people? What's it worth to be a part of something like that? It's priceless.

—*Millard Fuller*

∾

Doing the wrong thing, as many people do, will bring frustration, resentment, and misery. What your heart says you should be doing—what your passion says to do—is surely the right thing for you. Sometimes, a major change suggested by someone else produces positive results. Journalist **Pierre Salinger,** guided by his parents, chose a different road and reaped the rewards of change:

THE MUSIC OF LIFE

I WAS BORN IN SAN FRANCISCO TO A FRENCH MOTHER AND an American father, both of whom were very excited about culture—particularly music. My father had actually formed a symphony in Salt Lake City, Utah, before I was born.

By the time I was four years old, I was trying to play the piano. Of course, I didn't do it well, but I was excited about it.

In 1929, Wall Street crashed, throwing the United States into its worst recession in the twentieth century. My father lost his job as a mining engineer. But six months later, he found a new job in Ottawa, Canada, and in early 1930 our family moved to Toronto.

Not long after our arrival there, my parents enrolled me in the Toronto Conservatory of Music, where my teacher was a brilliant pianist, Clement Hambourg. I had the same basic instruction given to any beginning student of the piano, except that there was more concentration on the ability to move the fingers and hands around the keyboard properly. I started practicing hours a day; and over a year, my piano playing improved significantly and I was heavily into the music of Bach, Debussy, and Beethoven. On June 21, 1931—just a few days after I had turned six—I performed my first concert in Toronto, playing Joseph Haydn's Piano Sonata Number 2. I continued playing in Toronto, and then in 1934 returned to my home town, San Francisco.

In 1936, a big change took place. My father and mother were very concerned that I was becoming isolated from the world, that I had no friends, and played no sports while just concentrating on the piano. In a tape recording I heard later on in life my mother said, "His father and I talked it over and we both came to the same conclusion. We didn't want our son to be a concert pianist." She said, "He will not be able to have a family because he will be traveling everywhere and will never be home."

Telling me this, they suggested I quit the piano for a year since I was about to start high school. I thought about that decision. It was true that I had no friends my own age and had rarely swung a bat or thrown a ball. So even though I loved playing the piano, finally I agreed to make this big change for a year—so I thought. Well, it turned out to be the end of my career as a concert pianist because the moment I got to high school I got excited about journalism. I did spend some time learning music composition and how to conduct symphonies, but I never went back to playing piano concerts. While I regretted the end of my career as a concert pianist, I was starting into an entirely different life as a journalist, something I ended up doing for more than thirty years.

As much as I loved the piano, my heart was really in journalism. The decision I made years ago was not only life changing, but the right one for me. Even though that change happened many years ago, as I travel across the world today and attend parties, I still play the piano for everyone and have fun using those talents of mine as well.

—*Pierre Salinger*

∾

To know oneself, one should assert oneself.

—ALBERT CAMUS

∾

Many people not only embrace change as it comes into their life, but actually seek it out in order to create a richer life. If the happiness we seek is already inside us and events and people can trigger those good feelings, the way to be happier is to place ourselves in situations that bring out the best in us and be with people who make us feel good about ourselves. NBC News correspondent **Andrea Mitchell** believes in seeking out new challenges and receiving the rewards of that risk:

SNAPPING BACK

I HAD WONDERFUL FRIENDSHIPS, NEWS SOURCES, AND broadcasting experience in Philadelphia, a town where politics is very important. I was among the leading political reporters in that city and my life was very comfortable. For ten years I had the security of working for the same people and developing a great sense of confidence. Moving to Channel 9 in Washington and taking on a completely new job where no one knew me was scary. I left what had become a family to me in Philadelphia at the local news station to come to a very unforgiving city. A couple of years later, when I made another big decision—to leave Channel 9, a local CBS affiliate, and go to the NBC network, it was the second time in my life in which I've had to stretch myself professionally.

I tend to create families at work, so both of my decisions were clouded with the sense that I was leaving home for the unknown. That was what was so frightening. On the other hand, there was hope and an expectation that things—even though producing a lot of anxiety—would in some ways be better.

A NEW JOB IS AN ADVENTURE

In Washington, Channel 9 was an extraordinary place. It had an amazing news room. I was constantly learning new things and the people were so welcoming. Even though it was tough getting thrown into Maryland politics, covering the Governor Mandel trial and learning Annapolis and the legislature, it was all positive. Back in Philadelphia I knew everyone and his or her political background. I knew who had done what to whom. If a story broke, I was on top of it. In Washington I was covering some national stories, but also having to learn the nitty gritty of Maryland politics at the same time. I felt very insecure. A couple of times when I was out lost in Prince Georges County and wandering around covering a local sewage or land waste story, I was pretty miserable, but I never really thought of quitting.

Later, when I moved to NBC, there was a different style of writing and delivery. Again I had to find my way, and in that case, people were not as welcoming. The network was more competitive and the attitude was, "Who is this kid from local news and how is she going to prove herself?" or "Let's let her prove herself," or "See if she sinks."

FAILURE IS AN EVENT, NOT A PERSON

My absolute worst moment was during the energy crisis. I was supposed to do a story for a Friday night broadcast on gas lines and people's frustrations with them. It was supposed to have a lot of natural sound and I thought of it as hearing the voices of angry people and the feeling of shimmering heat with pictures of people waiting in lines. We got very carried away and the editor had not done a story like this before. The producer was new and we lost track of the deadline. The next thing I knew, we were at the crunch, people were screaming, and David Brinkley was introducing the piece on the air and the story wasn't ready. When it finally was ready and already pushed further back in the show, it was forty-five seconds too long. Now in the world of network news, five seconds is not good and ten seconds is a major federal case. Forty-five seconds over is unheard of! I was told the Washington producer got on top of a table in the control room and jumped up and down screaming and cursing. Of course, it was a Friday night so I had no way to redeem myself the next day. I went home and cried all weekend. Needless to say, I was not successful right away.

I think you have to pick yourself up off the floor when you fall and snap back. I've been behind the eight ball on a variety of beats and there were times that I was beaten on a story. There were times along the way when the technology was changing and it was not always easy to feed the story. I was at Three Mile Island on a Friday night when we never got the story out because someone had forgotten to order up the line. The recurring nightmare is not making the feed.

The truth is you never settle in. Something's always going to change. The management of the network will change and you have to start all over again proving yourself, or your assignment will change. Just when you think you're really covering the Reagan White House well, you discover that Iran-Contra has been happening right under your nose. None of us knew it until Ed Meese announced it in the briefing room. You have to constantly say to yourself, as I did recently, "If I didn't know that the CIA was involved in this way in Guatemala, what else is there I don't know?" That's also the excitement of the job—knowing there is so much out there that you don't know and need to explore.

It's tough for a woman. Part of it is internal—we demand so much of ourselves. We feel guilty for not doing everything perfectly. We feel we are shortchanging one side of life or another. Externally, it's also different because there are still a lot of barriers for women.

FIND SOME ASPECT OF ADVERSITY TO USE

My father always used to say to us when things were really rough, "You know, you're a Mitchell, you're strong. Nothing is going to stop you." He'd say, "We Mitchells are tough."

I think he meant that you have to keep challenging yourself, that it's not good to be complacent, and that you have to find some aspect of adversity that you can take and use to build character. I'm a survivor in the sense of not just enduring or surviving, but conquering and overcoming obstacles. You get the cards you're dealt and then try to play the hand as best you can. I was given some wonderful gifts. Brains and creativity I think I have; some other gifts I don't have. I'm not 5 feet 10, I wasn't born thin, and I'm not made for television as much I love it. But I like to think I can use my talents to communicate with an audience, express ideas, and do it within the limitations of a format and the time frame that I'm given.

The most startling recent change for me has been my switch out of the White House into foreign affairs. When you're on the White House beat, there are contacts, structure, schedule, and support facilities. What I've learned from this change is that I can be creative on my own. I am very proud of myself right now. I went down to Haiti last month, with veteran camera crews and producers.

They had no expectations that I could work in the field. Having been a White House correspondent for so many years, I wasn't sure that I could either. But we did some real reporting and produced, I think, some of my best work. That's very meaningful to me. I feel stronger and more alive today than I've ever felt before.

—Andrea Mitchell

∾

I love the therapeutic process, and over the years I have been blessed with the opportunity to work with excellent therapists. I've changed with their help and have received the rewards of our working together. Here's an example of a crucially important life lesson I learned the hard way and the rewards of learning it. It's a true story about me and a co-worker.

It was *my* office and I told myself the problem was *her desk*. By my standards (of perfection), her desk was out of control. I tried everything I could think of to get her to clean it and change her ways—which obviously worked for her. I begged and pleaded, used humor, got angry, employed sarcasm, expressed my feelings—all to no avail. This went on for months.

I took this "important" matter up with my therapist and the discussion lasted for too many sessions. My therapist should have gotten glassy-eyed, but didn't, when I returned to the topic of what I could do or say to get her to clean off her desk. Finally, one day when I had run the desk drama into the ground, my therapist asked, "Do you want to fire her?" "Of course not," I quickly responded. "She does terrific work, has a great sense of humor, is committed to me and the show, and I love her. Besides that, she's a great friend." And my therapist replied in that wonderful understated way that only therapists can, "Well it appears you're not going to change her; so if you want to work with her, you're going to have to live with her desk the way it is."

At the cost of roughly eight hundred dollars' worth of therapy, the lesson was:

The only person you can change is yourself.

I didn't understand it for a long, long time: I do now. Big change: many rewards. Today, I try to cut people a lot of slack. I'm sure others have been doing so for me for years. Since I'm not trying to change others, my relationships are much better. Ask my friends.

I was giving a speech one night to a predominantly couples audience and I invited them to turn to their mates, look them in the eyes, and say to themselves, "I am never ever going to change him" or "I am never ever going to change her." Then I asked them to add, "I must accept (him or her) exactly as (he or she) is right now, forever."

Light bulbs of truth and acceptance slowly lit up all over the theater. That simple idea received one of the longest laughs I've ever gotten during a talk. What a concept: *You can never change anyone else, ever.* Surprise!

∽

Bill T. talks about the changes he made—in himself—and the rewards they brought to him:

I AM FOREVER GRATEFUL

I OFTEN WONDER IF THE LIFE CHANGES I WENT THROUGH were the result of my own courage to change or if I simply painted myself into a corner—leaving myself no other options. The greatest change I've experienced has been in my thinking. At the age of eight I began to think like my older friends who were into drugs and alcohol. By the time I was twelve, I was smoking pot on a regular basis, and at eighteen I was in my first of seven treatment centers for alcoholism. By twenty-one my thinking was clearly blurred, to say the least. My concept of responsibility and any form of discipline was reactive: emotionally I was still a child.

My decision to join AA was not very difficult; once again my options were limited to jail or getting help. I chose the latter. I found many friends and much support in AA. My new AA friends taught me how to think differently and to act as an adult. They gave me the way to live a new life.

The most difficult decision I ever made was the decision to leave my support groups and discontinue therapy. After twelve years of counselors and ten years of meetings, I decided to begin using the tools given to me over the years on my own. I didn't make this decision because I was painted into another corner; I made it because I felt it was time for me to break away. It wasn't the group that had changed, it was me.

Today I am still using the tools AA and therapy have given me with great success. I don't know if I would offer my experience as advice to anyone in the first five years of recovery, but for me there came a time to leave the nest. AA gave me the courage to live life and I am forever grateful.

—*Bill T.*

❧

Abandoned, poverty-stricken, and labeled "mentally retarded" as a child, entrepreneur **Les Brown** is a wonderful
example of what determination can do:

DISCOVER YOUR SPECIFIC MISSION

ONE DAY I WAS IN A TEACHER'S CLASS WAITING FOR ANOTH-
er student. An instructor in speech and drama, Mr. Leroy
Washington, came in and said to me, "Young man, go to the
board, I want you to work something out for me." I said, "I
can't do that, sir." He asked, "Why not?" I told him, "I'm not
one of your students." He said, "It doesn't matter, go to the
board anyway." I said, "I cannot do that, sir." He asked, "Why
not?" I said, "Because I'm 'educable mentally retarded.'" He
came from behind his desk and said, "Don't ever say that again.
Someone's opinion of you does not have to become your
reality."

That was a turning point in my life. I was humiliated because
the students laughed at me, but I was also liberated. Most of us
live within the context of the opinions others have of us. No one
rises to low expectations. So I left there with a new vision of
myself and Mr. Washington became my mentor. I just latched
on to him and would not let him go because he looked at me,
perhaps in the eyes of Goethe, who said, "Look at a man the way
that he is and he only becomes worse; but look at him as if he
were what he could be, then he becomes what he should be." I
wanted to live up to whatever it was that Mr. Washington saw in
me. I didn't know what it was, but I was hoping that he was
right and I wouldn't let him go.

I believe we're born with greatness in us, but most people go
through life running away from their greatness. Following your
dreams is not just a choice, because as much as you have chosen
it, it has chosen you. At some point, it takes over your life. It
drives you. You've got to do it. It's not optional, it's not

negotiable, it is who you are. For this reason you showed up on the planet.

Everyone has a specific mission; some of us discover it, most of us don't. It's important for you to challenge yourself, to go beyond your comfort zone. Osborne said, "Unless you attempt to do something beyond that which you've already mastered, you will never grow." Life is about challenging, about growing. They say the wealthiest place on the planet is the cemetery. There you will find books that were never written, poems that were never composed, songs that were never sung. Most people take their good stuff with them.

Life is very hard. Easy is not an option. In tough times you discover a lot about yourself and about life. My mother passed recently and it's the most challenging thing I've ever experienced. Yet, I had to eulogize her. It was not an occasion for a minister to give a generic speech. I had to celebrate the life of Mamie Brown.

My twin brother and I were born in an abandoned building in Liberty City, a poor section of Miami, Florida. She adopted us when we were six weeks old. When I was in fifth grade and identified as educable mentally retarded, I was put back from the fifth grade into the fourth. They said to my mother, "This boy is educable mentally retarded." Momma only had a third-grade education but I've done many things in my life because of her vision for me.

Momma had cancer, but when I held her hand as she took her last breath and saw a tear come from the corner of her eye, I will never forget that peace. I was happy that she was no longer suffering. I never thought I would be able to speak at my mother's funeral, but I had to.

We will all have to go through pain in life. Viktor Frankl calls it "unavoidable suffering." Every day since I eulogized her, I've been out lecturing and I have not stopped. That fact dawned on me the other night when I was meditating, after a friend said to me, "Les, you can run, but you can't hide. The messenger of misery is waiting for you."

Even though I'm relieved that Momma's out of pain, I still need her. I did an interview the other day and after it was over, I ran to the phone to call her. And then I realized, "Oh my God, I'll never be able to call her again." I cried and I felt better but I had to face it. I've had to lean into the pain and handle it. There's no easy way out. I've just got to deal with it.

It's hard to face defeat again and again and pick yourself up. It's hard when you've been rejected, when you've lost a loved one, when you've gone through a devastating divorce, when you've lost your job—especially when you've been doing it for thirty years and they give you six weeks' severance pay and say, "You're out of here." It's hard to say, "How do I learn this new technology? How do I start all over again?" It's hard, but that's what life calls for. Charles Udall said, "In life you'll always be faced with a series of God-ordained opportunities brilliantly disguised as problems and challenges." Rather than lamenting the fact that it's hard, experience it as character building. Go through whatever you have to go through. You'll discover it's worth it.

—Les Brown

∾

I first knew of **Hazel O'Leary,** as most Americans did, as the newly designated Secretary of Energy in President Bill Clinton's Cabinet. As I found out later in a television interview we did together, "energy" was exactly the right department for her. She is energetic, enthusiastic, and optimistic—and convinced that believing in yourself and developing a strong code of personal values is the direct result of hard work and a lifetime of support from others:

A STRONG INTERNAL COMPASS

PEOPLE OFTEN ASK HOW I ACHIEVED SO MANY OF MY GOALS, particularly in the context of being an African-American woman. My answer is always the same: the harder the task, the harder I worked. This hard work, along with support from others, allowed me to become what I am.

I grew up as a minority in the segregated South, where opportunities appeared to be limited. But appearances don't tell the whole story. I had advantages, too, many of which are shared by others. My family, my church, my friends and advisers—all of them helped me develop a clear sense of who I am and the importance of a strong internal compass. This compass has kept me going, helped me make difficult decisions, and enabled me to take firm stands when needed.

EXPECTING THE BEST

I grew up in Newport News, Virginia. Segregation was the norm, but my parents nurtured, educated, and sheltered me and my sister. We spent our summers at camp in Massachusetts. When we entered high school, they sent us to live with an aunt in New Jersey to attend an integrated school.

Our entire family emphasized education and involvement in the community; they simply expected the best from my sister and me. We were raised with the sense that each of us had some bigger responsibility to give back to others. Education, hard work, and success carried with them a responsibility to others.

ROLE MODELS

Among my earliest and most significant role models were my grandmothers. One had a college education. The other didn't. Both valued hard work. My paternal grandmother fought to create the first library for black people in Portsmouth, Virginia. My maternal grandmother kept bags of clothing on the back porch so that she was always ready to help people in need. They created an environment where opening doors for others—figuratively and literally—was expected and practiced. It's notable that my role models were also ambitious women—which was a very unique characteristic at the time.

I wasn't perfect, of course. I tended to be rambunctious, take risks, and every so often, get into trouble.

Choosing Fisk University in Nashville, Tennessee, was an important step in my life. Fisk provided me with a supportive atmosphere where the leaders, teachers, and role models were African-American. I was never put in a position to question my race or my values. This was the university's tremendous gift. The people there instilled in me a strong sense of pride and confidence. Fisk reinforced the lessons I learned from my family, and I have carried those values and principles with me throughout my life.

Like many women, I found that balancing my family life with a full-time career was difficult but rewarding. I am enormously fortunate to have a caring and talented son, Carl Rollins. He is a lawyer who also cherishes the values that have moved from generation to generation in my family. Bright and sensitive, he believes in giving back to others. He is a mentor to young black men and a volunteer in his community. He is also my friend. I am extremely proud of him.

LESSONS AND VALUES

Working with many talented people, we have been able to largely accomplish our goals at the Department of Energy. I am proud of our work that allowed the United States to ban underground nuclear testing and lay the groundwork for an international test ban. We made government less secretive and more open and accountable to the American people. We cut costs. I am also proud of our success in developing clean technologies that will mean a better future in terms of the environment and the economy. The decisions we made—and the ensuing battles—were not always easy, but I drew from the lessons and values that my family taught me.

What next? Focus on the spirit. I look forward to reinvigorating old ties. But I also look forward to new professional challenges. All of us have conquered obstacles and met difficult times—particularly African-Americans and people with diverse backgrounds. We must be willing to make tough decisions and stand out. We can do it only with the support of others and when we trust our internal compasses. Each of us can make the path smoother for people who follow—enabling them to push the envelope of success and achievement even further. We owe this to ourselves and to coming generations.

—Hazel O'Leary

∾

REFLECTION

After a while you learn
The subtle difference between
holding a hand
and chaining a soul
and you learn
that love doesn't mean
leaning
and company doesn't always mean
security.
And you begin to learn
That kisses aren't contracts and
presents aren't promises
and you begin to accept your defeats
with your head up and your eyes ahead
with the grace of a woman
not the grief of a child.
And you learn
To build all your roads on today
because tomorrow's ground is
too uncertain for plans
and futures have a way of falling down
in mid-flight.
After a while you learn
That even sunshine burns
if you get too much
So you plant your own garden
and decorate your own soul
instead of waiting for someone to bring you
flowers.
And you learn
that you really can endure
that you really are strong
and you really do have worth
And you learn

and you learn
with every goodbye
you learn . . .

— "After a While," by Veronica A. Shoffstall

ↄ

PRAYER

Lord, make me a channel of thy peace: that where there is hatred, I may bring love; that where there is wrong, I may bring the spirit of forgiveness; that where there is discord, I may bring harmony; that where there is error, I may bring truth; that where there is doubt, I may bring faith; that where there is despair, I may bring hope; that where there are shadows, I may bring light; that where there is sadness, I may bring joy.

Lord, grant that I may seek rather to comfort than to be comforted; to understand, than to be understood; to love, than to be loved.

For it is by self-forgetting that one finds. It is by forgiving that one is forgiven. It is by dying that one awakens to Eternal Life. Amen.

— St. Francis

To be nobody but myself—in a world which is doing its best, night and day, to make you everybody else—means to fight the hardest battle which any human being can fight, and never stop fighting.

— E. E. Cummings

The real measure of success is to sit on the edge of a riverbank all day, do nothing, and really enjoy it.

— Loc Soo

11. SERENITY

Every now and then go away and have a little relaxation. To remain constantly at work will diminish your judgment. Go some distance away, because work will be in perspective and a lack of harmony is more readily seen.

—LEONARDO DA VINCI

A person should hear a little music, read a little poetry and see a fine picture every day in order that worldly cares may not obliterate the sense of the beautiful which God has implanted in the human soul.

—GOETHE

When my life was falling apart sixteen years ago, I was desperate enough and smart enough to pick up a phone and make an appointment to see Father Vaughan Quinn, a Catholic priest who at that time ran the Sacred Heart Treatment Center in Detroit. I had interviewed Father Quinn a couple of times on television program; and when nothing in my life was working and I couldn't stop drinking, I called him.

The day we met in his office was a typical Michigan December day—cold and gray. Father Quinn listened to me ramble on for what seemed like a couple of hours. I put my whole life on the table—all the anger, worry, depression, self-pity, fears, and thoughts of suicide. That's the usual profile of a drinking alcoholic. I talked about every aspect of my life from the time I was born. Father Quinn, a recovering alcoholic himself, listened to it all without interruption until I asked for his thoughts. He never missed a beat. "The problem in your life is alcohol. You get rid of that and the Valium, and your life is going to turn around quickly." He was right; it did. Other than a final "lost weekend" about three weeks later, I haven't had a drink since.

Calling Father Quinn and making that initial appointment didn't seem to have anything to do with courage. I was embarrassed to call him; and although I was ready to check into a treatment center, I certainly didn't want to go to his center in Detroit, a city where I was well known as a broadcaster. I wanted to go to a treatment center in Minneapolis where I could hide. Today I appreciate that my call and our meeting took a lot of courage on my part. I think I was able to find that courage because I had previous experience in asking for help when I needed it. Because I had gone to psychiatrists and priests when I had been in trouble before, I did what I had to do.

Father Quinn suggested that I meet each week with a group of his friends—all recovering alcoholics. He said, "Let's give that a shot and see how it works." In a very short time I looked forward to going to those gatherings. Eating out in public each week with members of that group—some of them publicly well known as recovering alcoholics—did take some bravery on my part since "you are known by the company you keep." It has taken discipline to continue that commitment over the years and I continue to do what I need to do to stay away from the first drink. So far, so good. Without question, my sobriety was and is the most important thing in my life.

No one can achieve serenity until the glare of passion is past the meridian.

—CYRIL CONNOLLY

Additional areas of continuing conflict for recovering alcoholics and addicts are often the daily living problems resulting from growing up in a dysfunctional home and codependency issues—the inability to relate to self and others in a healthy way.

For many of us in recovery, there are a range of debilitating, self-defeating behaviors that need to be addressed. This was the case for me. I needed and benefited greatly from recovery-related reading, therapy, and additional support group meetings.

Right from the beginning, my recovery included seeing psychologist Jack Gregory, who not only helped me get off pills, but introduced me to a new world of self-discovery and self-acceptance. That exciting growth process continued with work on adult children of alcoholics issues with Joan Pheney in Ann Arbor, Michigan, and codependency with Tarpley Mann Long in Washington, D.C.

Whether or not you need additional help in sobriety may be as simple as asking yourself whether or not you are happy.

Some years ago a friend sent me "the laundry list" of characteristics of adults who had grown up in alcoholic homes. The list included traits such as taking life too seriously, problems having fun, difficulty in making decisions, dependency in relationships, and addiction to excitement. I could identify with those things.

I worked on them through regular attendance at a support group that welcomed anyone with a "troubled" family history. Regardless of our specific family backgrounds—alcoholism, workaholism, compulsive gambling, suicide, sexual abuse, abandonment, or prescription drug addiction—the adult problems each of us in the group faced were pretty much the same.

∾

According to family-systems expert **Claudia Black,** all families experience trouble; in some families, however, the trouble is constant, traumatic, and chronic. Growing up in such an environment often leaves a legacy that deeply affects the adult capacity to make the normal life changes that bring about success, happiness, and serenity:

YOU'RE REALLY OKAY

WHEN SOMEBODY'S RAISED IN A TROUBLED FAMILY, THERE'S a lack of consistent support, affirmation, and validation—which are absolutely vital for children.

Sometimes the source of trouble will emanate from a dysfunction that is very blatant. It could be addiction, mental illness, abuse, or a long-term serious health problem on the part of a particular person. Usually we're talking about a parent. It's not a child-centered family; it's an "other person" centered family. To be in a chronically troubled family typically means to be in a family that is characterized by loss. For some children it's loss of childhood. It could be loss of innocence; it could be loss of hope. Probably, most significantly, it has to do with a loss of connection to other family members, not just to the person acting out.

FEAR, SHAME, AND ABANDONMENT

The legacy of living in these troubled families is fear, shame, and abandonment. Abandonment is experienced on a continuum—from absolute acceptance to absolute rejection. In between are varying degrees of parental indifference and emotional unavailability that teach children either that it's not okay to show who they are or that who they are is not acceptable; it's not acceptable to show needs or feelings; sometimes it's not even allowable to show your successes; and it's not permissible to make a mistake. You also may be held responsible for other people's behavior.

THE TRAUMA OF FEAR

Fear is the most basic feeling for a child who is raised in a troubled family. All the anger that people have is a response to their fear. Fear for many children comes with a lack of safety, especially psychological safety. Having experienced unmet needs of protection at a very young age, people have to compensate as adults to feel a greater sense of safety. That accounts for many defenses, particularly controlling behavior. Control and fear are very much connected to each other.

Fears can result from thinking that "It is not safe to talk about certain things because if I talk about them, I'm going to be told I'm wrong. I'm going to be told to shut up. If I speak, nobody's going to listen to me and I'm going to find out that I am really not of value," and that's going to create shame.

The ultimate fear is: "I'm not okay."

People manifest fear and shame on a day-to-day basis by manipulating other people, places, and things in a very rigid fashion. Sometimes this means moving into a victim posture, which may manifest itself in depression or tap into the potential for highly compulsive behavior. A victim comes from the belief system that says, "I'm not worthy, I'm not of value, other people are more important than I am." As victims, people get to the point where they don't even know what they want and need.

FEAR-BASED DECISIONS

When I run into someone who is very unhappy, fear and shame are the first things I look for. I do not know what happened in childhood, but typically, I find a person who's very frightened; and in defending himself or herself, the person has made things *not* happen. He or she has created an ongoing downward spiral of futility instead of experiencing a strong sense of healthy power. In a forty-five- or fifty-year-old adult you have the accumulated effects that come as a result of all the decisions that were based in fear.

Children have certain needs: warmth, security, validation, understanding, nurturing, and unconditional love. They have the right to be protected, the right to safety. Children have the need to play, to ask questions, to be able to take risks, to make mistakes. If these needs and rights are attended to by their parents children will grow up with a sense of who they are, what they value, and who is responsible for what; a sense of purpose, a sense of connection and bonding, and a sense of community— that they're not alone in this world.

On the other side of the coin are children who are abandoned. They will experience a host of problems that manifest themselves in physical, mental, emotional, or spiritual pain. One of the ways people attempt to control their pain is through rage. Rage is a holding tank for people with accumulated fears, angers, humiliation, and shame. Rage is a false way of garnering power for people who live with powerlessness, and rage tends to keep other people at a distance. That protects them and prevents us from seeing who they really are. Who they are is a very pain-filled, wounded person.

When you come from a history of fear and shame, you develop "survivorship" skills. One of the things you learn to do is to present to the world a false sense of self that says, "I am doing just fine," despite what is going on at home, despite the physical abuse, or the addiction, or the fact that your parent is chronically absent. A lot of people develop their survivorship skills during their growing-up years when they're not necessarily depressed. They move into adulthood and they're still relying on old defense mechanisms that have worked very well for ten, fifteen, twenty years.

DEALING WITH ADULT LOSSES

However, we will experience losses and changes in adulthood. It could be the loss of a job or the loss of a significant relationship—a partner, a lover, a spouse. It could be the loss of a child. It could be the loss of health as people age. Old defense mechanisms often don't work later in life and those people who have not developed new skills to attend to those adult losses may quickly succumb to depression. These people are what I call "the closeted depressed."

I worry a lot about recovering alcoholics who have only dealt with their addictions but haven't dealt with other complexities of their lives. Alcohol and other substances anesthetize their fears, and alcoholics and addicts often experience a false sense of courage and confidence. They take risks that they wouldn't otherwise take. That creates a sense of empowerment. Alcohol and other drugs—as an unhealthy response to pain—work from the standpoint that they are good medicators.

Other compulsive behaviors are very relevant to the recovering addict and alcoholic since any time they are involved in any process that interferes with their ability to be honest, it deserves attention. Some forms of compulsive behavior are sex addiction, problems related to gambling or money, chronic television watching or reading, or even list making (one of the most minor ones.) If a process interferes with the ability to be honest, that fear of being honest is about pain. The more removed you are from your emotional self, the less you have the ability to identify feelings and act appropriately.

Who we've come to believe we are—with all of our self-doubt—has to do with the shame we've internalized and the defenses we've created in response to our pain. One of the reasons people don't begin the process of change is that they don't want to face their emotional pain, their feelings.

LEARNING NEW SKILLS

The goal of recovery is to able be to live in the here and now without the past dictating who we are and how we make our decisions. It's living life without a script and with choice. The past always has an influence on us; but it shouldn't dictate how we feel about who we are and how we interact with other people. Recovery is not changing who we are but letting go of what we're not. Who we are is wondrous.

The four steps to freedom are exploring the past, connecting the past and present, challenging internal beliefs, and learning new skills. You have to see clearly where the past is impacting you today because that tells you where you need to challenge old beliefs.

Creating change and learning new skills takes effort, time, and willingness. It shouldn't be done alone. It's my belief that when you've lived in a troubled family, you've probably lived in isolation far too long. My hope is that you will allow others to be a part of your growth process. It's not something that you can change by reading about it or even by listening. You're going to have to actively participate in some kind of therapeutic process. It could be in a self-help group, a church support group, or professional counseling in group or individual therapy.

I don't know that people who are going to recover from family issues will find that the Twelve Step programs will be enough. People walk into Twelve Step or recovery programs and stay there for ten years. What they hang on to is, "Don't drink and go to a meeting." They don't hear anything else. I don't think that's what the program is saying. There are twelve steps. The first step talks about surrendering to the fact you're addicted but the other eleven steps go way beyond that. This isn't to be critical of the Twelve Step meetings. What I'm saying is that people can get more out of meetings than they do. Unfortunately, family issues interfere with their ability to get as much out of meetings as is available. It may very well take another kind of structure to make that possible. Recovering alcoholics and addicts will benefit by some additional help that allows them to attend to those issues, and ultimately, in doing so, they will get more out of their Twelve Step meetings.

FINDING THE COURAGE WITHIN

The rewards of change are a transformation from self-doubt to celebrating yourself and your uniqueness, a sense of security, knowing that you're really okay, and the comfort that comes with the acceptance of your humanness. When it comes to change, you have to take risks; and you've got to takes risks to be able to experience recovery.

In recovery you have the opportunity perhaps for the first time to connect with other people on an equal basis. In recovery you also have the opportunity to let go of the pain and the shame and enjoy intimacy with yourself. It's only when we know what we value, what we feel, and what we need that we have the ability to be present for a relationship with somebody else.

To embark on a course of change takes courage. People are going to find it within. It's there. Other people who are part of that process help you realize how courageous you already are. Often I've asked people to identify on paper all the risks they've taken in their life beginning as a young child. People don't acknowledge how much courage it took to run into the bedroom and to hide from a raging parent or how much courage it took to ask for help in a family where asking for help was not done, or how much courage it took to say, "No, I'm not going to stay home in this town, I'm eighteen years old and I'm going to go away to school." Whoever the person is, there have been some real important acts of courage already.

You've got to validate yourself in the recovery process. When you validate yourself for the little things, you begin to see your own power. "Today I called three resources as potential therapy options for me." "Today I went into a bookstore, went to the recovery section, and glanced at several books. I didn't buy one but I looked, and maybe the next time, I will buy one." It takes courage to pick up a book. It takes courage to stay with a book. It takes courage to walk into a meeting. Even if you didn't stay the first time, it took courage to walk into a second meeting.

Be willing to validate the change in behavior that is constructive, even when it's little. Recovery is about little steps. We don't experience recovery because we're sober for five years. We experience recovery on a daily basis with all those little acts of courage we do along the way.

Recovery is a spiritual process. We ask ourselves to let go of the controlling mechanisms of our pain and have faith in something outside ourselves. A lot of people who've been in an active recovery for three, four, seven, eight, ten years speak a lot of the spiritual language and yet there is unhappiness still in their lives. They may have a smile on their face when they show up for group therapy, but the unhappiness is there. They're not happy at home and other people aren't happy with them.

You don't experience life in a spiritual way by continuing to hold on, manage, and control pain and shame. Spirituality is an active practice. It means having faith in a power outside of yourself; but that power also resides within. It's a Higher Power, it's God. Making the connection with the Higher Power brings about a sense of peace, a serenity.

—Claudia Black, Ph.D.

࿇

There is no joy but calm.

—ALFRED LORD TENNYSON

There is an old saying that goes, "If you sober up a drunken horse thief, you get a sober horse thief." Obviously, there's more work to be done. In that context, there is a huge difference between sobriety (not drinking) and serenity (happiness, peace of mind, and contentment).

For some of us, our lives were a mess with the abuse of alcohol and drugs, and with obsessive behaviors. These addictions and compulsions killed our emotional pain, temporarily made us feel good, and distorted our reality. We thought that if we put the cork in the bottle, got rid of the drugs, or stopped acting out, our lives would be normal. We found out soon enough that whatever we were drinking, snorting, smoking, buying, debting, eating, loving, or having sex with was our medication to hide the pain.

∾

Addiction counselor **Pia Mellody** believes a vital area that may need extra special attention in recovery is our primary relationship with our self:

LIFE ON LIFE'S TERMS

A FAIR PERCENTAGE OF ALCOHOLICS AND ADDICTS ARE using drugs to medicate a reality that they are finding too difficult to face. When they stop drinking or using, they don't have a crutch. It's not that life gets worse, it's their *perception of life* that gets worse, because they're not medicating that perception anymore. The human species can use almost any substance or process to put itself in a trance. Work, sex, spending, debting, and gambling can also be used to medicate. A lot of process addictions create internal intensity and adrenaline rushes.

When addicts and alcoholics stop using, they have to face life on life's terms. What becomes very obvious is they don't have the wherewithal, because they haven't fully developed or matured. That's when codependency issues surface.

Codependence is about a failed relationship with self. It's a personality disorder. The codependent person lacks *intrapersonal* skills.

A lot of recovery is learning how to relate to self in a healthy way. Recovery is learning how to love the self, protect and contain the self, own the self and take care of it, and be moderate. When you don't love yourself, when you don't have good boundaries, when you don't know how to be politic or interdependent, you'll experience a lot of stress. A lot of people use substances or processes to medicate that stress.

I've been working in a treatment center for a long time. I've seen a number of alcoholics and addicts who sobered up, felt better, behaved better, and life went on. They didn't have a lot of trouble and they didn't seem to be suffering from anything.

Their recovery wasn't that complicated. They stayed away from booze and drugs and they did fine. Now there was another group we investigated who had trouble staying sober. When they gave up alcohol or drugs, they switched to another substance or process. A lot of people got into compulsive overeating or they may have been sexually at risk when they were drinking, but when they sobered up they started using that process to medicate and it got completely out of control.

Over the years it has been amazing to see how inventive people are at keeping themselves medicated. Smoking and using caffeine are very mood altering. Instead of dealing with the depression that some people feel over losing their alcohol or drugs, they'll start using caffeine to medicate. There are plenty of recovery meetings where people are smoking themselves to death and drinking tons of coffee.

THE IMPORTANCE OF SELF-ESTEEM

The most important thing children need to learn is that they are absolutely good enough in spite of the fact that they are imperfect. Self-love is the single most powerful lesson a child will ever learn. Self-esteem affects everything about your whole life. If you don't have enough, or if you barely have enough, you will not do very well. If you don't have any, you will die. You'll probably kill yourself either consciously or unconsciously. **How you feel about yourself determines what kind of people you associate with, what you choose to do, how well you take care of yourself, and how you perceive the environment. If you don't love yourself, you're probably going to pick somebody for a relationship who also doesn't know how to love himself or herself, and you'll pick somebody who more than likely will not treat you very well. This person will treat you the way you feel about yourself.**

Some people who are at one extreme of the codependent spectrum of self-esteem think they are "better than." They see everybody as worthless. These people actually do quite well because they step out in the world with a fair amount of confidence even though what they're doing is relatively dysfunctional. When you're on the "worthless" end, you have trouble. The ones who are arrogant and grandiose, generally speaking, succeed in work but their interpersonal relationships are terrible. But people who have no self-esteem, if they do survive, have terrible work issues and pretty crummy relationship issues too. They're not offensive, they're more the victim.

To the extent you love yourself, you'll set boundaries. To the extent you love yourself, you'll be politic. To the extent you love yourself, you'll take care of yourself. To the extent you love yourself, you'll be able to love others, contain yourself, and be moderate and nonoffensive.

The job of a parent is to teach the child how to love himself or herself unconditionally and to model self-esteem for the child. A lot of recovery from codependence is about unlearning dysfunctional habits and learning what is functional. You often have to unlearn what you saw modeled and learn something new.

THE LEGACIES OF CHILDHOOD TRAUMA

Unlearning the results of childhood trauma is very difficult. If your mother died and there was nobody to replace her, you may learn that women won't be there for you, they'll abandon you. When children grow up in a house where there is a lot of negativity, criticism, and judgment, they learn life's a bitch or the way to feel good about yourself is to put other people down. When children grow up in a house where there is a lot of anger and rage, they learn to be irresponsible with their own anger and not contain it. There is a connection between power and a sense of value and anger. When you make yourself angry, as your sense of power goes up, your sense of value goes up. People use raging as a way to **esteem** themselves.

When children grow up with an addict, their basic experience is that they're worthless and people will abandon them. With sexual abuse children usually learn that others have a right to use their body and they have a right to use other's bodies inappropriately. They will take on either a victim or an offender stance and act that out. They've learned that their bodies are to be used by other people and they won't be able to tell people "no" when it's in their best interest to do so on many levels, not only sexual.

Adult men who have not dealt with these past issues feel lonely, overly responsible, tired, and alienated. Women seem to feel unloved, fearful, and worthless. It isn't that men aren't afraid but they don't experience it as consciously as women do. They both have pain and fear.

THE REWARDS OF MY OWN RECOVERY

Right now some things have been going on in my own life and it's been really hard, but I have the mechanisms to deal with the difficulty. I have ways of resolving these issues today even if it's only to accept that there's no way to resolve them. Before I had no way at all. I just floundered, made inappropriate decisions, oftentimes made things worse, and could never feel confident or right. It was all a mess and getting worse. Now, when things are difficult, I deal with them. Sometimes I win, sometimes I lose, but I'm okay with what happens. I can roll with the punches. The problems created by my own behavior are certainly fewer and I stop other people from creating problems for me. I also know I can't control anybody, and that makes life a whole lot easier. When you get internal boundaries on board, the blaming has to stop and that makes you much more responsible.

There was a money issue going on between my husband Pat and me this morning. He was really upsetting himself, making himself miserable. He wanted something from me. A few years ago I would have been a total lunatic over it, developing resentments, feeling like a victim, being terribly upset and wanting to punch him. Instead, I was watching him and thinking, "Pat is really distressing himself and he's wanting something from me that I don't think I can give him. I don't think it's possible, because I don't think it's about me giving. I think it's about what Pat's doing to himself."

He really wanted something from me and I wanted to

resist but I decided, "I don't have to resist this. I'll give him what he wants. It's probably not going to work, but I'll give it to him anyway. I can just let Pat be who he is." So instead of agitating myself and hating him, I sat there in active love. I wasn't saying, "Oh, I love you, I love you," but in my head and my heart I knew that I was appreciating where he was and not having to get involved in it. I was there just listening.

Later on I gave him what he wanted. I doubt it helped in the long run. But I can be there with him as he's in a struggle rather than struggling against it or blaming myself or telling him what a jerk he is. That's what recovery is about. If I ignored the core symptoms, I would sit there and hate him, or I'd sit there and call myself names about what a jerk I am or think that I am a terrible person because he's upset about something I've done; or perhaps I would not use my internal boundaries while I was listening to him and I would take in things that weren't really true and try to bend myself into a pretzel so I could be in his truths. Or I would be sitting there thinking some pretty intense thoughts and tell him, when I really should have held them in because they wouldn't be helpful.

In the end I was loving. If I'm not too whacked out—if I'm not too hungry, angry, lonely, or tired, and have exercised properly—I generally can stay out of the core symptoms. The minute I get in them, then I become part of the problem and I want to drink. Recovery from addiction and recovery from codependence is about becoming conscious so you can have the opportunity to truly love and be part of the solution rather than part of the problem.

TAKE CARE OF YOURSELF

I was traveling yesterday and I was up until almost two in the morning. My flight got delayed, I was sitting in airports, lugging my baggage, transferring from one flight to another, and I'm exhausted. One of the things I am going to do shortly is to lie down. When I did not love myself, I wouldn't do that; I would just push on. I'd probably have some coffee or drink a bunch of soft drinks and I'd push through my exhaustion until about nine o'clock at night, and then I'd drop. Today I really consider myself to be worth taking caring of and I base decisions that I make daily on that.

When I'm uncomfortable, when I'm experiencing primary powerlessness or the resulting unmanageability, what's really going on is that I have been unable to love or it's an issue of boundaries. It's always around the core symptoms. When I'm uncomfortable I ask myself five questions:

- Is this an issue of loving myself or others?
- Is this an issue around boundaries?
- Is this an issue about being politic?
- Is this an issue about engaging in self-care?
- Is this an issue of moderation or containment?

If I'm uncomfortable, if I'm miserable, it's because I'm not taking care of myself in one of these five areas, or somebody else isn't and I want to "fix" or change them.

THE JOY OF LOVE

In the end, life is about whether you love yourself and others or not. That's what dictates whether a life has been well lived. To love unconditionally is a spiritual process. Being spiritual is about being in conscious contact with a Power greater than yourself. It's a relationship. It's being God conscious. When you're truly God conscious, you experience the Holy Spirit; you can feel the presence. There are two emotions that you feel when the Holy Spirit is with you: One is joy and the other is pain. It's really intense. You feel like laughing and crying at the same time.

Love starts with the thought: *I'm enough, I matter, in spite of the fact that I'm imperfect. I'm enough in the face of my issues of imperfections.* Self-love presents a feeling of warmth and the sense of swelling and pressure in your heart. When you feel that, you are loving yourself. In recovery you get what you want, and in doing so, you experience joy. With that joy, you have hope and a feeling of abundance, which gives you a sense of a well-lived life.

—*Pia Mellody*

∾

In struggling against anguish one never produces serenity; the struggle against anguish only produces new forms of anguish.

—SIMONE WEIL

∾

Throughout our book members of various Twelve-Step programs have shared their "experience, strength, and hope." All are identified by their first name and last initial. The following essay on acceptance as a stepping stone to serenity was so personal that the writer requested I list its author as simply **Anonymous:**

ACCEPTING MYSELF

THINKING ABOUT SERENITY BRINGS TO MIND A PARAGRAPH from the Big Book of Alcoholics Anonymous:

"And acceptance is the answer to all my problems today. When I am disturbed, it is because I find some person, place, thing or situation—some fact of my life unacceptable to me, and I can find no serenity until I accept that person, place, thing or situation as being exactly the way it is supposed to be at this moment. Nothing, absolutely nothing happens in God's world by mistake. Until I could accept my alcoholism, I could not stay sober; unless I accept life completely on life's terms, I cannot be happy. I need to concentrate not so much on what needs to be changed in the world as on what needs to be changed in me and my attitudes."

This past year I've experienced a process that I would never have described as acceptance. In October my lover of four years told me she wanted me to move, that I wasn't there for her. I felt shock. Betrayal. Anger. And blamed myself. In spite of our problems, I was committed to the relationship yet knew I had been troubled and couldn't figure out what to do about it. I had become withdrawn. While in our relationship, my life consisted of my full-time profession, part-time undergraduate course work, Twelve Step recovery, therapy, and a small amount of time allotted for friends and family.

I felt numbness as I moved to my sister's while I looked for a place to live. I wanted to hide my pain and wished I could. On December 31, I shut the door to my beautiful, affordable apartment and slept peacefully on the couch. It was important for me to wake up New Year's Day in my new apartment. A new beginning.

Shortly thereafter I began my next class and was required to read portions of Elisabeth Kübler-Ross's book *On Death and Dying*. Through the readings, I began to recognize my own feelings of denial, anger, bargaining, and depression. Daily I wrote my feelings and thoughts in my journal. I also began jogging and saying affirmations while I jogged. I continued to feel the loss. When I thought I'd explode from the pain I was in, I prayed. I went to the cathedral and lit a candle for myself and one for my lover and visualized the two of us as babies being handed over to a loving Higher Power. At work one day while in a meeting with my boss, I teared up unexpectedly. He asked if my job was okay, was my mother okay, and was there anything he could do to help. Embarrassed, I responded, "Just a friend problem, thank you." My depression seemed to get heavier, and I felt despair I have never known before. I stepped up my therapy, kept writing, and began to draw and write a few poems expressing my feelings. I just wanted to get over it.

Somewhere in this pain I very gradually began to feel a presence, a dimension of some kind, a sense of knowing. I was told this sense was a part of me, an emerging true self. I thought I was working very hard at accepting and grieving the failure and loss of my relationship. I didn't know consciously that I was beginning a process of giving my self the gift of my feelings.

The presence of my self wasn't as strong when I stopped hurting so much. However, something was left as a gift that remains. Acceptance of my self. Gradually, day by day, I find myself being more gentle and patient with me, my flaws, my mistakes. I try hard to be kind to me. Sometimes I see my unkindness and have compassion. I'm acknowledging that my emotional self exists.

All I was trying to do was "just make it through" and unexpectedly I have found love for myself. I think that's what I was grieving for all the time.

—*Anonymous*

❧

A Twelve Step program member referred to AA as shorthand for "Adolescence Anonymous." Recovery, he said, was really about "growing up." On the ladder of growth, maturity is reaching a much higher level of personal development and through it attaining serenity. The changes we experience pave our road to maturity.

REFLECTION

Maturity

. . . Is the ability to handle frustration, control anger, and settle differences without violence or destruction.

. . . Is patience. It is the willingness to postpone gratification, to pass up the immediate pleasure or profit in favor of the long-term gain.

. . . Is unselfishness, responding to the need of others.

. . . Is the gift of remaining calm in the face of chaos. This means peace, not only for ourselves, but for those with whom we live and for those whose lives touch ours.

. . . Is perseverance, sweating out a project or a situation in spite of opposition and discouraging setbacks.

. . . Is the capacity to face unpleasantness and disappointment without becoming bitter.

. . . Is humility. A mature person is able to say "I was wrong." He is able to say "I am sorry." And when she is proved right, she does not have to say "I told you so."

. . . Is dependability, integrity, keeping one's word.

. . . Is the ability to disagree with being disagreeable.

. . . Is the ability to make a decision, to act on that decision, and to accept full responsibility for the outcome.

. . . Is the ability to live in peace with that which we cannot change.

—ANN LANDERS

GRACE PRAYER

For Thee I thirst.
Into Thy hands
I commit my spirit
Thy will is my will.
Thy will be done through me.
Heal me at depth.
Reveal that which needs to be revealed.
Heal that which needs to be healed
So I can glorify you, God
And live in the fullness of grace.

—WINGS OF SPIRIT FOUNDATION

Forgiveness is an eminent form of giving, which affirms the dignity of the other by acknowledging him for who he is beyond what he does.

—POPE JOHN PAUL II

12. WISDOM

Wisdom lies neither in fixity nor in change, but in the dialectic between the two.

—OCTAVIO PAZ

Youth is the time to study wisdom; old age is the time to practice it.

—ROUSSEAU

CHANGE HAS GOTTEN A LOT OF BAD PRESS. THE NEGATIVI-
ty surrounding it has had a great influence over me—over us.
I've learned though my own experience and in compiling and
editing this book that I should—and we should—not only
expect change, but recognize that change is not the enemy. For
too long, I believed that change was to be feared.

I've learned to let go at least as far as people are concerned.
That has been a very important step forward in my growth. I've
learned that lesson the hard way, living through painful and
lonely times after I had tied my security to others. Often I tried
to control others for my sense of worth or benefit or became
overly dependent on them for my security. If you do either of
these things, people will flee. They must. Today my center is
within me. Now I have my security where it belongs. This vital
change has rewarded me with better friendships and more of
them.

∾

One of the by-products of pain is learning to relate to other
people's difficult times and suffering. It took me a lot longer,
however, to get comfortable with the notion of compassion
directed toward me. Take to heart as I have the following
thoughts on compassion and humility by **Dr. Theodore Isaac
Rubin:**

THE FREEDOM OF COMPASSION

COMPASSION MAKES CHANGE POSSIBLE. IF YOU DON'T HAVE compassion, how can you take the risk of change? How can you move? If you have no compassion for yourself, you are paralyzed. You live with an enemy who is constantly watching your every move; who's judging you and whose judgments are terribly harsh; and who dictates terrible punishments such as nobody else can. That enemy knows all of your vulnerabilities. If you have compassion, you neutralize that enemy and you can move. Then you're not so concerned about performance. You can be spontaneous. Spontaneity as opposed to compulsivity is crucial.

Compassion frees you from loads of dictates that are supposedly there to keep you safe. Actually, they don't keep you safe at all, they keep you paralyzed. If you want to have the courage to change, you must be very good to yourself. Compassion is love, but it's not narcissistic love. It's more in the line of self-acceptance. For example, if you found yourself envying some person you might say, "Now I don't like this feeling, but being human there are times when I am envious." That's compassionate. Let's say somebody died and you have the peculiar reaction: "Even though I'll miss her and wanted her to live, I feel kind of happy." Of course you're happy, you didn't die. You don't say, "Oh, what a monster I am." You say, "This is human."

One of the most valuable qualities an individual can have, which aids the cause of compassion, is humility. With it, you don't have to live up to such high standards that will always demean you because you'll fail to meet those standards constantly. The man who says, "I know, I know" has no humility. You can't teach him anything. Humility is the antithesis of arrogance. Alexander Reid Martin, the famous analyst, said, "When I stand on the ground, there is not far to fall."

—*Theodore Isaac Rubin, M.D.*

❧

The first test of a truly great man is his humility.

—JOHN RUSKIN

I had been complaining to a friend about a bad investment I'd made. It had cost me some money and I was blaming the guy who had put the deal together. "Take a look at your hand," my friend said. "When you're pointing your finger at somebody else, three of your fingers are pointing right back at you."

It took a lot more conversation, some deep soul-searching, and yes, humility for me to finally admit that what had really caused my trouble in the first place was my desire to make an easy and quick dollar (greed), my need to look good in the eyes of the dealmaker (false pride), and wanting to be a big shot investor (grandiosity). In the end, I had to see the problem was *me* and it was I who needed the work.

Some of us haven't learned enough about personal responsibility, or perhaps we're just lazy and want an easy way out. On the other hand, it could be human that we deny our own role in creating some of the messes into which we get ourselves and look outside ourselves for the answers and someone to blame.

We can be excessively hard on ourselves. So, as we were encouraged by Dr. Rubin, we need to treat ourselves with compassion. It's human to make mistakes and have failings, and it's courageous to begin any examination of conflict by asking yourself these questions:

- **What's my part in this mess?**
- **What can I change in me to improve the situation?**

When you see a noble man, try to equal him. When you see an evil man, examine yourself thoroughly.

—CONFUCIUS

෧

Many of us spend a lot of time trying to *fix* people and situations. We're convinced it's him, or her, or it that needs changing. According to radio therapist **Dr. Laura Schlessinger,** the reality may be that we are really trying to avoid personal responsibility.

The great religions offer a similar message: Judaism teaches "Live by God's laws and you will live a righteous life"; Christians pray, "Thy will not mine be done"; Buddhism states that "Unhappiness is caused by selfish cravings"; and Islam means "submission" to Allah's will.

> *Whoever submits his whole self to Allah and is a doer of good, he will get his reward with his Lord, on such shall be no fear, nor shall they grieve.*

> —THE HOLY QUR-AN 2:112

To live a quality life, the good life, the godly life that Dr. Laura talks about is not easy, but it is what we are asked to do. It's the price for happiness:

A QUALITY LIFE

PEOPLE HONESTLY BELIEVE THAT IF THEY COULD MOLD THE world to their whims and wants, everything would be okay. Just today, a woman called my radio show whining that her live-in boyfriend is not legally divorcing his wife. His wife and eleven-year-old daughter live in Texas. He has relocated to California. The caller gave up school in Texas and moved to California to be with him. Before she could ask me how to get him to file for the divorce, which was why she'd called, I stopped her and demanded, "Explain to me why you want to take a man into your life, heart, and body when he's abandoned his child?"

She replied, "I have no answer."

"This call should not have been about 'I love him, I want him, and nothing else matters,'" I told her. "It should have been about your character."

This kind of call suggests the texture of my show. I get a variety of complaints about callers' unhappiness at somebody else's actions, but we inevitably end up dealing with personal issues of character, conscience, and courage. You see, what I've learned after twenty years on-air is that people's primary method of relieving unhappiness usually is blaming another person's actions.

PEOPLE ACT IN SPITE OF THEIR FEARS

We all tend to want somebody else to change so we don't have to put all that effort into being responsible for ourselves. We want interpersonal conflicts to resolve themselves automatically and spontaneously so we feel comfortable.

Most of us really do want things either to go away or spontaneously get better. Whatever personal investment and suffering that it takes to improve a situation is cause for avoidance. People want to change how they feel, but they think that's done by changing somebody else. They say, "I'm intimidated by my sister. Change her!" as opposed to understanding how they aren't capable as individuals of dealing with a particular situation involving a sibling. That makes the guilty party the sibling, the mother, the boss, the wife, the boyfriend, the children, you name it—the whole world of others.

How do you begin to take responsibility for yourself, to act courageously? I'm sure some people will give you a clever answer about breaking through the wall of denial and suddenly seeing that the problem they're trying to solve may very well be about themselves. Well, I simply don't believe change is automatically rendered by a flash of revelation. I think an individual decides to do something constructive in spite of fears, discomforts, and ennui.

Recently I was on the Oprah show discussing this issue of personal responsibility and asked her, "When did you decide to eat only nonfat pretzels without salt? That meant giving up something that tasted good. Why did you do it?" Oprah looked at me in a searching way and answered, "Why, I knew I had to. I guess I just did it." Her action took courage, but it also took good sense. It's good sense that initially motivates people to start doing the right thing, and it's courage that helps them persist because behaving with character is difficult.

INVITE FEAR IN

Anytime anyone sets out to make a big change, there's going to be fear and a tremendous amount of pain and discomfort. Sometimes change means you have to be alone, sometimes you have to tread water in a sea of self-doubt for a long time. Only people with guts make it through difficult change. We must learn to act despite our fear. It doesn't go away. You can't push it from you and then act. You must permit the fear to coexist with your best efforts at changing. Frankly, there is no need for courage if there is no fear. A true test of moral fiber is not running from the fear but inviting it in as you would a guest at dinner.

It seems to me that when we don't muster up the guts to change, when we don't value ideals and struggle toward them, our lives are full of crappy little situations we're always wondering how to magically make better.

Remember my caller. She hadn't even considered that she was pinning her sense of self on a man who abandoned his child. As we were talking, I felt she was suddenly aware of a whole new way of looking at her predicament. I told her, "Ideals are not only about what touches you. An ideal is there if nobody else is in the room." I had the feeling she was beginning to realize she'd been seeing herself as the victim when she was really the perpetrator.

DON'T PAY THE PRICE FOR BEING A VICTIM

And there is indeed a payoff for seeing yourself as a victim. Victimization means you don't have to do anything. I remember one guy on the show I challenged by saying, "You know, I get a sense that what you do is whine," and he admitted he'd been accused of it before. So I asked him to tell me the good part about whining, and he recited a whole litany of things: when you whine, people give you sympathy; when you whine, you're not responsible or obligated to do anything; when you whine, it's "Poor me," not "What should I do?" As he saw it, "Whining just gets you off the hook from all sorts of obligations, responsibilities, and efforts. But," he added, "then you're stuck with things you don't want. Anyway, they don't happen all the time, so it works itself out." At least he had the courage to tell the truth, which was that he refused to stand on his own. People go to unbelievable lengths not to change. They're so afraid of the pain involved that they willingly sacrifice the opportunity for genuine, long-term happiness.

HAPPINESS IS A QUIET REACTION

Too many of us define happiness as feeling good, not doing good, which is absolutely backward. And doing good doesn't only mean you simply send a check to charity. Let me give you an example.

A while ago, I was a regular on a local television show. I was, in fact, their only regular, and it was my appearances that got them ratings. Another local show called me and said, "Don't go there anymore, and we'll put you on here." And I told them, "I can't do that. These people gave me my first break, and I owe them." So I didn't leave but I never mentioned that other offer to my employers.

Some time later I was doing a pilot for another show that wouldn't have competed with my regular show. But the station figured it would, and dumped me. Still, I wasn't unhappy because I felt secure in the courage of my convictions.

I guess most people in that situation would have defined happiness as leaving one show and getting the better one. Of course I was crushed by my station's actions because I never would have behaved the way they did. I try to surround myself with people who put the same stock in the things I do. Sure, I yelled and screamed and slammed a few doors and shouted "those SOBs," but I was aware that acting honorably never implies your behavior will be reciprocated. You have to be really naive to imagine it will.

Honorable behavior is its own reward, and people have to understand that joy in life does not come from eschewing obligations. Owning up to your responsibilities as a human being creates the texture that gives your life richness. This is what brings happiness. By the way, happiness is a quiet reaction. You rarely jump up and down and scream when you're truly, deeply happy. Usually, when you're deeply, profoundly happy, you weep. Happiness is a truly deep emotion that comes from the exercise of one's courage, character, and conscience. Name me a happy victim!

I have been known to come down pretty hard on many therapies and support groups because I think they too often keep people in the victim mind-set. In my opinion, they should be reserved for times that are personally apocalyptical—which is to say, when your life has sunk to the point where you're nonfunctional and have lost hope. Unfortunately, in our current society, people seek professional help as if they were getting their nails done. If you just sit there and marinate in the negative, which is often what happens, negative thinking and feeling settle in. I would much rather a troubled person first seek out something spiritual, which is a lot more positive and uplifting.

A GODLY LIFE

A predominant amount of people's problems are the result of not living a godly life. For instance, a Jewish woman called to say she was enraged at her future mother-in-law who was insisting the caller and her boyfriend move close to the family synagogue, since they're Orthodox and can't drive on Saturday. I told her, "You mean you're living with him and having sex with him before marriage, and you're worried about walking to the synagogue on the sabbath." Her argument was with his mother's demands, and she was not leading a godly life herself. Amazing.

In life, you get ill, people betray you, stuff happens. Somebody rear-ends your car, and your neck is hurt forever. This is the reality of life. Generally speaking, however, if the people who call me with their problems had led a godly life with more honor, dignity, and attention to ethical matters, they wouldn't be in the predicament about which they're calling me. A Catholic man phoned in to tell me he was dating a Catholic woman, a divorced woman with a child. He was troubled by the fact that she was divorced. I did my same old, "Are you having intercourse with her?" and of course he was. I asked him if the Pope hadn't had something to say about sex outside of marriage, and he responded by saying, "Yes, but I want to tell you something. I've only been listening to you in the last two weeks, and I've heard you discuss these things about character and respect for morals and values. I've decided not to have intercourse again until I am married because I realize that's what's causing my problem. We have intimacy on one level and no real life agreements on many other levels. So we have an expectation that things should be a certain way because we're getting naked and having sex, and it's not real life. I've learned that from you." I've got to tell you that call made me so proud.

There are no shortcuts to a quality life. It requires ideals, and that's where religion always comes in. Religion requires you follow ideals that you don't fluff off by saying, "Nobody's perfect." To me, that's denying that there are worthy ideals and meaningful changes that one works toward. Sometimes you hit it, sometimes you don't, but to me it's the effort you are constantly expending that's important. People would have more satisfying lives if they pursued these ideals rather than immediate gratification.

WHAT WE DO, WE ARE

Ethics and religion come together in the area of appropriate judgment. If you've been bad, you've been bad. I don't believe in judging the action and not the person. The person is what they do. We're not a composite of what we would like to have done. What we actually do, that's what tells us who we are. So there are good people and bad people. There are decent people and evil people. But I don't think there is a good person alive who hasn't made mistakes. The laws of ethics and religion exist to show us where we erred and how we can avoid taking the low road a second time.

ASK YOURSELF "WOULD I BE PROUD?"

Every day, I talk to 15 to 20 million people who are listening and learning about morality and values at a profound and pragmatic level. At the end of each hour, I'll always give a little thought, a meditation, that lasts about twenty seconds while the end music is playing. Today at the end of one of the hours, I said something like, "When you're planning to do something, project yourself ten years into the future, look back, and ask, 'Would I be proud to watch me do this?' If the answer is yes, go for it! If it's no, cease and desist immediately. That's my rule of thumb. It instantly erases all rationalizations." Would the caller with the undivorced boyfriend who deserted his child look back and be proud that she let herself be swept away in the amoral undertow? I don't think so.

"Would I be proud?" That's a simple yes or no. But it can help you gather your character, courage, and conscience to face a future of positive change and lasting happiness. On that I give you my word, and as you must know by now, my word is my bond.

—*Laura Schlessinger, Ph.D.*

∼

Wisdom has its root in goodness, and not goodness its root in wisdom.

—Ralph Waldo Emerson

∼

The words of Pulitzer Prize–winning author **Tracy Kidder**—his tone, style, pace, and content—beautifully recap our examination of personal change. While his names, faces, places, and realities are totally different from those in my story, there are enough similarities in Tracy's story and my own to allow me to identify with his thoughts and feelings about change.

All of us are very much the same, aren't we? Tracy's story is mine and my story is yours. While the details are different, each of us lives a human life and change is a big part of all of our stories:

THE CAPACITY FOR CHANGE

I'VE NUDGED FIFTY AND I'VE BEGUN TO NOTICE THAT I'M past that time when I can maintain the illusion that my body isn't changing—that I can always shed this extra weight; but as far as personality goes, I do think it's possible for people to change. You see examples all the time.

What fascinates me is the old question of predestination and free will. There's probably a whole bunch of behaviorists or whatever they are called who say that things are pretty much established by the time you're five or ten. I don't want to believe that's true. It would be really counterproductive as far as civilization goes, and measuring these sorts of things is impossible. To what extent the external world is making changes in a person or to what extent a person changes by acts of will, I don't know.

TRYING TO BECOME A BETTER PERSON

Changes seem to have so much to do with motivation or the illusion or the goal of becoming a better person. Where does that come from? Why does anyone have that as an objective? We have to be careful about lamenting the sins of youth since that has been going on for thousands of years. But there is that question when you're confronted with, say, the men who killed Michael Jordan's father. In the absence of a desire to be a good person, awful things can happen. How does that desire get laid down? Why does it misfire?

Do we get that from our parents? Do we get that from education? Do we get that from our peers? Can things be subsumed under the heading of good or back luck? I don't know. Yet I remember kids from school days who had perfectly wretched, cruel, and terrible parents who turned out quite wonderfully well—kids who did have that desire.

My decision to become a writer was mediated by a couple of things, I think, in retrospect. My mother, though she'd never said it, had always encouraged me to do something in the arts. Also I tried my hand at writing some short stories in college. They were well received, and to be honest, some of the young women in the class seemed to like them and it to occurred to me that this was a way of meeting and impressing girls. Then I got into a class taught by a man named Robert Fitzgerald, who was really an inspirational teacher. It was quite a coup to get into his class, and it didn't take very long before I began to realize that writing is a very high calling indeed. After that there was just nothing else I really wanted to do.

As far as my decision to get married goes, I feel I was lucky. It's easy enough when you're a young man to make a decision to do something, go into the military, become a writer, get married. What's harder, of course, is to sustain those decisions.

I could have quit being a writer and I felt quite a lot of pressure to do that. I wasn't making a living, and my wife was supplying most of the income. For quite some time, I found that humiliating and scary but writing was what I loved to do, I wanted to do it, and I felt I could. I loved the work and I was not going to give it up that easily. As far as my marriage goes, I love my wife. If anyone was going to pull out, it was going to be my wife, Frances. In my case, as far as being married and writing went, the two decisions sustained each other. What I'm suggesting is that the initial decision is in many cases less important than the long-term commitment.

ASK FOR HELP

I guess I've relied on other people a lot to help me make decisions. An important ingredient is knowing from whom to ask for help—finding people in the world you really can trust.

I remember someone making an almost offhand remark that I have no doubt he forgot within five minutes. It absolutely changed my life. It stuck with me forever. I was struggling to write fiction and I was really at a loss. My friend, Sam Toperoff, who is a fine writer, often gave me advice at a certain point in my life. One evening he said, "You know the world is so interesting right now and so bizarre and strange. If I were a young guy I'd go out there and do some real reporting." I don't know that he meant it actually as advice to me but it really clicked and I thought, "There's a direction I can try to follow."

How people find meaning in life is the real question. I'm sure it varies from person to person. I think it has to do with the kind of work that leaves something behind. The quest is not just to leave your mark but to have done good, conscientious work—

the best you could do. That seems to me to be one of the things that people really crave.

Part of what I've tried to do in going after the lives of ordinary people is to capture a real reflection of human character on the page. It happens to be what interests me. I'd like to get better at it.

—*Tracy Kidder*

∿

The greatest thing in the world is to know how to be oneself.

—MONTAIGNE

∿

Habitat for Humanity founder **Millard Fuller** offers some thoughts on appreciating the gift of life and the responsibility we have to develop our God-given talents:

THE GIFT OF LIFE

LIFE IS A GIFT. YOU APPEARED. YOU HAD NOTHING TO DO with it whatsoever. You had nothing to do with the color of your eyes, the color of your hair, the color of your skin, or how tall you were going to be. You stand with this gift of yourself. What are you going to do with it? God in his infinite wisdom decided to give us free will, so life is an absolute gift with no strings attached. You can gorge your body with too much food and make yourself fat. You can smoke and contaminate your lungs with all sorts of toxicants. You can stuff drugs in your mouth and make yourself groggy. Or you can go to school and train yourself. You can educate yourself and learn about the world in which you are living. God gave you self, gave you life, and gave you the world to live in. What are you going to do with that gift?

I say we have a responsibility. We were not given this gift of life just to amuse ourselves and run around wondering what titillating new thing we can do to amuse our bodies, our minds, and our spirit. What can we do to express some measure of gratitude for this gift we've been given?

When somebody hands you a present at Christmas, you wouldn't think of grabbing it out of his or her hands, saying nothing, and walking away. But some people treat life like that. They snatch the gift of life away from the Creator and walk away without any words of gratitude. That's a sad way to live. It's tragic for the person involved, for their neighbors, and for the world.

We're called to be cocreators with God, take what we've been given, and make it grow. It's an obligation and responsibility to develop the God-given talents we have. Most people tiptoe through life hoping to arrive safely at death.

—*Millard Fuller*

∾

A human being is a part of the whole, called by us "Universe," a part limited in time and space. He experiences himself, his thoughts and feelings as something separated from the rest—a kind of optical illusion of his consciousness. This delusion is a kind of prison for us, restricting us to our personal desires and to affection for a few persons nearest to us. Our task must be to free ourselves from this prison by widening our circle of compassion to embrace all living creatures and the whole of nature in its beauty. Nobody is able to achieve this completely, but the striving for such achievement is in itself a part of the liberation and foundation for inner security.

—ALBERT EINSTEIN

Love is, above all, a gift of oneself.

—JEAN ANOUILH

∾

Author and teacher **Marianne Williamson** believes the key to a happier life is love:

THE UNIVERSAL SPIRIT

WE ARE HEADING INTO THE FINAL STRETCH OF THE TWENTI-
eth century. There's a world view that has dominated this entire
century and it's been very scientific, analytical, and mechanistic.
This is the century in which mankind felt it could pretty much
fix everything; but it's been a century without heart. We are
seeing the limits to that thinking. We are seeing that we pushed
passion aside. We pushed poetry aside. We pushed intuition
aside. We pushed aside human values and with them our capacity
to feel and be tender with one another. Now all of a sudden
there is an effort to retrieve some lost part of ourselves. There's
one social order that's disintegrating but there's another giant
wave of hope, enthusiasm, and revitalization that's being born.

According to *A Course in Miracles,* there are only two human
emotions, love and fear. Every emotion that does not stem from
love is derived from fear, which is merely the absence of love.
The relationship of love to fear is the same as the relationship of
light to dark. In the presence of light, dark can't exist. So you
don't fight darkness, you just turn on the light and the darkness
is gone. Similarly, you stop fighting your fears. You fill your
mind with love and all fear is gone. Hate, anger, sadness,
disappointment, and violence are all derived from fear. In the
presence of love, however, those things don't exist.

In the Western mind we always think in terms of how to
attack a problem. The Eastern religions say, "Seek God and all
that is not authentically you leaves." The shift, psychologically,
has to do with the notion that we can embrace the answer.

Embrace light. Embrace love. As we do, we begin to make
love more of a participatory emotion in our lives—something
we "do" every day. A miracle is a change in perception from
seeing through the eyes of fear to seeing through the eyes of love.

I can look at something you do and I can judge you, criticize
you, or blame you. Or I can say, "Wait a minute, I'm going to
live my life from a different place. I'm going to focus on the fact
that you tried your best and I'm going to give you the benefit of
the doubt. I'm going to open my heart instead of closing it."

Regardless whether you find your truth and sustenance in the Bible, or in the Koran, or in the Talmud, or in the Seth material, or in the *I Ching,* or in Lao-tzu, or in *A Course in Miracles,* what's important are those universal spiritual themes that are in all the great religions. That, I believe, has to do with how we connect to one another as human beings. For me the spiritual path has to do with that journey from the fearful places in myself to the loving places in myself. God is love. God is the love inside of us. That Higher Power is the essence of what it means to be human.

—*Marianne Williamson*

❧

Time moves slowly, but passes quickly.

—ALICE WALKER

❧

Senator William S. Cohen opened his Bangor press conference by saying, "The people of Maine were kind enough to send me to the House of Representatives when I was thirty-two years old and then to the Senate in 1978. During that time, I've won six elections, served with six presidents, cast more than 11,500 votes, and been at the center of the two great Constitutional crises of Watergate and Iran-Contra." He went on to say, "Of the many decisions I've made during the past two decades, this one has been the most difficult. I am announcing today that I will not seek a fourth term to the Senate in 1996."

On my THIS IS AMERICA television program, I asked Senator Cohen why he had chosen not to run. His response: "The time has come for me to move on. I've been here for almost a quarter of a century. I hear the ticking of the clock and it's time for me to try something else."

Senator Cohen ended the program by reading one of his own poems from his collection, *A Baker's Nickel:*

TO LOOK BACK

To look back
might mean never
to go on.

To see the pile
of shattered glass
and broken days,
the horror of
time that's lost.

To listen for
the voices of sons
that ran once
like laughing brooks,

To hear the echo
of footfalls when
they walked into
mustaches and manhood
before I turned.

If I should thumb
through photographs that
remind me how I've
lived in the margins
of my life,

I might never go on,
climbing Jacob's mystic ladder
into the night,
searching for a place
to rest in some
perfect light.

I might stop.

And what then?

—WILLIAM S. COHEN

❦

Life is a simple journey for complicated people. A philosophy for living it well was written by the late Bessie Anderson:

To laugh often and much,
To win the respect of intelligent people
and earn the affection of children,
To earn the appreciation of honest critics
and endure the betrayal of false friends,
To appreciate beauty,
To find the best in others,
To leave the world a bit better
whether by a healthy child,
a garden patch or a redeemed
social condition,
To know even one life has breathed
easier because you have lived—
This is to have succeeded.

Change. For the most part, we hate it, fear it, hide from it. Yet without it, where would we be? Think back to a year ago, five years, ten. Good, bad, and so-so. We are wiser in every way, even if we choose to ignore what we have learned and know to be true. Even that bit of stubbornness will give way to change some day.

Change is always upon us and we muddle through. Amazing to think, to believe, to know that even as we trip all over ourselves to be better or different, God loves us exactly as we are at this very moment. We cannot begin to fathom His unconditional love for us. Yet deep in our hearts we know we are in need of change, we are ripe for that change, and we should seek it. For it is the miracle of change that leads us to our destination: to know and love ourselves, and to love others, life, and God.

The slogan says, "Don't quit before the miracle happens." Of course, there is no quitting in life until it's done—and *you* are the miracle, the miracle of change. Can you deny it?

REFLECTION

A man's liberal and conservative phases seem to follow each other in a succession of waves from the time he is born. Children are radicals. Youths are conservatives, with a dash of criminal negligence. Men in their prime are liberals (as long as their digestion keeps pace with their intellect). The middle aged run to shelter: they insure their life, draft a will, accumulate mementos and occasional tables, and hope for security. And then comes old age, which repeats childhood—a time full of humors and sadness, but often full of courage and even prophecy.

—E. B. WHITE

It is not the mountain we conquer, but ourselves.

—SIR EDMUND HILLARY

TO THE READER

If you have experienced The Miracle of Change in your own life, please write and tell me about it:

Dennis Wholey
The Miracle of Change
1615 H. Street, NW
Washington, DC 20062

The Contributors

CLAUDIA BLACK, PH.D., became the first well-known figure associated with the Adult Children of Alcoholics movement upon publication of her classic book, *It Will Never Happen to Me.* Her other best-selling books are *My Dad Loves Me, My Dad Has a Disease,* and *Repeat After Me.* She is a past chairperson and current adviser to the National Association for Children of Alcoholics.

LES BROWN, author of *Live Your Dreams* and *It's Not Over Until You Win,* is a rare example of what determination can do. Abandoned, poverty stricken, adopted, and labeled "mentally retarded," he has pursued his life's goal to make a difference in the lives of others. Best known as an award-winning motivational speaker and entrepreneur, he was the host of his own nationally syndicated television series, *The Les Brown Show.*

MARY HIGGINS CLARK, "The Queen of Suspense," has written sixteen best-selling books, including *Moonlight Becomes You, Let Me Call You Sweetheart, Silent Night, Remember Me,* and *My Gal Sunday.* She has nine honorary doctorates and has served as president of the Mystery Writers of America.

WILLIAM S. COHEN (Republican/Maine) retired from the United States Senate after serving there for eighteen years. A former mayor of Bangor, he also served three terms in the U.S. House of Representatives. Writing has been Senator

Cohen's avocation for many years. He is the U.S. Secretary of Defense in the second Clinton administration.

WAYNE W. DYER, PH.D., is an internationally known author, lecturer, and psychotherapist. He is the author of ten books, including such best-sellers as *Your Erroneous Zones, You'll See It When You Believe It, Real Magic,* and *Your Sacred Self.* He has coauthored three textbooks, and numerous professional journals, and he lectures extensively in the United States and abroad.

BETTY J. EADIE, the mother of eight children, is celebrating her thirty-fourth year of marriage. The seventh of ten children, she was raised in rural Nebraska and on the Rosebud Indian Reservation in South Dakota. Her personal near-death experience was the subject of her book, *Embraced by the Light,* which was number one on both hardcover and paperback lists of *The New York Times* for more than sixty-five weeks.

ALBERT ELLIS, PH.D., is a fellow of the American Psychological Association and has served as president of its Division of Consulting Psychology. He holds the top award granted by the American Humanist Association. He served as chief psychologist of the New Jersey State Diagnostic Center and is the founder of the Albert Ellis Institute in New York City.

MARY FISHER is the founder of the Family AIDS Network, Inc., a nonprofit organization that supports her role as an HIV/AIDS spokesperson by expanding the network of concerned individuals and organizations. She speaks publicly about her own experience of being HIV positive and the AIDS crisis. Two collections of her speeches have already been published: *Sleep with the Angels* and *I'll Not Go Quietly.* She is also the author of her memoir, *My Name Is Mary.*

MICHAEL J. FOX currently stars in the hit ABC television series *Spin City.* He is also known to television audiences worldwide for his Emmy-winning performance as Alex P. Keaton in the weekly series *Family Ties.* At the peak of the seven successful seasons in which he starred in that series, Fox received twenty thousand fan letters a week. He began acting professionally at fifteen in the Canadian Broadcasting series *Leo and Me,* and among his many movie credits are starring roles in the popular *Back to the Future* films (Parts I, II, and III), *For Love or Money,* and *The American President.*

MILLARD FULLER, former president of the Fuller and Dees Marketing Group, is the founder and president of Habitat for Humanity International, the eighth largest builder of homes in the United States. Habitat volunteers have built homes together with fifty thousand families in need in twelve hundred U.S. cities and forty-five countries. Habitat's headquarters are in Americus, Georgia.

FATHER JOSEPH GIRZONE began his writing career after retiring from the active priesthood for health reasons. His first novel, *Joshua,* the story of a modern-day Christ figure, became a bestseller without a publicity campaign or major book reviews. It has now sold over 1.5 million copies and has been translated into seven languages. Fr. Girzone's other works include *Joshua and the Children, Joshua and the City, Never Alone,* and *What Is God?*

SHAD HELMSTETTER is an author and lecturer in the field of motivational behavior. His books include *What to Say When You Talk to Yourself, You Can Excel in Times of Change,* and *Network of Champions.* Shad is the chairman of the Self-Talk Institute in Tucson, Arizona, a nonprofit organization that develops programs for schools, businesses, and other organizations nationwide.

ARIANNA STASSINOPOULOS HUFFINGTON is a senior fellow at the Progress and Freedom Foundation in Washington, D.C., where she chairs its Center for Effective Compassion. Her books include *The Fourth Instinct: The Call of the Soul; The Female Woman; Maria Callas: The Woman Behind the Legend;* and *Picasso: Creator and Destroyer.*

JOHN JAKES is the author of more than a dozen best-selling novels, including *The Kent Family Chronicles,* an eight-volume series depicting the nation's history through the lives of a fictional family. The series currently has over 45 million books in print. John Jakes was the first author ever to have three books on *The New York Times* best-seller list in a single year. His most recent books are *Homeland* and *California Gold*.

JUDITH JAMISON is the artistic director of the Alvin Ailey American Dance Theater and the Alvin Ailey American Dance Center. Her autobiography, *Dancing Spirit,* tells of her career as a principal dancer and choreographer, teacher, and artistic director. She has also served as a presidentially-appointed member of the National Endowment for the Arts.

BILL T. JONES is an internationally celebrated dancer and choreographer. Together with his late partner and companion, he founded the Bill T. Jones/Arnie Zane Dance Company in 1982. His works often deal with such themes as racism, homophobia, sexism, and human mortality. Across the United States he has conducted "survival workshops" for people with terminal illnesses.

TRACY KIDDER was awarded both the Pulitzer Prize and the American Book Award for *The Soul of a New Machine,* a study of the eighteen-month-long struggle of engineers to create a competitive super-mini-computer. His other works include *The Road to Yuba City, House, Among Schoolchildren,* and *Old Friends.* He is a contributing editor of *The Atlantic Monthly.*

DENNIS KIMBRO, PH.D., is the coauthor (with Napoleon Hill) of *Think and Grow Rich: A Black Choice.* When Hill died, he left behind an unfinished manuscript with a positive message aimed for African-Americans. The Napoleon Hill Foundation chose Dennis Kimbro to complete it. He is also the director of the Center for Entrepreneurship, Graduate School of Business, at Clark Atlanta University, and author of *Daily Motivations for African-American Success* and *What Makes the Great Great.*

LONNIE MACDONALD, M.D., is a psychiatrist in private practice in New York City specializing in the treatment of addictive disorders. He served as the first Chief of Community Psychiatry at Harlem Hospital.

HARVEY MACKAY, marketing genius, civic booster, and super-salesman, is the best-selling author of *Swim with the Sharks Without Being Eaten Alive, Beware the Naked Man Who Offers You His Shirt,* and *Sharkproof.* He is one of the most popular business lecturers in America today and an avid marathon runner and former golf champion, and has been elected to the Senior Tennis Hall of Fame.

REBECCA MADDOX is the president of Capital Rose, Inc., a company that provides women business owners access to financing, information, and related products, and works with Fortune 500 clients to capitalize on the growing opportunities in the women's market. She held senior executive positions at Capital Holding, Citicorp, and Comp-U-Card of America and is the author of *Inc. Your Dreams.*

OG MANDINO wrote eighteen books that have sold more than 33 million copies in twenty languages. His first book, *The Greatest Salesman in the World,* has sold more than 12 million copies. Other books include *Og Mandino's University of Success, The Choice,* and *The Spellbinder's Gift.* His work as a lecturer has been recognized by the National Speakers Association and the International Speakers Hall of Fame.

KELLY MCGILLIS, who trained as an actress at the Juilliard School of Drama in New York, is probably best known to film audiences for her roles as Rachel in *Witness,* Charlie in *Top Gun,* and Kathryn in *The Accused.* Equally at home on stage in the classics, she has portrayed Helena in *All's Well That Ends Well,* Viola in *Twelfth Night,* and Portia in *The Merchant of Venice* at the Shakespeare Theatre and Nina in *The Seagull* at the Kennedy Center, all in Washington.

MICHAEL MEDVED is a film critic and commentator on media and society. For more than ten years, he served as cohost with Jeffrey Lyons for *Sneak Previews,* which was aired nationally on

PBS stations. He is the author of seven books, including *What Really Happened to the Class of '65?* and *Hollywood vs. America: Popular Culture and the War on Traditional Values* and *Hospital.*

PIA MELLODY, R.N., is a certified addiction counselor and registered nurse who has worked in the addiction recovery field for twenty years. She is the author of three books: *Facing Codependence, Breaking Free,* and *Facing Love Addiction.* She and her husband, Pat, are the cofounders of The Meadows treatment center in Wickenburg, Arizona. Pia Mellody lectures on all aspects of recovery, including codependence, love addiction, and shame.

ANDREA MITCHELL is the chief foreign affairs correspondent for NBC News. Prior to that assignment, she was chief White House correspondent, covered Bill Clinton's 1992 presidential campaign, and worked on Capitol Hill as chief congressional correspondent. She is a regular panelist on NBC's *Meet the Press.*

THOMAS MOORE is a writer and psychotherapist who has become a leading teacher and lecturer in the area of archetypal psychology. In 1987, he founded the Institute for the Study of Imagination, a nonprofit educational organization. His most recent books are *Care of the Soul, Soul Mates, Meditations,* and *The Re-Enchantment of Everyday Life.*

GEORGETTE MOSBACHER is the chairman and CEO of Georgette Mosbacher Enterprises, Inc., and is the author of *Feminine Force: Release the Power Within to Create the Life You Deserve.* Among her honors are the Distinguished Humanitarian Award from Brandeis University and Entrepreneur of the Decade from the Touchdown Club of Washington, D.C. Her husband, Robert Mosbacher, is a former Secretary of the U.S. Department of Commerce.

DENNIS E. O'GRADY, PSY.D., is the author of three books on personal growth, including *Taking the Fear out of Changing.* In addition to his private practice in Kettering, Ohio, Dr. O'Grady writes a syndicated newspaper column and conducts professional workshops and training seminars on change, communication, and conflict resolution.

HAZEL O'LEARY is the former Secretary of the U.S. Department of Energy and the first woman and African-American to hold that position. She served in key energy posts in both the Ford and Carter administrations. In the private sector, she most recently was president of Northern States Power Company in Minnesota.

JAMES REDFIELD, a therapist who has specialized for fifteen years in the treatment of adolescents, is the author of *The New York Times* best-selling books *The Celestine Prophecy* and *The Tenth Insight*. More than 5.5 million copies of *The Celestine Prophecy* are in print in forty languages.

SALLE MERRILL REDFIELD is the author of *The Joy of Meditating: A Beginner's Guide to the Art of Meditation* and the audio tape *Meditations for the Tenth Insight*. With her husband James Redfield, she lectures throughout the United States.

ANN RICHARDS served as governor of Texas from 1991 until 1995. Prior to that, she was Texas state treasurer for two terms. She gained national attention for her famous keynote speech at the 1988 Democratic National Convention. She is now a senior advisor to the law firm of Verner, Liipfert, Bernhard, McPherson & Hand in Austin, Texas, and is in great demand as a public speaker.

SOGYAL RINPOCHE was born in Tibet; raised as a son of one the most accomplished spiritual masters of this century, Jamyang Khyentse Chokyi Lodro; went to university in Delhi and Cambridge; and began to teach in the West in 1974. Rinpoche, author of the highly acclaimed *The Tibetan Book of Living and Dying,* is the founder and spiritual director, along with H. E. Dzogchen Rinpoche, of RIGPA, an international network of centers and groups that follow the teaching of Buddha under his guidance.

THEODORE ISAAC RUBIN, M.D., former president of the American Institute for Psychoanalysis, is a practicing psychiatrist in New York City. Dr. Rubin is the author of more than twenty-five books, including *Compassion and Self-Hate, Overcoming Indecisiveness: The Eight Stages of Effective Decisionmaking,* and *Lisa and David.*

TIM RUSSERT is the senior vice president and Washington bureau chief of NBC News, and has been moderator of *Meet the Press* since December 1991. He is political analyst for the *NBC Nightly News, Today,* and MSNBC.

PIERRE SALINGER has maintained public prominence since the early 1960s, when he worked as President John F. Kennedy's press secretary. In 1968 he directed Robert Kennedy's presidential bid. A long career in broadcast journalism culminated with work at ABC News as chief foreign correspondent and senior editor for Europe. He continues to serve as an ABC international consultant and is also vice president of the public relations company Burson-Marsteller. His autobiography, *P.S.: A Memoir,* was published last year.

DR. LAURA SCHLESSINGER is the author of the best-selling *Ten Stupid Things Women Do to Mess Up Their Lives* and *How Could You Do That? The Abdication of Character, Courage, and Conscience.* Dr. Laura is the host of an internationally syndicated radio show heard on more than two hundred stations via SMI Broadcasting. Dr. Schlessinger received her Ph.D. in physiology from Columbia University and a postdoctoral certificate in marriage and family and child therapy from the University of Southern California. She is licensed as a marriage and family and child therapist. She has taught at both Pepperdine University and USC.

NATALIE SHAINESS, M.D., has worked as a psychiatrist and psychoanalyst for over fifty years. She has written over two hundred papers and professional book reviews, as well as a best-selling book on masochism, *Sweet Suffering: Woman As Victim.* Dr. Shainess is a lecturer at Columbia University in New York.

MARTIN SHEEN first achieved prominence in the Broadway hit *The Subject Was Roses.* His extensive film work includes starring roles in *Apocalypse Now, Gandhi, Gettysburg,* and *The American President.* On television he has portrayed John Dean in *Blind Ambition,* John F. Kennedy in *Kennedy,* Robert F. Kennedy in *The Missiles of October,* and the title role in *The Execution of Private Slovik.*

CAL THOMAS writes a twice-weekly syndicated newspaper column distributed to over two hundred papers nationally. He is the author of eight books, including *Book Burning* and *The Things That Matter Most.* He has also been a regular contributor to National Public Radio's *All Things Considered,* worked for public television and NBC News, and hosted *The Cal Thomas Show* on CNBC.

NINA TOTENBERG is an ABC television news and National Public Radio correspondent. Her reports air regularly on NPR's critically acclaimed news magazine *All Things Considered, Morning Edition,* and *Weekend Edition.* She is a regular panelist on the syndicated weekly public affairs program *Inside Washington* and a frequent reporter on the *ABC Evening News* and *Nightline.*

TOMMY TUNE is an actor, dancer, singer, choreographer, and director and the winner of nine Tony awards. He is the only person in theatrical history to win Tony awards in four different categories and to win the same two Tony awards two years in a row. His works include *My One and Only, Grand Hotel,* and *The Will Rogers Follies.*

JACK VALENTI has led many lives: a wartime bomber pilot, advertising agency founder, political consultant, White House assistant, and author of four books. He is currently the president and CEO of the Motion Picture Association of America.

ANDREW WEIL, M.D., is currently associate director of the Division of Social Perspectives in Medicine and director of the Program in Integrative Medicine at the University of Arizona in Tucson, where he practices natural and preventive medicine. Dr. Weil says, "My mission is focused on two things: one is to work to build the confidence of both doctors and patients in the body's own natural healing abilities; the other is to try to reform medical education and the way we train doctors." Dr. Weil's latest book is the best-selling *Spontaneous Healing.*

BETTY WHITE is best known for her five-time-Emmy-Award-winning roles on *The Mary Tyler Moore Show* and *The Golden Girls.* Most recently she starred in *Golden Palace* and *Maybe Next Time.* She is the author of four books, including *Here We Go Again: My Life in Television,* and has been honored by numerous organizations for her dedication to animal health and welfare.

RABBI HAROLD WHITE is Jewish chaplain at Georgetown University in Washington, D.C. Rabbi White served as U.S. Navy Chaplain at Parris Island, South Carolina, and with the Seventh Fleet in the Pacific. He has served as a congregational Rabbi in Dublin, Ireland, and Ann Arbor, Michigan. For nine years, Rabbi White was associated with American University before his appointment at Georgetown University. He is the first rabbi to be appointed to a full-time campus ministry by a Catholic university.

ARMSTRONG WILLIAMS is the author of the book *Beyond Blame: How We Can Succeed by Breaking the Dependency Barrier.* His weekly television show, *The Right Side,* is seen on NET and his nightly radio show, also called *The Right Side,* airs on the USA Radio Network. He is CEO of Graham Williams, an international public relations firm.

MARIANNE WILLIAMSON is an internationally known lecturer and teacher, as well as the author of the best-selling books *A Woman's Worth, A Return to Love,* and *Illuminata.*

JUDY WOODRUFF is a news anchor and senior correspondent at CNN, where she also cohosts the programs *Inside Politics* and *The World Today.* A veteran Washington reporter, she also has served as the White House correspondent for NBC News and as a Washington correspondent on both NBC's *Today* show and PBS's *The MacNeil/Lehrer NewsHour.*

ZIG ZIGLAR, one of the most sought-after motivational teachers in the country, has shared the platform with presidents Ford, Reagan, and Bush, generals Schwarzkopf and Powell, Dr. Norman Vincent Peale, Dr. Robert Schuller, and Margaret Thatcher. He is the author of the best-selling books *See You at the Top, Raising Positive Kids in a Negative World,* and *Over the Top,* as well as chairman of The Zig Ziglar Corporation.

ANONYMOUS—More than one hundred different support programs use the basic philosophy of Alcoholics Anonymous. The term *Twelve Step,* which is used to identify these groups, refers to the twelve steps or principles of AA. The practice of those steps is called *the program.* Some of the groups that are represented here by the contributors are Alcoholics Anonymous, Narcotics Anonymous, Al-Anon, Adult Children of Alcoholics, Overeaters Anonymous, Debtors Anonymous, and Sex and Love Addicts Anonymous.

~